Contents at a Glance

KU-607-400

Part I   The New E-Conomy

1   E-Commerce Thinking   11
2   Business Models for the E-Conomy   25

Part II   Deploying E-Commerce

3   The Plan Is the Thing   47
4   Customer Touch Points   65
5   Content Will Always Be King   83
6   Instant Global Presence   99
7   Outsourcing Is Always an Option   119

Part III   Maintaining Momentum

8   New Expectations for Customer Service   137
9   Managing the E-Commerce Organization   155
10   Ongoing Internet Marketing   171
11   The Law Catches Up to E-Business   195

Part IV   E-Volving the Future

12   Shifting Markets   211
13   A View from the Real World   225
14   Change Is Constant, Change Is Good   245

Part V   Appendixes

A   Case Studies   273
B   E-Commerce Primer   297
C   Resources   301
D   End Notes   301

Index   315

Table of Contents

Forewords   xv

Introduction   1

Part I The New E-Conomy

1	E-Commerce Thinking	11
	From the Industrial Age to the Internet Age	12
	The New Internet Customer	13
	Current Philosophy Toward Integrating the Internet	15
	The Holistic, Internet-Enabled Entity	16
	True Internet Integration	17
	Failure Is a Good Thing	18
	Thinking Outside the Box	18
	Current Trends That Affect Thinking	20
	E-Volutionary Tactics	23
2	Business Models for the E-Conomy	25
	In the Beginning...	26
	Virtual Value Webs	28
	The Customer Drives the Model	30
	Partnering on the Rise	31
	New Partner Selection Criteria	32
	Marketing Partners	33
	Distribution or Channel Partners	35
	Supplier and Vendor Partners	36
	Fulfillment Partners	37
	Business Infrastructure Partners	39
	The Economics of the Value Web	40
	Integrating the New with the Old	41
	E-Volutionary Tactics	43

Part II Deploying E-Commerce

3	The Plan Is the Thing	47
	Planning in the Business Context	49
	The Big Picture and the Vision	50
	The Measure of Success	51

The Roadmap   53
Keeping the Processes Moving   54
Ensuring Customer Value   54
Stakeholders   56
Partner Involvement   57
Plan Creation and E-Volution   58
The Tactics of Planning   59
The Objective: A Smooth, Empowered,
    Self-Running Entity   61
E-Volutionary Tactics   62

4 **Customer Touch Points**   **65**

The Role of the Customer Is Changing   66
From Customer Satisfaction to Customer Retention   68
Customer Relationship Management   69
The Five Major Touch Points   70
Stratifying Your Customer Base   71
Individual and Personalized Interactions   73
Who Interacts with the Customer?   74
E-Volving Your Business Processes Around Your
    Customer   74
From Customer to Process to Business Model   76
Delivering Value on an Individual Basis   78
E-Volutionary Tactics   80

5 **Content Will Always Be King**   **83**

Content Must Provide Value to the Customer   84
Organizing and Designing Content   88
Valuable Content Is a Differentiator   91
Competitive Advantage Means Constantly
    E-Volving Content   92
Measuring the Effectiveness of Content   92
Who Creates Content?   94
E-Volving Content in Context   95
E-Volutionary Tactics   97

6 **Instant Global Presence**   **99**

Being Global   101
The Case for Globalization   102
Your Vision Determines Your Global Presence   103
Thinking Globally   104
Legal Barriers   105
Worldwide Logistics   106
Online Currencies   107

Multilingual E-Commerce 107
Acting Locally 108
E-Volving Your Processes 110
The Global Plan 112
Global Operations in Action 114
Options for E-Volving Your Global Operations 115
E-Volutionary Tactics 116

7   **Outsourcing Is Always an Option** 119

You Can Outsource Almost Anything 120
ASPs, BSPs, and Other Service Providers 121
A Starting Point 123
Deciding What to Outsource 124
Control and Access: The Differentiating Factors 126
Keeping Your Customer Touch Points Alive 127
Selecting Outsourcing Vendors 128
Managing Your Outsourcing Partners 129
E-Volving the Outsourcing Plan 131
E-Volutionary Tactics 132

Part III Maintaining Momentum

8   **New Expectations for Customer Service** 137

The Customer Service Organization 140
Metrics 143
Incentives 144
The Role of Partners 145
Revisiting the Plan 146
Service Level Agreements and
   Customer Stratification 147
E-Volving the Processes for Customer Service 147
The Universal Customer Database 148
An Infrastructure Made for Customer Interfaces 150
Maintaining Service Levels As You Grow 152
E-Volutionary Tactics 153

9   **Managing the E-Commerce Organization** 155

A Blueprint for Organizational Alignment 157
Aligning with Your Vision 158
Organizational Structures for the Internet-Enabled
   Entity 159
Transitioning to a New Structure 162

People and Processes   163
Legacy People   164
Transforming People   164
Self-Directed Work Groups   165
Collaborative Management   166
Walking and Talking the Vision   167
E-Volutionary Tactics   168

10   Ongoing Internet Marketing   171

New Ways to Market and New Buzzwords   172
No Field of Dreams Here   174
The Basics of Internet Marketing   175
A Memorable URL   177
Site Navigation   178
Give Away Something of Value   179
Content and Related Content   179
The Omnipresent URL   180
Signature Tags   180
The Search Engine Game   180
Online Newsletters and Magazines   182
Direct Marketing Online   183
Branding and the Web Site   183
Market Research   184
Conventional Marketing and Internet Marketing   185
Everyone Is a Marketer   185
Your Holistic Marketing Strategy   187
E-Volutionary Tactics   192

11   The Law Catches Up to E-Business   195

The Status of the Statutes   197
Regulatory and Enforcement Issues   198
Global Differences   200
Privacy   200
Intellectual Property   201
Contract Law   202
International Trade Policies   203
Taxation   203
The Desire for a Holistic Internet-Enabled World   203
What All This Means for Your Business Today   205
Staying Current   206
E-Volutionary Tactics   207

12	**Shifting Markets**	**211**
	The Internet Is Here to Stay	212
	The Shift to Customer Focus	214
	New Products and Services	214
	New Types of Markets	215
	Finding New Opportunities	215
	The Role of Experimentation	218
	Market Development	219
	Partnering and Collaboration	220
	The Future of Branding	221
	Metrics for Dynamic Markets	221
	No More Dinosaurs	222
	E-Volutionary Tactics	223
13	**A View from the Real World**	**225**
	1. The More Things Change, the More They Stay the Same	227
	2. The Hybrid E-Conomy	228
	3. Everything and Everyone is Connected	230
	4. Customers Rule	232
	5. Better, Faster, and Maybe Cheaper	233
	6. Business Models and Value Webs	234
	7. New Standards and Rules Create Opportunity	235
	8. E-Volving End-to-End Infrastructure	237
	9. The New Face of Marketing	238
	10. New Dimensions for Growth and Evolution	239
	E-Volutionary Tactics	242
14	**Change Is Constant, Change Is Good**	**245**
	Dealing with Constant Change	246
	Catalysts of Change	247
	Change Management	248
	Trends That Create the Need for Change	249
	Managing the Future	250
	E-Commerce in the Year 2025	250
	Back to 2000	260
	Boldly Setting Forth...	261
	E-Volutionary Tactics	262

Part V Appendixes

A   Case Studies   **273**

        United Parcel Service, Inc. (UPS)   274
            Key Concepts from This Book   274
            History of Transformation   274
            Products and Services   274
            Catalyst for Change   275
            Vision and Strategy   275
            Changes Made/E-Volutionary Process   276
            Main Lessons   280
            Roadmap for Continuing E-Volution   280
        Office Depot   281
            Key Concepts from This Book   281
            History of Transformation   281
            Products and Services   282
            Catalyst for Change   282
            Vision and Strategy   282
            Changes Made/E-Volutionary Process   283
            Main Lessons   286
            Roadmap for Continuing E-Volution   286
        Cardinal Health   287
            Key Concepts from This Book   287
            History of Transformation   287
            Products and Services   288
            Catalyst for Change   289
            Vision and Strategy   290
            Changes Made/E-Volutionary Process   290
            Main Lessons   294
            Roadmap for Continuing E-Volution   295

B   Recommended E-Commerce Glossaries   **297**

C   Resources   **301**

D   End Notes   **305**

        Index   **315**

About the Author

Mitchell Levy is:

- ▲ President of ECnow.com.

- ▲ Executive Producer of ECMgt.com.

- ▲ The founder and program coordinator for the San Jose State University Professional Development's (**http://ecmtraining.com/sjsu**) Electronic Commerce Management (ECM) Certificate Program.

- ▲ A conference chair at the Fall 2000 ECMsym.com Symposium, the Comdex Spring 2000 / ECMgt.com E-Commerce Management Symposium, and the Comdex Fall 2000 Comdex.biz Core Conference.

- ▲ A regular contributor to CommerceNet's research department.

ECnow.com works with start-up, medium, and large corporations helping them transition from the Industrial Age to the Internet Age and is engaged in strategic ECM consulting, training, and Internet marketing activities for both domestic and international corporations. Mitchell sits on the boards of various dot.com's and is on retainer at medium- to large-sized corporations. Mitchell lectures, writes about, and is asked to judge the ECM efforts of companies on a global level, and has been actively involved with numerous industry consortia.

Mitchell spent nine years at Sun Microsystems during the key infancy period of the Internet, and managed the e-commerce component of Sun's $3.5 billion supply chain. Since leaving Sun, he has put together the e-commerce strategy for the $2 billion revenue-based Bay Networks (both the buy and sell side), and has run a privately held Web Presence company founded in June 1995, which consulted, designed, created, and hosted Web pages for clients.

In addition, Mitchell currently speaks at conferences (including Comdex, Miller Freeman's Web Design and Development, Thunderlizard's Web Design, DCI's Internet Expo, CommerceNet's Annual Conferences, and C/Net's Web Builder, plus other Silicon Valley-based and individual client events worldwide). Mitchell also lectures at San Jose State University on both strategic e-commerce and Internet marketing. He chairs the Silicon Valley-based Software Development Forum's E-Commerce SIG. He has been actively involved with Commerce.Net, is currently a member of their research staff, has served as chair of their Marketing Working Group, and was an active participant of their Members Advisory Committee.

Dedication

I dedicate this book to my wife (Alex Debra) and son (Duncan Xavier). Her unwavering support and belief in everything I do made this book and the other ECM activities I'm involved in possible. She is the foundation I draw my strength from. And to my 2¼ year-old son, Duncan, whose joy is unending and who reminds me every day to open my eyes and look at the world with a new set of lenses.

Acknowledgments

I wish to thank and acknowledge Catherine Kitcho, whose dedication and amazing efforts made this book a reality. The difference between a good idea and an accomplished task lies in the execution. Thanks for executing and thanks for figuring out the best way to work with me.

I also wish to thank Yann Pecha, who created the wonderful illustration concepts that livened up many of the chapters. Thanks for burning all the midnight oil to make that happen.

In developing the content, it was necessary to gather together the views and perspectives from the best thinkers and leaders in today's world of ECM. More than 50 people took the time and made the effort to provide me with chapter input and quotes. Thank you for making time in your otherwise overloaded schedules to do this. A complete list of their companies appears in Appendix D, "End Notes," and at the E-Volve-or-Die.com Web site, but here is a list of these wonderful people:

> Alan Amling, Director of E-Commerce, UPS
> *Christina Cheney, President and CEO, Simmedia.com
> Leo Clarke, Principal, Techrisklaw
> Russ Cohn, CEO, Brigade Solutions
> Bill Daniel, Senior Vice President, Products, Vignette
> *Don Davis, Director of Worldwide Business Development,

Ricoh-Silicon Valley

*Dave Deasy, E-Business consultant

*Todd Elizalde, Director, E-Commerce, Cisco

Brooks Fisher, Vice President, Corporate Strategy and Marketing, Intuit

Clyde Foster, CEO, eConvergent

Neil Gardner, Vice President, Technical Operations, Navisite

Rip Gerber, Chief Strategy Officer and Vice President, Marketing, Commtouch

*Love Goel, CEO, Personify

Mark Grossman, Chair of Computer/E-Commerce Law Group, Becker-Poliakoff

Ben Horowitz, President and CEO, Loudcloud

Norm Hullinger, Vice President, Sales and Operations, Egghead

*Barbara Jones, Director, Customer Service, Cisco

Sean Kaldor, Vice President, E-Commerce, NetRatings.com

*Brian Kellner, Development Manager, Zoho Corporation

Andrew Krainin, Senior Vice President, Marketing, Sameday.com

Steve Larsen, Senior Vice President, Netperceptions

Monica Luechtefeld, Senior Vice President of E-Commerce, Office Depot

Mohit Mehrotra, VP & GM, American Express Corporate Services Interactive

John Mumford, Founding Partner, Crosspoint Venture Partners

Alan Naumann, President and CEO, Calico Commerce

*Doug Nelson, President, Seabright Group

Peter Neupert, President and CEO, drugstore.com, Inc.

*Peter Ostrow, CEO, Testmart

Dave Perry, President and CEO, Ventro

*Tom Popek, Principal, Strategic Internet Consulting

Mark Resch, President and CEO, CommerceNet

*Maria Luisa Rodriguez, Co-Founder and Director, e-co consulting

*George Roman, CTO, diCarta

Ashu Roy, CEO and Chairman, eGain

Lisa Sharples, Chief Marketing Officer, Garden.com

Michael Silton, CEO, Rainmaker Systems, Inc.

Narry Singh, Vice President of Global Trading, Rapt Inc.

Peter Sisson, CEO, Wineshopper

Steven J. Snyder, President and Chief Executive Officer, Net Perceptions, Inc.

Rick Steele, President and CEO, kinkos.com

Dave Steer, Director of Communications and Spokesperson, Truste

Jim Sterne, President, Target Marketing

Don Swenson, Vice President, Marketing and Business Development, SAQQARA

Michael Tilson, Senior Vice President of Technology and IS, Rainmaker Systems

*Dan Todd, Director, Marketing Strategy, Keynote Systems

*Dylan Tweney, Writer and Consultant, Tweney Media

Atul Vashistha, CEO, neoIT

Mark Walsh, Chairman & Chief Strategy Officer, VerticalNet

Eric Ward, President, The Ward Group

Kathy White, Executive Vice President & CIO, Cardinal Health

*Jorden Woods, Chairman and CTO, Global Sight

Monte Zweben, CEO, Blue Martini Software

*is a current or past instructor or guest lecturer in the premiere ECM program at San Jose State University Professional Development **http://ecmtraining.com/sjsu**.

Finally, I want to thank the management and editorial team at New Riders who were willing to push the envelope on this project. Steve Weiss, Theresa Gheen, Jennifer Eberhardt, and Michael Thurston brought this book through the final stages in record time—consistent with the pace of this crazy New E-Conomy that we are all living in today.

A Message from New Riders

As the reader of this book, you are our most important critic and commentator. We value your opinion and want to know what we're doing right, what we could do better, in what areas you'd like to see us publish, and any other words of wisdom you're willing to pass our way.

As the Executive Editor for the Graphics team at New Riders, I welcome your comments. You can fax, email, or write me directly to let me know what you did or didn't like about this book—as well as what we can do to make our books better. When you write, please be sure to include this book's title, ISBN, and author, as well as your name and phone or fax number. I will carefully review your comments and share them with the authors and editors who worked on the book.

Please note that I cannot help you with technical problems related to the topic of this book, and that due to the high volume of mail I receive, I might not be able to reply to every message. If you run into a technical problem, it's best to contact our Customer Support department, as listed later in this section. Thanks.

Email: steve.weiss@newriders.com

Mail: Steve Weiss
        Executive Editor
        Professional Graphics & Design Publishing
        New Riders Publishing
        201 West 103rd Street
        Indianapolis, IN 46290 USA

Visit Our Web Site: www.newriders.com

On our Web site, you'll find information about our other books, the authors we partner with, book updates and file downloads, promotions, discussion boards for online interaction with other users and with technology experts, and a calendar of trade shows and other professional events with which we'll be involved. We hope to see you around.

Email Us from Our Web Site

Go to www.newriders.com and click on the Contact link if you

▲ Have comments or questions about this book.

▲ Want to report errors that you have found in this book.

- ▲ Have a book proposal or are interested in writing for New Riders.

- ▲ Would like us to send you one of our author kits.

- ▲ Are an expert in a computer topic or technology and are interested in being a reviewer or technical editor.

- ▲ Want to find a distributor for our titles in your area.

- ▲ Are an educator/instructor who wants to preview New Riders books for classroom use. In the body/comments area, include your name, school, department, address, phone number, office days/hours, text currently in use, and enrollment in your department, along with your request for either desk/examination copies or additional information.

Call Us or Fax Us

You can reach us toll-free at (800) 571-5840 + 9+ 3567 (ask for New Riders). If outside the U.S., please call 1-317-581-3500 and ask for New Riders. If you prefer, you can fax us at 1-317-581-4663, Attention: New Riders.

Note

Technical Support and Customer Support for This Book   Although we encourage entry-level users to get as much as they can out of our books, keep in mind that our books are written assuming a non-beginner level of user-knowledge of the technology. This assumption is reflected in the brevity and shorthand nature of some of the tutorials.

New Riders will continually work to create clearly written, thoroughly tested and reviewed technology books of the highest educational caliber and creative design. We value our customers more than anything— that's why we're in this business—but we cannot guarantee to each of the thousands of you who buy and use our books that we will be able to work individually with you through tutorials or content with which you may have questions. We urge readers who need help in working through exercises or other material in our books—and who need this assistance immediately—to use as many of the resources that our technology and technical communities can provide, especially the many on-line user groups and list servers available.

▲ If you have a physical problem with one of our books or accompanying CD-ROMs, please contact our Customer Support department.

▲ If you have questions about the content of the book—needing clarification about something as it is written or note of a possible error—please contact our Customer Support department.

▲ If you have comments of a general nature about this or other books by New Riders, please contact the Executive Editor.

To contact our Customer Support department, call 1-317-581-3833, from 10:00 a.m. to 3:00 p.m. U.S. EST (CST from April through October of each year—unlike the majority of the United States, Indiana doesn't change to Daylight Savings Time each April). You can also access our tech support Web site at http://www.mcp.com/support.

Forewords

by Michael Silton, CEO, Rainmaker Systems, Inc.

Alan Naumann, President and CEO, Calico Commerce, Inc.

Alfred Chuang, Founder, President, and Chief Operations Officer, BEA Systems, Inc.

Peter Neupert, President and CEO, drugstore.com, Inc.

Peter Sisson, Vice-Chairman and Chief Strategy Officer, wine.com

John Mumford, Founding Partner, Crosspoint Venture Partners

Rob Wrubel, CEO, Ask Jeeves, Inc.

Steven J. Snyder, Ph.D., Co-Founder, President, and Chief Executive Officer, Net Perceptions, Inc.

Monte Zweben, CEO, Blue Martini Software

Rick Steele, President and CEO, kinkos.com

Love Goel, CEO, Personify

Jim Sterne, President, Target Marketing

This is no ordinary foreword because—perhaps—this book is no ordinary e-commerce resource. As I've shared my thoughts and various drafts of this manuscript with my colleagues in the industry, many have graciously offered to write the basic foreword, so many, in fact, that I've included the thoughts of these people as a collection of testimonials to the strength of the ideas presented herein. To each of these contributors, I offer my heartfelt thanks.

Mitchell Levy

September 7, 2000

By Michael Silton

CEO, Rainmaker Systems, Inc., (NASDAQ: RMKR)

Two choices: E-volve or die! Clearly, you bought this book because you have chosen to e-volve. Good choice. How will you get the most from this book? And why should you trust what it has to say?

You have probably formulated questions that you hope this book will address. And, most likely, they revolve around understanding what your customers want and what actions you can take. By asking questions as you read the book and, even more importantly, as you implement your e-volving e-strategies, you find out what works, what is out of date, and what you can add to make your results even better.

The first thing to realize about the Internet is that you are out of control. I am not talking about the rate of change and all the confusing technologies. I am talking about power in a relationship—the relationship between you and your customer. In the old world, you sold to customers. In the new world, a customer buys from you. The center of power has shifted. If you understand this and take it to heart, you'll figure out how to win when the center of power or action has shifted to your customer. A great relationship, by definition, involves two-way communication. So, how do you let your customer have the power, but still play a proactive role in helping them create successful transactions with you and your company? That's your magic question. Answer it, and you've applied what you've learned from this book.

To discover the answer, why not learn from someone who has already helped hundreds of e-companies, someone who has already seen thousands of mistakes and hundreds of intentional and accidental successes? No one is more connected with e-commerce management than Mitchell Levy. In *E-Volve-or-Die.com*, Mitchell takes us on an exploratory journey through the key issues in this area. On each page, he shares the practical experience of someone who has tried something new. Get behind the scenes to see the thought process, not just the end results. There is no better, more independent source of ideas to help you as you build your e-volved and e-volving strategy than *E-Volve-or-Die.com*.

The radical change that placed the customer at the center of the relation-ship is undeniable. Companies today are still struggling with the basics of turning all their systems, processes, and especially thoughts inside out to ac-commodate and take advantage of this change. In the true spirit of the Internet, Mitchell has also made available a Web site for continually up-dated ways to e-volve. But most importantly, this book will get you ready to e-volve your own thoughts on an ongoing basis, as long as you keep ask-ing the right questions.

I look forward to reading about your questions and successes on the *E-Volve-or-Die.com* Web site.

Michael

September 8, 2000

By Alan Naumann

President and CEO, Calico Commerce, Inc.

The next wave is coming. And it will no doubt carry some to the promised land of success, while others drown in its wake. The Internet, we know, is not a tsunami, and e-commerce was no flash flood. Rather, the Web is a series of waves that continue to roll in, fundamentally changing the velocity and experience of business.

In this book, Mitchell Levy has captured a pattern in motion and gives us both the strategic underpinnings and the practical tools we need to ride the wave of e-business success. While it's easy to become overwhelmed by the sea of information about the Internet today, Levy has sifted through the clutter. He gives us the insightful analysis necessary to anticipate what to think about next and how to implement strategies that will beat the competition.

More than ever before in business, competition is fierce. Continuous improvement is no longer merely an advantage—it is a requirement. Only those companies that e-volve will survive, and evolution now happens in real time. The most successful corporations today are those that e-volve through experimentation—they make bold moves quickly, they aggressively seek feedback from all directions, and they reinvent and adjust constantly. The most successful corporations of tomorrow will refine this process and will strike a balance between staying focused on a vision for the future and unceasingly seeking new paths by which to realize it.

The path of e-business success is shared, and companies who win in the Internet economy can't do it alone. Increasingly, customer and partner relationships are a critical element in compelling business plans, and this cooperation will continue to build momentum. While e-business does significantly shift several of the previously accepted fundamentals, one key business principle remains steady: There has to be something in it for everyone.

In e-business, this means that buyers and sellers alike must reap tangible benefits from their participation in online marketplaces and Web-based commerce channels. In the early days of e-commerce, the focus was on the buyer. Indeed, one of the most dramatic changes the Internet has to date affected is the transfer of power to buyers, in the form of information, choices, and value. The next wave, though, is empowering sellers. Technology now enables sellers to better know their customers, their competition, and themselves.

Whether selling in Net Markets, direct over the Web, or through existing channels, corporations engaged in e-business today can, more than ever, control the key factors of their own success. As technology itself has shifted from being internally to externally focused, so have the businesses who use it. Customer-facing applications are defining the next generation of software, and customer-focused organizations are those that will be most successful in e-business.

The ultimate goal, obviously, is to increase sales and grow profit margins. The means to this end, though, has more to do with creating a personalized experience for the buyer and customizing products, promotions, and pricing to meet the unique needs of each individual customer. The Web is the driver for this new approach—both to buying and selling—and the infrastructure and applications that enable it are the building blocks for the strongest business models currently under construction.

Levy has recognized this reality, and he helps readers maximize the opportunity. Opportunity is abundant. E-business is still very much in its infancy. In 1999, only 1 percent of business transactions were conducted online. By 2004, however, industry analysts expect this number to increase to 25 percent. And it certainly won't stop there. The companies who move the fastest and work the smartest right now are the companies that will reap the wealth the Internet offers.

During the next five years, we will experience the greatest degree of change in business that our economy has seen since the days of the Industrial Revolution, a transformation that spanned 30 years. This time, the change is happening globally. Indeed, international e-business opportunities will fuel many of the coming waves of change. By definition, Web-based selling channels are, to a degree, open to the world. But the same sites and the same strategies that have worked in the U.S. market do not directly translate internationally.

Again, companies looking to globalize their e-business efforts will survive only if they focus clearly on specific customer segments and incorporate real-time feedback in the effort to continuously improve. The principle behind this is simple: Businesses have to sell what, how, when, and where buyers want. Fortunately for sellers, technology now gives them the capability to achieve their own goals within the buyer-centric world.

Fortunately for all of us, visionaries like Mitchell Levy can gather, digest, and relay the principles, opportunities, and strategies most critical to e-volving with the Internet. *E-Volve-or-Die.com* is a must-read for anyone compelled to succeed in the New E-Conomy. It is the first book I've found that so closely aligns itself with my own convictions about content, customers, and change in e-business as we'll come to know it.

Alan

By Alfred Chuang

Founder, President, and Chief Operations Officer, BEA Systems, Inc.

If we learned anything from the NASDAQ meltdown in spring, and if we take anything to heart from the dot.com shakeout that continues in its wake, it should be this:

> Giving your brick and mortar company a facelift with a pretty Web site does not make an e-business.

Customers are king, yes, but if you spent all your pennies on flashy marketing and Super Bowl ads to bring them in, but you neglected to build a reliable and scalable infrastructure that could give them—*all* of them—the service they demanded when they came, you would not only dethrone your customers but also pauperize your company in the process. It's not enough to get customers to come at any cost. You must give them what they want when they come—or say goodbye forever.

While you can't predict change, you must be prepared for it. Whether it's the next Napster popping out of nowhere, a guerrilla company deciding to knock on the door of your industry from the industry next door, or a 500-point plunge in the stock market the day after tomorrow, you must quickly adapt to changes, any changes, whether they come from your internal or external environment. And if you can't, well, hey... maybe we'll see you in the next revolution.

Mitchell Levy has it right in the title of this new book: *E-Volve-or-Die.com*. The Internet is an incredible opportunity for all of us, but it is also an unforgiving place if you're not ready for prime time. Because of its global reach and instantaneous communication, customers, partners, competitors, investors, distributors, and employees all know at the same instant that your systems failed, or that your business model is reportedly unsound, or that you failed to make your numbers this quarter, or that you angered a customer who is eager to tell the world through his own tailor-made I-HATE-YOUR-COMPANY Web site. Harsh? You bet it is. Depressing? Not if you learned the lessons listed above.

In this book, Mitchell Levy addresses these lessons and more in his own inimitable style borne of a rare combination of experience and vision. He knows that the Internet requires fundamental changes in the way business is done and the way businesses are built. It's not enough to throw up a Web site and think your job is done.

In Part One of this book, Mitchell stresses the need to move beyond legacy thinking. Only by thinking out of the brick and mortar box can we develop new strategies and business models that are in tune with the global instantaneity that the Internet has created. In Parts Two and Three, Mitchell turns to a discussion of how to successfully deploy e-commerce applications and how to maintain momentum after your initial deployment. He rightly focuses on the primacy of the customer in these two sections because, no matter what else you may do well, if you don't win *and retain* customers, it's all for naught.

Our customers have always been the number one focus at BEA, and that is why 6,500 of the most successful companies in the world have trusted their business to BEA in just five years of operation.

Part Four of Mitchell's book, "E-Volving the Future," might just be the most important. At BEA, we certainly are focused on enabling companies, with our e-business infrastructure, not only to adapt to change, but *to leverage change as a competitive advantage.*

If your business is built on proprietary technology, it is set in cement. If your business is built on point products that you've wired and superglued together, you are trusting numerous vendors to update their diverse products in synchronicity (and we wish you loads of luck—you'll need it). If your business is built on a patchwork platform that requires hand-coded integration, you are racing in a rickety vehicle that may be unsafe at any speed.

What you need in order to flexibly and nimbly adapt to change is an e-business platform that provides the essential infrastructure for building an integrated e-business that can *reliably* service customers; *scale* to handle unpredictable levels of growth across the entire chain of commerce; *personalize* services for customers to capture their loyalty; *collaborate* flexibly with partners, suppliers, and customers; and *adapt* nimbly to an increasing rate of change.

That's what we believe as a company. I personally believe Mitchell's book is an essential primer for the Internet Age—and one that comes at a critical time. The dot.com hype has been brought down to earth, and e-business has finally gotten serious. What should you focus your business on? How can you refine your strategy so it works? What stages should you follow as you plan your e-commerce initiatives? How can you provide the level of service e-generation customers demand to give your e-business a real chance to succeed? Are you ready for life on the global stage? What outsourcing issues should you consider? How can you best manage legacy people, processes, and systems? And what steps must you take to "future-proof" (as we say at BEA) your business? Mitchell addresses these important questions and more in this compelling read. Enjoy, learn, and e-volve. It's a whole lot better than the alternative.

Alfred

By Peter Neupert

President and CEO, drugstore.com, inc.

In these pages, Mitchell Levy spotlights three of the imperatives of the world of e-tailing—constant experimentation, collaborating with the right partners, and keeping the customers at the center of every decision. We didn't have the benefit of his primer during the drugstore.com garage days but with the ever-sharp focus of hindsight, I can vouch that his imperatives are consistent with the guideposts we have followed in our quest to create personal relationships with consumers. Our team has learned every one of the lessons. We've made mistakes, we've stalked industry giants as partners, and we've committed thousands and thousands of hours to creating a superior customer experience. And with all of our accomplishments, we're still learning every day.

With a respect for and an intimate understanding of the many unknowns of the Web, Levy has written an insightful travelogue of emerging business principles. Will his words guide future entrepreneurs to success? No one can predict the evolution of the economy, yet I believe Levy is on target with his prescription for building a successful long-term business in today's fast-paced world: The winners must approach the endeavor holistically and comprehensively.

At drugstore.com, we focus our efforts on doing the best job we can for our customers, partners, and investors. In less than two years, we have defined an entirely new Internet category and seized market leadership. By any measure, the tenets Levy discusses are working for us. We have more customers than our competitors, and we continue to show healthy growth in all areas of our business. Using technology in unprecedented ways, the drugstore.com team works daily to empower consumers to make better, more informed healthcare decisions.

As Levy prescribes in his discussion of the critical elements of a sustainable business model, drugstore.com constructed a network of strategic partnerships, meeting consumer demand at every point where consumers interact with their drugstore.

By leveraging the Internet to enhance the customer experience, we are achieving economies of scale through alliances that offer widespread access to millions of new customers as well as co-marketing opportunities with partners that consumers know and trust.

In addition, Levy emphasizes the value of failure. At no other time in my career—be it my role leading the development of the (ultimately) ill-fated OS/2 at Microsoft, to the first days of MSNBC—have the lessons been so marked in their immediacy and poignancy. Like most of the team at drugstore.com and many of our peers in the e-commerce world, I am attracted to solving problems. I love that this revolution has attracted some of the most passionate, dynamic, and fearless personalities on the globe and I love that I have the chance to work with them everyday. No doubt, as you read Levy's chapters, you will feel a similar sense of familiarity or epiphany if you are working in the e-commerce world. For those who have yet to enter it, I suspect it will touch you sooner rather than later. And when it does, you will be glad for having read the fundamentals by Levy.

Peter

By Peter Sisson

Founder and former CEO of WineShopper.com, now Vice-Chairman and Chief Strategy Officer, wine.com

Change. Scary for some, a challenge to others, and chock full of opportunity for those who understand that building a business is about solving problems—and if nothing changes, there are no new problems to solve!! Typically, these "problems" are those of your customers, future or potential. Sometimes the problems are obvious, like the need for sharpeners after pencils were invented. Sometimes consumers do not know they have a problem, and demand needs to be created—for example, when it dawns on someone that they need a Palm V organizer.

But other problems involve the changing circumstances in which businesses operate. Often the change is technological, and certainly much of the opportunity spawned in the New E-Conomy has been the result of technological change. But other things change as well. Economic prosperity, worker skillsets, consumer preferences, access to capital, internationalization—the list of change factors is long. The constancy of change (and the need to respond) is a persistent theme in this book, culminating in the final chapter.

The need to adapt is something of which I am particularly aware. When I first met Mitchell, I was trying to get him to work at a startup I was thinking of founding called WineShopper.com. Our competition would be a sleepy company called Virtual Vineyards, with limited venture backing and a limited selection of wines. By the time Mitchell started working on this book, WineShopper.com was a company of 80 with $14 million of venture funding in the bank. A few months later, Virtual Vineyards became wine.com, and raised $30 million. The race was on, and this was late 1999, when venture capital for consumer e-commerce flowed like water. By the time Mitchell asked me to contribute to this book, WineShopper.com was a company of 200 with a total of $46 million raised, and wine.com had $90 million in their coffers! Now, as I finally write this foreword in the second half of 2000, wine.com and WineShopper.com are one company—we agreed to merge just a few weeks ago. Although there were many good strategic reasons for the merger, the sudden disappearance of venture capital support for consumer e-commerce was a sudden change we needed to address. So we adapted, taking off our boxing gloves and joining forces, instead of wasting scarce capital trying to kill each other.

Neither company could have predicted this outcome a year ago—but that is exactly the point.

If you want to learn how to figure out what type of change is in store for your company, you must read this book.

Peter

By John Mumford

Founding Partner, Crosspoint Venture Partners

From my vantage point as a venture capitalist, there has never been a more exciting time to help entrepreneurs realize their dreams. My passion for companies, as living, growing, and adapting entities, has never been stronger. The challenges and opportunities for all companies today relates to how the Internet brings power, energy, and new equations to the relationships of all the constituents of a successful business. Customer service, outsourcing, and building new and dynamic business models are three key areas where the Internet has fundamentally changed and built new relationships among these constituents, from customers to vendors. I have three deep beliefs that speak to any firm, traditional or Web-centric, that plans on being successful in the next five years:

- ▲ The Internet, combined with high-bandwidth digital transmission, will stimulate a reinvention of human commerce.

- ▲ Marketing, sales, distribution, and support functions for almost every type of business will be re-tooled.

- ▲ The e-volution will be rapid. Many existing businesses will perish. Many new ones will be born.

What is exciting about the Internet, especially to an investor, is how it is helping redefining how businesses relate to customers, partners, and suppliers. Just staying alive in this environment is like crossing the country in a '34 Ford roadster at 100 mph. You have technology that is just barely adequate to keep you on the ground, as the countryside rushes by at speeds that push every piece of your business machine to its limit. The truly brave push the metal even harder, just to hear the roar of the wind on uncharted road even faster and to see their competitors in their mirror. But do you have the strategy to match your unbridled courage? Even light speed isn't everything.

At Crosspoint, we have helped launch new Net-centric businesses that will allow existing companies to communicate, serve, and transact more effectively with their customers, employees, vendors, and channel partners. These new business-to-business networked solutions offer dramatic economic benefits to all parties and improve customer and partner relationships and satisfaction. The key to their success has been integrating internal business processes with outward facing relationships, not just to strengthen business, but to build networked e-Business. Integral to continued success is examination of success and failure, and its distillation into knowledge and e-wisdom.

Joining a startup while at Stanford Business School changed my life irrevocably. The growth of the Internet, especially e-commerce, has been driven by similar startups with the courage and conviction of an idea, a vision, and a team with the will to bring it to life and adapt in the tornado of growth. Startups today face added challenges, as well as the virtual sea of opportunities of the Internet that accelerates business relationships that make or break a company. But only at the helm of a master who knows that strategy, tactics, and constant introspection, not luck, bring fortune.

Ventures like Ariba, Hello Direct, Inmac, and Office Club (Office Depot) have ridden this sea and transformed, as well as given birth to new companies, even within themselves. Our latest vision, E2 Open, will provide a global marketplace where any computer, consumer electronics, or telecommunications company can plan, collaborate, manage, and execute supply chain transactions over the Internet. Intelligent collaboration, planned and managed successfully, ensures that a good business today will continue to thrive in a world where business relationships blossom and wither in barely a moment. E-volution and the natural selection in e-business will be measured in the strength of the relationships and combined strategies that global marketplaces create and marshal. Learn to build e-strategies.

As an investor, I watch the flurry and pace of change so close to home from my ranch in Woodside. I also see the opportunity that the Internet revolution can bring to almost anyone who can dream, work hard with undying commitment, and prosper. In a world with such cultural and economic diversity, we live in a time where individuals excel without bias, that only the greatest economic revolution in history can bring. For those born of less advantage, the knowledge gained by learning and relearning the principles of the New E-Conomy will reshape the distribution of wealth and opportunity across the entire globe—and in a time measured in years, perhaps barely a decade.

A book like this can have the impact as it did for me. Inspirational, moving, and deeply personal, showing you a direction that is clear and a path moving forward. The ideas, advice, and inspiration in this book come from the experience of being there, going there, and taking along as many people as your business can marshal.

E-volve or die—because light speed is not enough.

John

September 25, 2000

By Rob Wrubel

CEO, Ask Jeeves, Inc.

For the last decade, business has adopted the mantra of putting customers at the center of everything we do. But the Internet has challenged us to live up to this pledge in ways we never expected. Today, we're closer to our customers than we've ever been before: We have the opportunity to listen to and know them with an immediacy that was unimaginable only a few years ago.

Some managers may find themselves thinking of the old adage to be careful what you wish for.

E-Commerce leaders, however, will recognize a vast opportunity to rethink and reorganize how they respond to changing customer needs and expectations. We've seen, for example, that some of the greatest opportunities appear in less-than-obvious places. Dell completely reinvented the supply chain model and came out of nowhere to conquer the giants of computer manufacturing. eBay stitched together an international marketplace from the totally improbable fabric of garage sales and swap meets. And at Ask Jeeves, we looked at the Internet's phenomenal store of information and decided to make it accessible to anyone who had a question. By leveraging what we discovered about people's concerns and needs, we expanded into a service helping companies listen to and learn from the questions their customers ask.

Today's business mantra may be that all the rules have changed. Like a lot of slogans, this saying contains an important element of truth. But the most successful companies in the Internet age will balance a rapid adaptation to change with a solid commitment to core values. Revolutionary rethinking has to be backed up with careful planning and flawless execution. And, yes, the customer should be at the center of our offices, our supply chains, our product design and marketing sessions, our board meetings, and our Web sites.

In this demanding and exhilarating environment, Mitchell Levy's book offers valuable, practical steps to understanding how to build and manage an e-commerce company.

Rob

September 8, 2000

By Steven J. Snyder, Ph.D.
Co-Founder, President, and Chief Executive Officer, Net Perceptions, Inc.

Do you get it yet? Have you seen the light?

The business world is in the throes of a catharsis that's moving at an Internet-driven pace. Buying and selling opportunities now regularly come and go in microseconds, and that means businesses that plan to be among those that endure must be positioned to assess the landscape quickly, act decisively, and move rapidly to ensure they are making the most of every possible contact.

This book by Mitchell Levy offers provocative insight into how this new world is shaping up and what is required to make sure your company survives, adapts, grows, and thrives. It lays out well what we who have been in the industry for years have learned through experience—that success depends on the ability to change before change becomes necessary.

I invite you to pay particular attention to Chapters 5, 8, and 10, in which Levy focuses on the significant elements of content, customer expectations, and marketing. The reality of constant change is a common thread that ties these sections together.

As Levy notes in Chapters 5 and 10, the ability to constantly maintain and e-volve content that is fresh and appropriate for individual customers is an art and a science. It requires the ability to deeply analyze the relationships between each customer, your products, and your promotions. You have to analyze that information quickly, and your infrastructure must allow for on-the-fly content change that is meaningful to the user. The good news is that the merger of this art and science is achieved through the application of advanced technology.

Chapter 8 deals with customer expectations. Who doesn't acknowledge that customer desires are always in flux? But this nuance of business is magnified because the Internet has not only created a new channel for interaction, but it has now established the ability to link all the points of contact a business has with its customers. The customers know this, and they're demanding a response. Again, the technology is there to handle this integration.

Someone once said, "To change and to change for the better are two different things." This book presents guidance on how to make sure your business does the latter.

Steven

By Monte Zweben

CEO, Blue Martini Software

With *E-Volve-or-Die.com*, Mitchell Levy has captured and distilled the essence of today's e-commerce practices. The following chapters explain exactly what businesses need to enact successful commerce on the Internet. I recommend that you pay especially close attention to Chapter 1, in which Mitchell sheds new light on the latest mindset that is required to be successful on the Internet, and Chapter 4, in which he really zeroes in on the critical issues involved in successfully interacting with customers. Mitchell leaves no stone unturned in his powerful story, but let me try to draw out a few points that I feel are especially significant.

When e-commerce first emerged, most observers thought that it would become a powerful marketing force that operated independently of existing channels. This impression was reinforced by the seeming success, especially in the capital markets, of Web-only retailers such as Amazon and eToys. As traditional businesses recognized the strategic importance of the Internet and began to follow suit, they naturally tended to follow the same strategy that had been established by the e-tail pioneers. The results of this disconnected effort were dissatisfaction when online customers realized purchases could not simply be returned to a local store, reseller resentment as they were cut out of the supply chain, and brand dilution in the online marketplace. Even established brands, when first getting online, felt the pull to develop separate on- and offline operations, where the online operations operated in a vacuum from the physical stores with separate inventory, separate information systems, and separate exchange and return systems.

The notable move away from a Web-only e-tailing business model in a number of prominent cases has led both click and mortar and click-only retailers to the realization that their approach to e-commerce should be consistent with and coordinated to their other marketing channels. Companies should present a single face that is personalized to their customers' individual requirements and unique characteristics. After all, a company's online customers are, for the most part, the same people that come into their stores. For example, a customer should be able to browse, compare, and purchase products on a company's Web site and then choose to pick up the goods at the store to avoid shipping costs and wait time. Similarly, a business-to-business customer should be able to identify the product through an email campaign, then establish mutually agreeable terms with a salesperson on the telephone, and subsequently execute recurring transactions on the company's Web site according to the negotiated terms.

Polaroid is a company in the B2B space that has successfully addressed channel conflict issues. The company's Polaroidwork.com site delivers business and professional users access to real-time imaging solutions through resellers and is the cornerstone of the Polaroid B2B business model. The site addresses the fact that individual resellers need the support of a well-recognized branding campaign to help translate buyers' needs into solutions. Without this, there can often be a considerable time lag between the Web site visit and the sale. To streamline the sales process, Polaroid's site performs a needs analysis to suggest solutions to customer problems. Extensive product content is provided to the end-customer to accelerate the purchase decision. The customer is then redirected to the reseller's Web site to complete the order. Polaroid has also found an easy way to manage content and product information and to personalize each interaction with business-to-business customers. Their business users can easily update content without the involvement of IT resources and use data warehousing, data mining, reporting, and personalization capabilities to create a tailored customer experience.

And this is only the beginning of a new generation of e-commerce that typifies the term "e-volve." For example, visionaries are working on collaborative shopping applications that allow two or more friends to shop online together, even when sitting halfway around the world from each other. Just as shopping in a retail store is usually a social experience, collaborative shopping will help to socialize e-commerce by giving friends the opportunity to convince one another to buy things. The result should be substantially higher conversion rates.

The bottom line, and one of the most important things that can be taken away from Mitchell's comprehensive book, is that the first generation of Web-only retailing has provided extremely valuable lessons about customer interaction. You need to respond by making sure your business takes advantage of multiple touch points, including integration with traditional channels. Mitchell's book also makes it crystal clear that businesses today have zero time to lose in implementing these lessons.

Monte

By Rick Steele
President and CEO, kinkos.com

Survival of the fittest. Most of us were taught about Darwin's theory in early science classes, which suggests that the survival of groups of animals and plants is contingent upon their ability to successfully adapt to their environments. Darwin's theory of natural selection is no less valid in the world of business, where those companies that are slow to adjust to change—whether mandated by Wall Street, competition, or customers—are often removed from the landscape by the same ruthless imperative that governs their biological counterparts.

Whereas Darwin studied change that occurred over many centuries, today we are forced to look at the evolution and survival of businesses in terms of years, months, and even days. When technological advances and competitive demands are coming at a pace so dizzying that businesses sometimes feel they have their hands full just keeping up, change is constant and must be looked upon as an opportunity.

Without a doubt, the Internet, and the resulting "E-Conomy," has been the catalyst of change in today's fast-paced high-intensity business climate. In just a matter of years, the E-Conomy has had a phenomenal and profound impact on so many facets of our lives, from the way we work and play to the way we shop and communicate. The emerging trends, explosive market conditions, and e-volving technologies of the 1990s provided tremendous global opportunities for those of us who were—and are—willing to seize them.

And, because the Internet is here to stay for the foreseeable future, those businesses that don't take heed and that ignore the advice presented in the pages that follow, risk becoming the next victims of the Internet Age. For survival in today's competitive environment requires a total rethinking of the old ways of doing business—from marketing and customer service to establishing business partnerships and managing employees. In chapter after chapter, Mitchell Levy does an excellent job of examining how business leaders are transforming strategies and operations in response to the growing impact of the Internet on their companies.

It seems that today's fittest companies are those that are in a constant state of careful, honest re-evaluation and are able to adapt to their changing environments. In this book, Mitchell's examination of management challenges provides readers with emerging trends and thought-provoking cases, which will encourage the re-thinking that is necessary to succeed. One thing you will find is that many industry leaders approach this exercise with an open mind, a flexible plan, and a commitment to two things: change and the customer.

Every day, I apply these very principles to my own company, which has seen numerous changes over the years and has e-volved from a contract-based multimedia design company founded in 1994. While I am not ashamed to say that the business model, product line, customer base, and marketing strategies have changed drastically throughout this e-volution, I am proud to tell you that two things have remained untouched every step of the way.

You guessed it, they are my commitment to 1) changing the company in response to market, competitive, and customer demands and 2) doing what is best for the customer every single time.

Rick

By Love Goel

CEO, Personify

If I were to make one observation about the human condition, and the state of companies in America today—I would have to say we are in the midst of an e-volution revolution. Companies and leaders are e-volving at an exponential rate compared to even twenty years ago, when the PC was being invented. A new breed of entrepreneurial ventures in the late twentieth century are breaking the old paradigms by capitalizing on technological innovation, speed, customer focus, availability of venture capital, and a creative workforce. They created new businesses and new business rules and are at the dawn of a new age that has redefined successful companies, the leaders who run them, the leadership styles that work, and the personal rewards bestowed on those who succeed.

Amidst all this change, there are some constants. For example, there is no substitute—as a lot of the new breed of entrepreneurs are discovering—for profitability, strong leadership, integrity, and talented people. Some knew this and built their companies to last, some have learned this lesson the hard way, and yet others have learned it too late or not at all.

The old breed has taken a roller coaster ride (not for the weak of heart) where the fear of God was basically put into them—the fear of being Amazoned (Retail), Yahooed (Media), Etoyed (Toys), or what-have-you for your particular sector. Today they breathe easier knowing they are not yet extinct, but they are losing dollars, mindshare, and most importantly customer relationships to the new breed of players. The old breed is too large, too disorganized, unable to galvanize resources to focus, unable to attract world-class talent, and unable to free up the capital to compete effectively. Their time might not have caught up with them yet, but the wheels of e-volution are turning at an ever-furious pace. There is still too much venture capital chasing good ideas that will kill the old breed—and this time around, the threat will come from even more credible players with better business models, better leaders, and even more effective execution.

As an observer and a participant in this e-volution, I have had an opportunity to learn and experience firsthand the ups and downs of the ride we are on. I've had the tremendous opportunity to work in transforming and building enterprises among the old breed. Early in my consulting career, I helped large companies like Cargill, Carlson, Sears, Supervalu, and Prudential prepare for the future; then, in 1998, I had the privilege of helping launch and build, in a Fortune 1000 company, Fingerhut Business Services, the nation's largest fulfillment and direct-to-the-consumer services provider that helps clients like walmart.com, etoys, Levi's, and Pier 1; and then, in 1999, I helped create one of the largest e-commerce networks in the world for Federated Department Stores, the parent of Macy's and Bloomingdale's, where our 17 properties did more than $200 million in e-commerce revenues. Recently, I have had the privilege of serving as CEO of Personify, a San Francisco-based profiling, analytics, and personalization software company that is helping e-business better understand their business and customers in order to rapidly accelerate growth and profitability.

From this perspective, I found the book quite engaging, introspective, and candid. I know you will enjoy and appreciate this collection of first-hand insights from so many leaders in the e-volution revolution. Whether you are a CEO leading the old economy charge or a lieutenant helping build a New E-Conomy venture, you will find timeless truths about the (r)e-volutionary challenges in developing new business models, the leadership experience, and the e-volution process that will lead to the extinction of many companies we know and love.

Love

By Jim Sterne

President, Target Marketing

When asked for examples of truly great customer service, one of my seminar attendees told the story of a recent visit to Amazon.com. He recounted how easy it was to find the book he wanted… how easy it was to make the purchase… how delighted he was when the item actually showed up on his doorstep the very next day. Another participant pointed out how sad it was that the first man was delighted because a company he was doing business with made a promise and actually stuck with it. The rest of us chuckled, but then we realized our level of expectation in most stores is rather low. Our online expectations are considerably higher.

You've been thinking about and working on your Web site and Internet integration for years, but you don't expect to see the end of the tunnel anytime soon. The competitive landscape continues to change at a dizzying pace. *E-Volve-or-Die.com* gives you a current bird's-eye-view of the lay of the land—something you are going to need to keep up with customer expectations.

Keeping your customers no longer rests in their willingness to stay with you out of blind loyalty or inertia. Consumers and business buyers are becoming more and more sophisticated and getting used to better and better service. People expect instant access to product information, order status information, and specific account information. Customers know that you keep information about them in computers. The expectation is that your computers can talk to each other and customers can access every bit of account information.

What was the last order I placed?

Has it shipped yet?

When will it be delivered?

When will my backorder be filled?

Are there any alternative products I can get faster?

Expectations continue to rise dramatically. If you have a real-time database with all that information in it, customers expect you to have a Web server capable of fetching that information and dynamically delivering it at the click of a mouse.

Who is my sales rep?

How much have I ordered in the past six months?

When will I hit the next discount level?

How many frequent flier miles do I have?

When will I need my next tune-up?

When will my membership expire?

Who is authorized to place an order over $5,000?

What is my current credit aging?

What do you mean I can't find out on your Web site? What do you mean you haven't linked your Web site to your back-end corporate data center? I can get that information 24 hours a day, seven days a week from your competitor...

Chapter 8, "New Expectations for Customer Service," zeroes in on this customer expectation inflation and how online customer service has changed from a unique new feature to a competitive necessity. Learn what you need to do within your company to manage new customer's expectations and e-volve your company.

In October 1998, Ford Motor Company put out a memo to its suppliers that was pure Back-to-the-Future. "Allow them to buy supplies and raw materials over the Internet by June 1999," said the memo, "or they will take their business elsewhere." Companies like Snap-On, the makers of high-end hand and power tools, woke up and smelled more than 10 percent of their income at risk. It was time to move from curious to serious about the Web.

Making your company easier to do business with is today's great competitive edge. Customers expect the best price. They expect fast service. They expect to get answers instead of being put on hold until dawn. They will flock to buy from you if you can save them ten minutes here and twenty minutes there.

Take a moment to look at your competitors' efforts on the Web. Take a moment every week. It's the only way you're going to stay ahead of the game. What can you offer that your competitors cannot? If you can't improve your products any more and you can't lower your price any more, you can only improve your service.

Why do your customers need service twenty-four hours a day, seven days a week? Because that's when they're working. Engineers, operations managers, human resource workers, marketing executives, and others have always burned the midnight oil to finish projects. More and more virtual corporation partners are working at home and getting online after the kids are asleep. These people need answers at all hours, not just from nine to five, and certainly not just in your time zone.

Successful customer service always means looking at your products, your company, and your customer-service methods through your customers' eyes. The customer doesn't care if your company is organized by product line, business unit, or spheres of political influence. The customer wants his or her question answered or problem solved—and now.

The most important task for a customer service Web builder to undertake is figuring out what the customer will want to see, want to learn, and want to get out of the experience—every time they contact your company.

Chapter 4, "Customer Touch Points," offers insight into capturing the attention of your customers and walks through the five phases of customer/company interaction. Customers are starting to get accustomed to CRM (customer relationship management) and expect you to provide more and more and better and better service. Even if you outsource the touch point, you can't lose control of your customer interactions.

How do you continue to cater to customers on an ongoing basis? It may be well worth the effort to ask them directly, "As you do business with us via our Web site, what additional information would you like us to show? What functionality would you like us to add?"

As your and your competitors' Internet integration continues, your customers are going to have higher and higher expectations. You'll need to stay one step ahead of them. You need to e-volve or die.

Jim Sterne

Introduction

Thanks for picking up this book. Once you see what's inside, I'm sure you won't be able to put it down. The book is about e-volution, it's about survival, it's about the transition from the Industrial Age to the Internet Age, and it's about the change that will occur in the business world for which most of us are unprepared.

I have a passion for educating and, in particular, helping people and companies understand how they can make change work for them; in other words, helping people and companies e-volve. As President of ECnow.com, my goal is to help companies transition from the Industrial Age to the Internet Age. I do this through public and private speaking, teaching, and strategic consulting, as the content aggregator for the San Jose State University Professional Development (SJSU-PD) E-Commerce Management (ECM) Certificate Program (**http://ecmtraining. com/sjsu**), as chair for Comdex Spring and Fall, as well as my own Symposiums (ECMsym.com), and the author of my monthly ECM newsletter (ECMgt.com). If you're curious, you can view a more detailed biography at this web location: http://ecnow.com/ml_bio.htm

I decided to write this book for three reasons:

> Because this vehicle (a physical book) is still a great mechanism for communication and I want to reach as many people/companies as possible

> I thought it would be fun—and it was—to interview and share opinions with some of the best practitioners in the ECM world

> I wanted to document, as best as I can, my thoughts on the issues that need to be raised and the questions that need to be asked in making this transition

The book is about deploying, managing and e-volving e-commerce within corporations. It's about change. The e-volve-or-die.com books series will be a continuous stream of books focused on various aspects of ECM told by some of the best practitioners in the field. Let me know if you have suggestions for future titles and what book you'd like to see next. You can e-mail me at Mitchell.Levy.E-volve@ecnow.com.

I'm sure you noticed the multiple forewords for this book. Although this is a bit unusual for a business book. I wanted to let you hear directly from a number of the top business people their views on managing, deploying, and e-volving e-commerce. I'm glad they decided to take the time to contribute to this effort and we are all better off from their wisdom and stories.

This book is divided into four main sections and three appendices. Throughout the book I have strategically placed provocative questions for you to think about as you go through each chapter; look for these in the side margins. I have also added illustrations to help guide you through the content. More than 50 executives from companies all over the world have contributed content and you will find numerous quotes throughout the book. The company descriptions of executives interviewed can be found in the end notes section at the back of the book. A more detailed description of the companies, the quoters' biographies and all quotes can be found on the *E-Volve-or-Die.com* Web site.

The content is arranged in four parts that characterize the New E-conomy, address the issues involved in deploying e-commerce and maintaining momentum, and e-volving into the future. Part One is focused on the New E-Conomy, and is a starting point for exploring new ways to think about business and the many ways to configure effective business models that include customers, partners, and often competitors. In Part One, I set the foundation for the transition from the Industrial Age to the Internet Age and the changes that may be required to legacy systems, legacy processes, and legacy people. Survival in the Internet Age will require thinking outside the box. Constantly changing business models represent challenges and opportunities, and they are explored in detail in Chapter 2, "Business Models for the E-Conomy."

Part Two is focused on the work required to deploy e-commerce from a management perspective. Any business transformation must begin with planning, and the key elements and a proven approach are addressed in Chapter 3, "The Plan is the Thing." Customers must be at the heart of any company, and the role of the customer is becoming even greater in the New E-conomy. Customer relationship management and customer touch points are addressed in Chapter 4, "Customer Touch Points." Content and its relationship to successful e-commerce deployment is the focus of Chapter 5, "Content Will Always Be King." Globalization and related business challenges are addressed in detail in Chapter 6, "Instant Global Presence." Chapter 7, "Outsourcing is Always an Option," looks at outsourcing as an option for fast deployment and competitive advantage. By the time you complete Part Two, you will have a good idea of some of the decisions you will need to make regarding the e-volution of your company.

In Part Three I have included content that is critical for maintaining and managing e-commerce. The changing world of customer service is explored in Chapter 8, "New Expectations for Customer Service," along with its impact on your business processes. People management is one of the biggest challenges and the key to success in transforming the company into the Internet Age, as addressed in Chapter 9, "Managing the E-Commerce Organization." Marketing must e-volve and change in order to survive, and much creativity and focus is needed, as addressed in Chapter 10, "Ongoing Internet Marketing." Legal issues have always impacted how we do business, and e-commerce is no exception. Chapter 11, "The Law Catches Up to E-Business," covers the legal issues that every executive must be aware of as we move forward in the Internet Age.

Part Four is about surviving and e-volving into the future. This section is about what is likely to happen in the future, based on current trends as well as real-world people's opinions. Chapter 12, "Shifting Markets," is about opportunities that are created by shifting global markets and technology, and includes suggestions on how to capitalize on these opportunities. Chapter 13, "A View From the Real World," is a candid collection of predictions from people who are in the midst of transforming their companies into the Internet Age. Chapter 14, "Change is Constant, Change is Good," is all about change and adapting to it as we move into the future. I have also included my view of e-commerce in the year 2025, to stimulate thinking about what you can do now to prepare for this new world. Chapter 14 concludes with a series of pages where you can begin to plan your e-volutionary path.

Appendix A, "Case Studies," contains three exciting case studies from companies who are successfully e-volving. UPS, Office Depot, and Cardinal Health share their experiences and lessons learned that relate to nearly every chapter in this book. Appendix B, "E-Commerce Primer," identifies the best sources for e-commerce terminology. Appendix C, "Resources," is a summary of printed and online resources that will help supplement the content in this book.

In terms of using this book, I have 10 different suggestions on how to read it:

> Sit down with a pot of coffee, kick back, and enjoy the entire book.

> Read the first paragraph and concluding paragraph for each chapter.

Read the "E-Volutionary Tactics" at the end of each chapter.

Go online **http://www.e-volve-or-die.com** and read just the quotes from more than 40 ECM strategists and practitioners interviewed for this book.

Read Chapter 13 and the middle section of Chapter 14 to see the predicted trends for 2001 and for business in the year 2025 (if you know the future, or have a glimpse of it, you can start preparing today).

Read Appendix A, which contains case studies of three companies who are applying various concepts covered in the book (UPS, Office Depot, and Cardinal Health).

Randomly read chapters that catch your interest

Utilize Appendix B as a primer and Appendix C to beef up your day-to-day knowledge of ECM.

Don't forget to use the worksheets that are located at the end of Chapter 14.

Check the web site for updated content (**www.e-volve-or-die.com**).

Please apply one or all of these suggestions.

Will the book change your life? I don't think so. Will it help? Absolutely, if you want it to.

At the SJSU-PD ECM program, I have seen the change that occurs in people that are introduced to the concepts and workings contained in this book. Actually 75 percent do. They change their attitudes and perceptions toward the Internet age, typically resulting in a change in everything they do, including their interests at work and home and how their companies should approach this transition. It's absolutely amazing.

I wanted to close this introduction with a story of my son, Duncan. For those of you who have kids, you will know exactly what I'm talking about. For those who don't, you'll have to work with me. Let me start off by saying, kids are amazing. Duncan has forced me to see life through a whole new set of lenses. He's fun to be around, and it's amazing that at the age of two, he causes me to rethink everything. I won't talk about the obvious stuff, but maybe the not so obvious. To Duncan, when he receives a gift, the wrapping paper and box is as exciting a gift as whatever is inside. Trying to rush the unwrapping experience kills Duncan's joy of playing with the box. It makes one wonder what treasures we walk by and pass up every day, expecting the pay off to be something else.

The most exciting thing he does is when he walks into a pristine room. He'll look around, envisions the state he'd like the room to be in (he does this by rolling his eyes), and then declares his intentions. He says the word "mess," which acts as both a verb and a noun. It is a declaration of what he is about to do as well as the fact that he has the authority to do this. The onslaught that follows must be seen to be believed. For those of you reading this book, it's very simple—you need to do the same thing. You need to look at the shape and structure your companies are now in, and you need to change it all—your legacy systems, processes, and people as well as the relationships with your customers, partners, and employees. Everything needs to be re-evaluated through the "new" lenses of the holistic Internet-enabled entity. To do so, you need to start by creating a mess. So, in the words of Duncan Levy, go out and create your own "MESS." Then, restructure your organization around the holistic Internet-enabled entity.

Mitchell Levy
December 2000

The New E-Conomy

1 E-Commerce Thinking   11

2 Business Models for the E-Conomy   25

E-Commerce Thinking

NO ONE KNOWS what the future of e-commerce will bring. It's up to

you, the reader, to figure it out. Think about it, experiment, and make it

happen. Every organization and company will find its own way of

e-volving e-commerce. You have the answers…you won't find them in

the back of the book. However, in this chapter, you will find a few guide-

lines on working through the thinking process. More importantly, I will

continually challenge you with the questions you need to ask in order

to think creatively. If you are prepared to set aside all preconceived

▶▶

notions or definitions of what the industry says e-commerce represents, you will be able to create the future. It's time to get started.

What's your definition of e-commerce?

What is e-commerce, anyway? Is it the same thing as e-business, or any other term with an "e-" prefix in front of it (or "m-" for mobile or "c-" for contextual or "d-" for dynamic or "g-" for global or "xyz-" for the next great idea)? E-Commerce and e-business are synonymous, at least in this book. When the term "e-commerce" was first used, it implied secure financial transactions over a public or private network. But it's more than that, just like commerce is more than conducting financial transactions. It encompasses all the interactions that businesses engage in: between a company and its customers, between a company and its partners, between a company and its employees, and between any participants in the company's value chain. Not all of these interactions involve the exchange of money. That's why e-commerce means e-business, which really means business—it encompasses all aspects and functions of a company. With this expanded degree of interaction, we now have more complexity to manage. That's the downside (and if you're not scared yet, you should be). There's also a tremendous upside: in terms of the future of e-commerce, there are no limits. If creative thinking is employed, there will be an endless supply of new business opportunities. It is a new frontier—the beginning of the Internet age. But are we there yet, or are we still stuck in the Industrial Age?

From the Industrial Age to the Internet Age

Are we really in the Internet Age yet?

At the start of the 21st century, we are at the beginning of a tremendous new social and economic phase. The Internet has created a completely new way of interacting with people in both our professional and personal lives. To try to understand the magnitude of the transition we're in, picture a farmer tilling crops with a team of oxen at the turn of the 20th century. How could that 19th-century farmer possibly imagine the industrial revolution that would transform the world in the 20th century?

We are at a similar point today, facing forward to the Internet Age. However, with the exception of a very few companies who are experimenting, we are not there yet. We can only see the path (see Figure 1.1). In order to move down this path, we need to adjust our thinking.

E-Commerce and the Internet have enabled huge amounts of information never before assembled to be transmitted and distributed universally, with tremendous economic value to everyone concerned. This phenomenon has brought economic pressure as well as opportunities. Internet-related technology spending (to develop infrastructure) cuts across just about every industry sector today: manufacturing, financial services, government, communications, retail, health care, utilities, education, and construction. No sector of the economy is left untouched by the influence of the Internet. Any industry mired in paperwork and inefficient processes that skew the natural order of supply and demand is open to change.

But most companies who have embraced the Internet so far see the Internet as a technology or a productivity improvement tool, not as a model for transforming business and the way we think about it. The Internet should be thought of as an invisible engine for our business and processes—integrated so that it becomes second nature to what we do. The Internet has created the path. Although a few early adopters have started, the rest of us must choose when we will start the journey, how far we will go, and what we will do when we're on the path.

The New Internet Customer

Customers are adopting e-commerce technology at an unprecedented rate. As a result, customers now wield more power than ever before. The bar has been raised in terms of customer

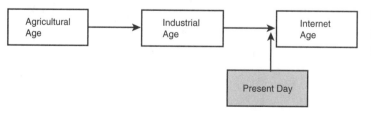

Figure 1.1

We are just beginning to see the path of the Internet Age.

satisfaction and expectations of service—and that extends to both the online and offline worlds. This is true in the business-to-business (B2B) arena (such as Cisco Systems, VerticalNet, Ariba, Ventro, Rapt, Calico, and other companies discussed in this book) as well as the business-to-consumer (B2C) arena (Priceline, Mercata, Bluelight, Wine.com, Egghead.com and many other companies discussed in this book). Gone are the old days when companies could afford to lose a few customers here and there. Word of bad customer service now spreads online like wildfire.

At the most basic level, online customers expect service, speed, and easy access. They want a positive customer experience every time, and if they don't get that, they are one click away from your competitor. It's not enough to just have low prices or the convenience of ordering online. Customers want updated content and a site that is always functioning, is easy to use, and offers fast response time—from both the technology and the human elements. Doing business with a company via their Web site should be identical to or better than doing business with them via any other venue (in person, over the phone, by fax, and so on). Companies must focus their resources on creating the right online environment that presents a seamless, integrated presence in order to keep their customers coming back. It is necessary for survival. In a digital economy, all processes must be linked and integrated; customers expect this. Also, customer touch points should be considered assets of the firm.

To effectively compete, companies must offer their customers new ways to interact with the company and new business models, such as customers naming their own prices for goods and services (Priceline), or customers who expect to bid for goods and services in an auction (eBay), or a reverse auction environment (eLance). The new Internet customers want the flexibility to buy according to the universal supply and demand that exists on the Internet. Companies who embrace this philosophy and develop creative ways to engage customers and keep them coming back will be the winners. Catching up and reclaiming ground in the marketplace is brutal in the Internet Age.

Current Philosophy Toward Integrating the Internet

Most existing companies who have had to face the Internet have thought about it in one of these ways:

> "We'll just start a new division and let them worry about the e-commerce stuff."

> OR:

> "Have the IT department look into that—we'll just make it part of our existing operations."

> OR:

> "Let's start by just setting up a Web site and see how it goes. Maybe it'll be a passing fad, and then we'll get back to business."

Even some of today's new dot.com companies don't necessarily start up their operations with Internet-enabled e-commerce business models. Some of the same statements listed above have been uttered by people in new companies as well. This is the wrong kind of thinking. E-Commerce is here to stay—as a potent business tool for a company's survival and growth. After telephones, electricity, and running water, we never move backwards. The sweep into a digital world is irreversible. It must be thought of as the way a company does business. It needs to be integrated across all departments, across all functional areas, and this philosophy must be engrained in every employee. All functional areas in a company need to be redefined for the Internet Age (as discussed in detail in Chapter 9, "Managing the E-Commerce Organization"). Existing and mature companies must quickly adapt. New companies must adopt this new way of doing business from the outset. This new business environment requires renewed objectivity and creativity in strategic thinking and execution.

Are you really integrating the Internet?

E-Commerce can be simple to manage, but not within the simple paradigm in which companies do business—regardless of how long the company has been in existence. To envision the scope of managing e-commerce, think about who has responsibility for these business issues in the average company:

▲ What's the company's 30-second vision statement, and who makes sure everyone in the company's value Web can recite it?

▲ Does everyone in the company know his or her performance goals relative to delivering upon the company's vision statement?

▲ Does the customer have direct input to making changes in products, as well as access to executive staff?

▲ Who makes sure employees and partners in the value web are happy?

▲ Who listens to customer complaints?

▲ Who updates the Web content?

▲ Who makes sure the Web content is consistent with the company image?

▲ Who (or which system or process) changes price points dynamically as a function of new customer relationships?

E-Commerce touches all these areas in the company, plus a whole lot more. All the business processes and all the interface points among employees and with customers and partners are affected by these decisions. Integrating the Internet into the everyday business lives of the company is what it takes (see Figure 1.2). The corporate identity should become the company's URL and vice versa. That's the level of thinking that is required throughout the organization. Few companies are able to effectively do this yet, but some are trying hard, such as Amazon.com and HPShopping.com. This doesn't mean that the whole organization becomes a dot.com, but rather that the whole organization must become Internet-savvy. They need to understand how to e-volve going forward.

The Holistic, Internet-Enabled Entity

The most important part of e-commerce thinking is to think "big picture." According to Webster, *holistic* means "dealing with wholes or integrated systems rather than with their parts."

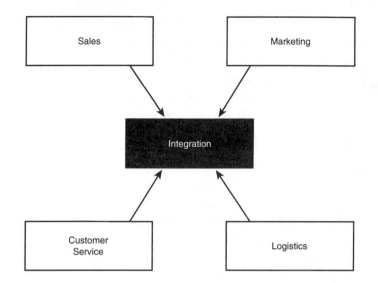

Figure 1.2

All processes in the company must integrate the Internet, where appropriate.

That is how you need to think about your company (your entity). *Internet-enabled* means that the organization is *able* to conduct business via the Internet. However, the business may choose to use or not use the Internet. Your goal should be to think through how your company can achieve this state. It will require integration of all your systems, processes, and people into a smoothly functioning organization for the Internet Age. And throughout this integrated organization, you need to maintain a 360-degree view of the customer.

True Internet Integration

Developing an Internet integration strategy and then implementing it successfully across the company takes commitment, resources, constant communication, training, and the willingness to change the way the company operates. It also requires creative thinking on the part of all the organizations involved. Several companies have accomplished this, as you will see throughout the book. In Appendix A, "Case Studies," you will learn how UPS, Office Depot, and Cardinal Health have put creative thinking into action. Sometimes it's done incrementally, and sometimes all at once. Hopefully the examples used in this book will offer some ideas of what you can do to achieve true Internet integration.

On the path to true Internet integration, you need to experiment with new ideas and new ways of doing business—with a focus on people, systems, and processes. These experiments will lead to positive and also negative results, but they will greatly contribute to the learning curve for the company.

Failure Is a Good Thing

The approach of trial and error may be an effective way to integrate the Internet and design an e-commerce operational scheme. A lot will depend on how flexible the organization is in terms of experimenting with new business processes. Employees should be rewarded for failing because it is through experimentation that creative solutions can be found. When failure occurs, the spending stops. People must regroup and go in another direction, with new knowledge of what some of the limits might be. However, it is also important to learn from experimentation and failure, and companies must take the time to do that as they go along.

Not only is it necessary to experiment in the initial phases of setting up and deploying e-commerce, but it is even more crucial to experiment after e-commerce is established as part of a business entity. Businesses who can learn to adapt and change through creative thinking will thrive in the Internet Age. Experimentation is required in order to maintain and e-volve e-commerce within the company, and all three stages (deployment, maintenance, and evolution) need to be managed effectively. (See Figure 1.3.)

Thinking Outside the Box

Companies must decide how and when they will make the necessary changes for business survival and growth—internally and externally. The e-volution of e-commerce forces creativity in that it requires entities who previously were separate to work together in different ways. Sometimes these entities include competitors, as well. Building and nurturing these new relationships requires creative approaches. It requires communication and creative thinking.

The old way of business thinking involved organizing an annual offsite meeting with key managers, bringing in a facilitator,

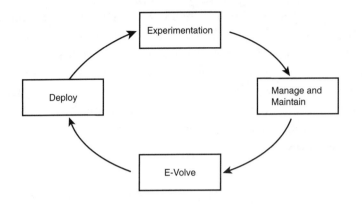

Figure 1.3

To effectively deploy, manage/maintain, and e-volve, e-commerce requires experimentation.

engaging in groupthink for a few days, and formulating a five-year plan. That approach doesn't work anymore. The new e-conomy moves too rapidly; it is now necessary for every key manager to constantly re-evaluate strategy. The re-evaluation process also requires constant gathering and analysis of business intelligence and assessing what's happening in the outside world. Evaluation of metrics and looking at results of business experiments are also key. Five-year plans have been replaced by small, nimble six- to twelve-month plans. And every department in a company needs to be nimble enough to shift course rapidly if necessary in order to remain competitive. It's difficult today to imagine a corporate strategy lasting longer than 18 months.

Creativity is becoming essential for success in the e-commerce marketplace. All employees should be encouraged to engage in creative brainstorming, including regularly scheduled sessions to develop new ideas and approaches to solve business problems. Everyone has the capacity to be creative, but individuals may differ in terms of how they access and express creative ideas. For some people, external cues in the environment may stimulate creativity, and for others, ideas may arise intuitively from within. Regardless of how people think creatively, they should be given opportunities and time to do this and should be encouraged to express their ideas in the appropriate forum. Ford, for example, recently gave all 300,000 employees a computer with unlimited access to the Internet for a couple dollars per month—a great step toward facilitating open/creative communication among all levels of the organization.

When was your last creative thought?

In recent years, a lot of attention has been given to the concept of "thinking outside the box." This phrase refers to a person's ability to use his imagination to find new ways of looking at things that lay outside the most widely accepted way of looking at things. It means throwing away boundaries and structure in order to find new points of view. Many people have written books on this subject; see Appendix C, "Resources," for a list of resources. (See Figure 1.4.)

With the advent of e-commerce, there really isn't a "box" yet. That's the good news. There is tremendous opportunity to be creative, and "no" constraints apply. Internet-related technology knows no boundaries, so the business opportunities are unbounded. The bad news is that you have to constantly come up with creative ideas before your competitors do, and that requires constant innovation, which is difficult to sustain, even in new companies. To do nothing—that is, to *not* e-volve—is to die!

Current Trends That Affect Thinking

Everyone in business and the media seems to have an opinion about where e-commerce is going. Many interesting trends are reported by people who are in the business of studying the business of e-commerce.

Figure 1.4

E-volving your company requires thinking outside the box.

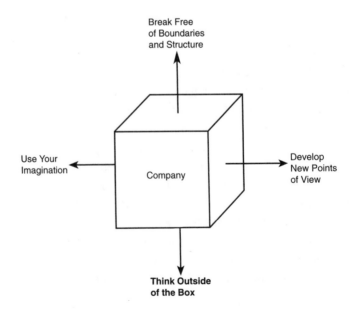

ECnow.com conducts online surveys to test the top 10 trends in e-commerce each year and writes about them monthly in the premier online ECM e-zine, ECMgt.com (**http://ecmgt.com**). Survey data is provided by real individuals and organizations who routinely practice and manage e-commerce.

What trends do you think will happen?

1999's Top Ten Trends

1. While consumer-based security concerns continue to decrease, privacy concerns will increase, leading companies to focus on the non-monetary forms of currency (time, attention, and trust).

2. Companies will begin to recognize that customer service will become the point of differentiation.

3. Outsourcing EC functions will become very popular.

4. More top-level executives will focus on and be responsible for EC.

5. There will be a dramatic increase in access speeds of technology that connects to the Web and integrates EC applications.

6. Growth of affinity groups will continue.

7. Price transparency will continue.

8. Shopping, impulse buying, and price-driven buying will take hold—special EC function keys will appear on keyboards.

9. A non-U.S. player will dominate some e-commerce space.

10. 1999 and 2000 will be the years of "show me the money" for EC enterprises.

2000's Top Ten Trends

1. **B2B Growth Continues its Dramatic Pace:** B2B growth will continue at its dramatic 1999 pace, leading to more liquidity in the B2B exchanges and inter-organizational virtual enterprises. Part of this growth will stem from the B2B practitioners borrowing successful techniques already proven in the B2C marketplace.

2. **M&A Activity Escalates:** Private, public, traditional and newly created corporate venture capital funds will increase the pace of mergers and acquisitions.

   We will continue to see the "dot.coms" snapping up physical real estate. In addition to technology and market share as reasons for acquisition, companies will be acquired for their employee base (technical and managerial).

3. **Privacy Concerns Increase:** Privacy concerns will increase in the U.S. as the public becomes more aware of how their Web site activity can be tracked, profiled, and merged with data collected from multiple offline sources to reveal very "personal" information about themselves.

4. **Dynamic Pricing Reaches Most Industries:** Dynamic pricing will extend into numerous industries via the name-your-own-price model (such as Priceline) and the Auction model (such as eBay).

5. **ASPs' Capabilities Expand:** ASPs (Application Service Providers) will continue to increase the quantity and quality of their customers and the robustness of their service offerings. The ASP model, as it becomes more pervasive, will lead to a dramatic change in how the software industry produces and distributes software.

6. **Wireless Applications Become More Common:** Wireless Internet access will rapidly be adopted in the U.S., possibly catching up to Europe. Wireless technology will be incorporated into standard business operations and will be used to deliver in-store competitive pricing and remote e-mail anywhere, contributing to a steep rise in online usage.

7. **Free Extends into B2B Space:** "Free" continues as a B2C e-commerce model and extends into the B2B world.

8. **Customer-Centric Corporate Restructuring:** For the Global 2000 companies that adapt and integrate the Internet into their businesses, a customer-centric view will start reshaping their culture and infrastructure.

9. **Executive Inability to Morph:** The majority of Global 2000 corporations will recognize that e-commerce is a reality they must embrace, but the majority of top executives will be unable to "morph" their corporations into holistic Internet-enabled entities.

10. **Expanded ECM Deployment:** Brick and mortar companies will continue to deploy e-commerce efforts that integrate with their core business. After Y2K preparation and cleanup, e-commerce will hit the business world like a tidal wave.

    Year 2000 will see a significant increase in the number of traditional companies that extend their brands onto the Web and meld on- and offline marketing activities.

Bonus Trend for 2000—Electronic Wallet Acceptance: Major in-roads will be made in the acceptance of electronic wallets. Driven by the success (and partial frustration) of the 1999 Christmas shopping season, consumers will be looking for an easier, quicker shopping experience.

Chapter 13 contains quotes from people in real-world companies regarding the top ten trends for 2001.

These trends focus on the real issues as observed by people who are actively experimenting with e-commerce solutions. Some of the 1999 and 2000 trends happened, and some did not. What's interesting about them is the magnitude of how e-commerce touches every aspect of a business. They indicate that we are just now beginning on the path of the Internet Age, and there's a lot more to come.

So... buckle your seat belt and hold on because the ride has just started!

E-Volutionary Tactics

→ E-Commerce encompasses all the business interactions of a company.

→ We are just setting out on the path of the Internet Age.

→ The Internet Age will spawn a new, more powerful customer.

→ The goal for your company should be to create a holistic Internet-enabled entity.

→ The Internet must be integrated across the entire company and all partners in your value web.

→ Failure and experimentation will be a necessary part of strategy.

→ Thinking outside the box will be essential for survival, growth, and evolution in the Internet Age.

Business Models for the E-Conomy

A BUSINESS MODEL describes a process by which a company conducts business, including how the company develops and produces their goods and services and how they deliver them to their customers. Quite often, business models involve other business entities who provide some service or goods to the primary company, including vendors, suppliers, distributors, or other types of strategic partners. In the New E-Conomy, new business models are being created every day that threaten the old ways of doing business and define new opportunities

▶▶

for all constituents in the economic value chain. Says Andrew Krainin, Senior Vice President of Marketing for Sameday.com, "In this new E-Conomy, customers *still* demand more for less, and it requires new business models to be more efficient at delivering just that—we are in a phase of Darwinism applied to the efficiency of business processes, and the companies that can adapt (and e-volve) their business models most rapidly will survive."

Welcome to the Internet e-conomy— it's all up for grabs! Where will your company fit in?

Companies who disassemble and reassemble business processes, those who work within or across vertical markets, and even those that are pure content plays are shaking up the old business models, transforming them into new models that will thrive in the environment of the Internet.

In the Beginning...

Some of the earliest experiments with the Internet stemmed from finding better ways to exchange information among established business partners, such as suppliers, vendors, and companies. In the early days, Internet-like tools such as access-controlled virtual private networks (VPNs) and extranets were widely used for already established supply chains, linking suppliers and vendors to companies. (Please note the use of the term 'supply chain' comes from the Industrial Age models; today it refers to a model that treats suppliers as a link in the chain, not as a partner. See Chapter 7, "Outsourcing Is Always an Option," for more information about the "new" supply chains and outsourcing.) Soon after, these same suppliers and vendors started collaborating with companies on manufacturing processes and product design (collaborative engineering) through the same network, increasing its potential value as an inter-enterprise communication tool. Additionally, Electronic Data Interchange (EDI) systems that operated over private encrypted networks enabled the secure processing and transfer of money among trading partners. For example, while I was at Sun Microsystems (1988–1997), a number of EDI transactions were conducted with suppliers to automate the procurement processes—all done over a private network. At first, the Internet was regarded as experimental, with many technology hurdles to be overcome, especially the perceived security issue. Networked trading partners insisted upon having protection of their confidential information as well as any financial transactions. Eventually, when robust and reliable encryption techniques became available for the Internet, those companies that were accustomed to doing business through VPNs or extranets were able to quickly move to the Internet environment. The ordinary, simple business supply chain and EDI models were simply transferred to the Internet, and for the most part, no fundamental changes were made—same process, different network.

In terms of marketing and selling, at first the Internet was largely regarded as a nice place to do some advertising or as "just another distribution channel" that might bring in more revenue someday but by no means would become a serious revenue producer for the average company. Sun Microsystems has been around for a while and has been one of the companies touting the benefits of distributed computing and the Internet. However, the introduction of MOSAIC in 1993 started people thinking. The commercialization of MOSAIC by Clarksdale and Andreessen in 1995 (at Netscape) really woke up the world. Yahoo and Amazon.com were two of the early pioneers that were initially laughed at, but today they are huge forces of change. Yahoo created a new industry, while Amazon caused havoc in an existing one.

In just five short years since 1995, many value chains and supply chains and basic business models have been rendered obsolete. Relationships that took years to establish and extensive management to maintain ceased to be a barrier to entry to the mass-market world of the Internet. Essentially, any individual with a good idea and enough money to buy a domain name can now come up with an entirely new way to do business—one that is capable of bringing a mega-giant competitor to its knees or at least make it think hard about how to react. Some examples are Dell in computers, eBay in auctions, Amazon in books, Carsdirect and Autobytel in autos, and eSchwab in online trading.

Virtual Value Webs

The traditional business models that have worked for decades are being turned upside down by the Internet e-conomy. In the past, the average company had a supply chain set up to facilitate the production of goods and services and had a value chain for the purposes of delivering and distributing these goods and services to the ultimate customer (see Figure 2.1). The only complexity was derived from multiple business partners that made up the chain. Essentially, the more you had, the more managing you had to do. You could diagram a simple value chain, figure out where the gaps were, and then find partners to fill those gaps. Now, those easily understood chains are being replaced by virtual value "webs," with multiple nodes and multiple paths for exchanging information, goods, services, and money—over a VPN and/or the Internet (see Figure 2.2). Companies trying to do this today include VerticalNet, Ariba, and CommerceOne.

Is your business model obsolete?

In virtual value webs, the players change often, as long as it makes economic sense for all parties involved. Every time a new node and link is added to the value web, new economic opportunities are created for the entities in the Web. What does this mean for your business? Whether you are an existing company or a new entrepreneur, it means that you have some decisions to

Figure 2.1

The traditional value chain. In the traditional model, the customer is at the end-point of the value chain, and only one entity interacts directly with the customer. The manufacturer must trust that entity to deliver value.

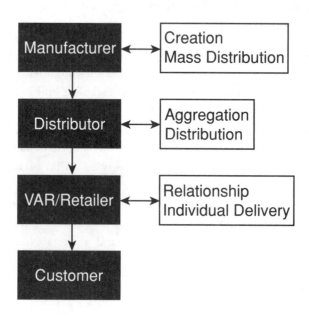

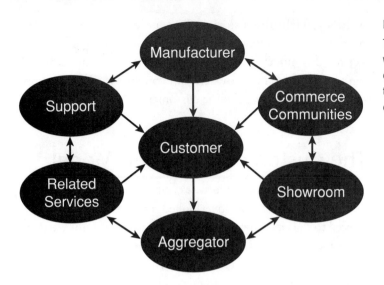

Figure 2.2

The value web. In the value web, the customer is in the center, and value flows directly to the customer through all other channels and entities.

make. The upside is this: You have many more opportunities to create value and to be profitable. Metcalfe's law illustrates this point. Robert Metcalfe is the founder of 3Com and the inventor of the ethernet. The law states that as each node in a network is added, the value to all nodes increases exponentially. This is certainly true for online business, and there are many benefits. The downside: Value webs require more management attention in order for the model to be effective. That means a solid organization must be in place to manage the value at each customer touch point (see Chapter 4, "Customer Touch Points") or node in the value web. Chapter 9, "Managing the E-Commerce Organization," examines these organizational issues in more detail.

Value webs are not created all at once. They begin with one or two entities and e-volve from there. It requires thought, planning, flexibility, and creativity to make the value web work. Where do you begin? First you must consider the most critical node in the value web—your customer. There have been a few successes with value webs, but many have failed. Among the failures were companies who were great at market making and creating a new model to connect buyers and sellers, but who couldn't achieve critical mass in the marketplace. Therefore, they were unable to complete the final transaction of building a value web: That of delivering value to all participants in the web—especially the customer. There needs to be constant focus on the customer along with attaining critical mass in the market for this model to work effectively. Your partners can help with this, too; many providers can combine their core competencies to deliver value to the customer.

The Customer Drives the Model

How does your customer define value?

When we talk about value webs, whose value are we talking about? The obvious but overlooked answer: It's the value delivered to the *customer*. In the e-commerce world, the customer is the focal point and, in fact, has become even more important and more powerful in terms of driving expectations for how companies should deliver their goods and services, as well as how they are treated during the process. How do you know what is valuable to your customer? You ask! You study them and do your homework, and you conduct formal market research. Remember to not only ask your existing customers who may stay with you over the long term, but also consider your potential future customers.

If you have existing customers, it's time to do some research or focus groups to discover what their expectations are when they do business with you and when they do business with your competitors. And if you are targeting new customers, you need to do a lot of research to learn all you can about them. Research may include psychographic and demographic profiles, past buying behavior, or any type of research that helps determine the customers' expectations regarding value. In addition to the traditional questions and information, you need to understand your customer and their familiarity, as well as their acceptance of Web-based interfaces, how Web site design and usability affects their customer experience, the value they place on digital brand, and how to more efficiently conduct business with you. This can save you a lot of time and expense later on, as was discovered by Digital Market, originally created as an online buying and selling marketplace for the electronics industry. Digital Market found out that their system was not consistent with the way large customers buy chips in volume, and that these customers expect to be able to negotiate. Their original offering didn't allow for that capability, which Digital Market realized when their revenue fell short of expectations. They eventually redesigned their online offering as an electronic parts procurement application for vendors instead. Perhaps if Digital Market had researched their target customer's business processes (especially the purchasing process) in advance, their initial offering would have accommodated the true needs of their customer.

When you have some idea of your customer's definition of value, you can create or produce the goods or services the customer wants. It's also necessary to figure out where you will find your customers—on the Web or in traditional locations—so you can market and deliver the goods and services. Then you need to market to these customers/potential customers with Internet-based and traditional tools. All three of these major tasks (production, delivery, and marketing of goods and services) are ripe opportunities for partnering. For example, think about how online brokerages, like E*Trade or eSchwab, have found the true value customers want (by doing trades, managing finances, and so on) and then designed a service offering that focuses on that particular value in a new cost-efficient way.

You likely will need partners in the New E-Conomy, but how do you retain customers if you outsource some of the components of the business models to partners? This is a common hurdle for some companies, which prevents them from participating in new ways of doing business. "What is often required," according to Don Swenson, Vice President of Marketing and Business Development for SAQQARA, "is a targeted, personalized relationship with established customers, *and* an excellent Web site to interact with these customers online. It allows you to still manage the customer relationship, and raises the level of personal attention. That goes a long way toward retention."

Partnering on the Rise

Driven by the connectivity opportunities afforded by the Web, partnerships are becoming more common than ever and are becoming a vital element of long-term business success. Reasons to partner include the traditional ones (joint marketing, co-development, distribution) as well as some new ones (faster time to market, customer retention, fulfillment, flexibility, and customization and post-sales support, to mention a few). When a new partner is added to the value web, it is crucial not only to choose the partner carefully, but also to manage the partner in order to make sure they are delivering the intended value to your customer. The more nodes there are in the value web, the farther removed your ultimate customer becomes. That's where careful management is required, because it's important to obtain and manage all information associated with all customer touch points (see Chapter 4).

New Partner Selection Criteria

In the old days, searching for compatible partners was like a human courtship ritual where the two candidates focus on their cultural compatibility and assess how they might work together. Building just one long-term partner relationship could take months or sometimes years. Now the criteria have changed. The primary criterion has become the customer's point of view: Will your customers view the end results of the partnership as being valuable to *them?* The experience of established retailers who have developed online operations (Lands' End, Nordstrom) suggests that partnering be done with great caution and that the proper amount of time be given to developing relationships. It's also imperative to keep your customer's interest at the top of the list of priorities. There is pressure for companies to partner because the consensus is that no company can be successful in a solo mode.

Portals function as an incarnation of a company's Web site, and attempt to create the starting point for customers to explore the Internet. For established companies needing portal partners, it is tempting to give up customer data in exchange. However, customer data and your relationship with your customers are one of your core currencies of the New E-Conomy. If you give away customer data, are you doing your customers a disservice? Will your valued customers receive unwanted junk email or advertising? If this "junk" is associated with your brand, you will be doing your company more harm than good because you can alienate your customers. Partnering for the sake of partnering is not wise, even if the pressure is on. As with any partnering relationship, you need to establish partnership agreements that mitigate risk while increasing benefits to all parties.

Another important criterion is the level of quality your partners provide in carrying out their role in the partnership. "Partnership performance should be measured by quality of the customer's experience, not by how many leads you obtained in your target market segment," says Dan Todd, Director of Marketing Strategy for Keynote Systems. "The key question has to be whether your customers will view the partnership as valuable to them." It's necessary to research partner candidates ahead of time. Is the candidate likely to be in business in the next few months or years? Are your skill sets and theirs compatible and complementary? Who are their reference accounts? What do their customers say about them? Is this what you want your customers to say about you if they become aware of this partnership? Partner relationships are critical in the world of e-commerce management, and it's critical to spend as much time studying your potential partners as you would spend studying your target customer.

Who will your new partners be?

Marketing Partners

Co-marketing programs among strategic partners have been around for years. Programs included a mutually agreed upon budget and a list of promotional activities with the objective of boosting sales for all concerned. These promotional activities would include sales incentive programs, bonuses, sweepstakes, rebates, print advertising, and events—all held live or in the form of print or by telephone. The Internet has created a new venue for cooperative marketing among value web partners.

What do these Internet marketing alliances look like? They are more than just shared Web links to one another's home pages or mutual banner ads. AOL, for example, has put together an alliance with Ritz Camera, and they will mutually promote one another's products and services through click and mortar as well as online. ("Click and mortar" companies are brick and mortar companies that are integrating online activity with their business.) A consumer can drop off film at Ritz Camera locations and have pictures delivered to his AOL account. While he is in the store, the customer can pick up AOL CD-ROMs to sign up for service. AOL visitors will have access to Ritzcamera Online's products and services.

Other types of business models and partnering (such as those discussed later in this chapter) also offer opportunities for joint or cooperative marketing, even if that's not the primary purpose of the partnership. For example, PurchasingCenter.com gives potential supplier partners marketing tools to use in order to attract them into the online marketplace.

"Affiliate marketing" is routinely practiced between companies and between individuals and companies. These programs consist of percentage commissions on sales or referral fees generated by links from the participants' Web sites. One of the first Internet companies to do this was Amazon.com, who received a patent on this business concept. Every entity participating in affiliate marketing becomes a node in the virtual value web, and each may have varying levels of commissions or incentives as well. Companies such as Amazon and CDNow with active affiliate marketing programs have hundreds of thousands of affiliates, and more are being added each day. Today, Web companies such as Referit.com and Clickquick.com rate the various affiliate programs so that companies or individuals can decide what is best for their needs. You can learn more about affiliate marketing programs in Chapter 10, "Ongoing Internet Marketing," or at this Web page: **www.ecnow.com/Internet_marketing.htm**.

There are companies, such as Vstore.com, whose entire business model and revenue stream is based on affiliate marketing through multiple commissions on multiple products—a Web version of multi-level marketing. Affinia is similar to Vstore.com, but they also provide Web site development services and earn commissions on affiliate programs through the sites they build. Schoolpop.com utilizes a slightly different model; they partner with merchants, take a commission, and donate a certain percentage of proceeds to schools and charities.

Pure content Web sites can realize a revenue stream through such programs, and the companies who provide links to these sites also enjoy increased revenue. Customers benefit because they receive additional value through the content provided at the time that they shop for and then buy the products through the Web. Adding affiliate links to one's site is a quick and easy way to add content and form partnerships in the New E-Conomy. More information about affiliate links can be found in Chapter 5, "Content Will Always Be King," and Chapter 7, "Outsourcing Is Always an Option."

Distribution or Channel Partners

It is said that the Internet is causing disintermediation of the value chain. Portals, Web communities, and Web exchanges are all part of the new laws of Internet supply and demand. Traditional distribution channels are busy trying to figure out how to survive when, in effect, companies and customers may not need them any more. If a customer can go directly to a company's Web site and configure, design, or order a product directly from a company, who needs a distributor? (Please don't be offended if this question makes you think.)

The only way these distributors can survive is to come up with ways to add value or services to what the company is selling, that is also valued by the customer, like providing direct customer service. Distributors are getting creative, such as providing inventory management or fulfillment services for their partner companies, or providing training and post-sales support for customers.

Another growing trend is for non-distributors to provide re-selling or distribution services. Many traditional retailers are pairing up with dot.coms to create new distribution relationships. One such example is Safeway and GroceryWorks. In this arrangement, Safeway actually becomes the wholesale distributor to GroceryWorks, who will sell co-branded Safeway products through their online store and grocery delivery service. Viewed another way, GroceryWorks is the online distributor for some of Safeway's products. As part of the deal, GroceryWorks receives purchasing services, wholesale products, and brand recognition. They provide fulfillment and delivery. Safeway, in turn, receives on online ordering and delivery service (along with an online presence). In another example, Hallmark has teamed up with Premiere Choice Award to sell gifts to corporations as employee incentives, and also has teamed up with GiftCertificates.com, who will sell gift certificates directly to consumers. Hallmark thus becomes a distributor of gift certificates and has another distribution channel for its Hallmark-branded line of gifts.

The lesson here is that distribution seems to be up for grabs, for remolding or evolution, and the roles are changing. For your company, you need to seek out distributors who can provide the most value for your Web (and those who aren't stuck in the dark ages), or you need to figure out another type of relationship that may involve your own company entering the distribution business.

Supplier and Vendor Partners

Supply chains have been in place for decades, but the Internet has enabled new ways for suppliers to do business with companies. Not only does the Internet speed up the traditional supply chain process, but also emerging supplier and buyer communities or portals reside on the Internet. Online marketplaces, exchanges, and buying cooperatives are becoming a new way to participate in buying and selling for companies in almost every industry. These marketplaces seem to work best in environments where there is a lot of fragmentation. By setting up a virtual marketplace, buyers and sellers can meet and transact business immediately. In 1999 and 2000, companies saved billions of dollars just by conducting online procurement.

eChemical supplies production chemicals more widely and more quickly (at better prices) to manufacturers through an open exchange. Another company is EqualFooting.com, a B2B exchange of building supplies for the construction industry. Shop2gether.com offers office supplies, health benefits, and other services to small businesses. The aerospace industry companies such as Boeing and Lockheed Martin have partnered with Commerce One to build an industry-wide exchange for goods and services. Ford, GM, and DaimlerChrysler are combining efforts for an automotive supply marketplace, and Cargill is building a vertical marketplace for food and beverages. These online marketplaces are being developed by industry leaders and insiders because they want to write the rules for how the business works, rather than have outsiders come in and manage it.

One of the more unique exchanges or "clearinghouses" is the Arbinet Global Clearing Network, focused on buying and selling telecommunications capacity. Arbinet's Web site acts as an online trading floor where sellers can post excess capacity, and interested parties can bid. This exchange gives telcos the ability to buy and sell capacity on a daily basis—yielding cost savings for both buyers and sellers. Arbinet takes a commission of each transaction.

Online marketplaces essentially operate as a partnership—but on a very large scale. Economies of scale and pooling of supplies benefit all the trading partners involved. But how can you find the best suppliers who will become reliable partners if the field is so open? Enter the watchdogs of the online marketplace world: companies who rate trading partners, such as OpenRatings.com. They base their ratings on cumulative reactions of customers and partners over time—using artificial intelligence software. VerticalNet, Ariba, IBM, and Commerce One also match up compatible buyers and sellers for certain markets, which increases the odds of partnering success.

Fulfillment Partners

For dot.coms selling tangible goods, one of the most critical types of partners is that of fulfillment. If a company's sales and marketing programs are effective, the delivery systems must be in place to cross "the last mile" to the customer. And the value must be there as well. There are countless tales from previous holiday seasons where goods purchased over the Internet were never delivered or were delivered late—especially critical for business to consumer enterprises. A great example here is how Toys 'R' Us was unable to fill consumer demand in the holiday season of 1999 and ended up providing $100 USD gift certificates to disappointed consumers. Forecasting demand has always been difficult, but the Internet brings inherent unpredictability, and companies must be able to deliver whether they are experiencing peaks or valleys. Allowing your suppliers direct access to your or your resellers' actual sales would certainly help them to do a better job of forecasting future production as well.

Certain shipping companies, such as UPS and FedEx, are faring quite well in the Internet economy. However, they are not standing still and just reaping the profits. All these companies are thinking of ways they can offer more value to their partner companies, such as providing warehousing and logistics management, while still providing the highest quality of services to the customer. UPS established a number of new businesses, based on their thorough understanding of their customers' needs, along with creative thinking about how they could provide more value at each customer touch point. All the new businesses that UPS created leverage their infrastructure and core competencies. These businesses include managing the entire back-end operations for their customers, from ordering and inventory management, to call centers, to processing and handling of returns. Even though UPS has been in business for 93 years, they have recognized the need to adapt to the New E-Conomy and are taking steps accordingly. More detail about the success of UPS becoming an enabler of global e-commerce can be found in Appendix A, "Case Studies."

There are new companies in this space whose core business it is to provide fulfillment. Examples are Kozmo.com, a home delivery service for consumer goods, and Sameday.com, which provides supply chain management services including fulfillment, returns, delivery, and customer support. WebVan, although focusing on groceries and prepared meals, could also deliver other items to households. Because of these new models, there are more choices for fulfillment partners.

For companies selling intangible goods or services (software, electronic media-based goods, or personal services, for example), fulfillment is still important. In fact, the line is beginning to blur between where the product ends and the service begins. Customers expect both, regardless of what they are buying… and they are raising the bar continuously in terms of quality expectations. This is true for services as well as tangible goods. Good examples are Intuit, which now provides the ability for customers to submit their taxes entirely online; and Ernst & Young, who pioneered an online offering of consulting services to businesses (called "Ernie"), provides small- and medium-sized businesses the access to the firm's knowledge base and partners through online interactions.

Business Infrastructure Partners

When examining business models, we should not ignore what goes on inside the company. The organization must function effectively to supply its goods and services to the customer, and its infrastructure must be in place to support the external value web. Back office systems should operate seamlessly with the front office systems that interface to your customers. Today, there are more choices than ever for outsourcing almost any aspect of business operations infrastructure: sales, logistics, fulfillment, customer support, information technology, accounting, telecommunications, and call centers. Several service providers known as ASPs (application service providers) or BSPs (business solution providers) are able to handle either individual parts of your infrastructure or the whole thing—and to handle it all over the Web. Most of the ERP vendors, such as SAP, Oracle, and PeopleSoft, have incorporated this business model and are providing outsourced services to dot.coms. Businesses today can truly focus on their core competencies and outsource everything else. Even with these choices, it is still critical that these providers be regarded and managed as partners. They, too, need to participate in adding value to your customer. The importance of customer value is also addressed in Chapters 4 and 7.

Several levels of ASP offerings are emerging, and some of them are based on old models that still work quite well. At the fundamental level, transaction processing, credit card merchant services have been around for many years. At a slightly higher level of complexity, there are ASPs that offer proprietary software packaged with business process transactions. An old version of this model includes online payroll services. Another type of ASP includes companies who merely provide their otherwise shrink-wrapped, packaged, or hosted software over the Web with no added technology or business value—they are offering it as more of a convenience for their customers. These categories, as well as completely new combinations of products and services, will continue to e-volve. Instead of paying $250,000 to $1 million USD for an ERP package plus the cost of hardware and people necessary to support it, you can rent one for a fraction of the cost.

The Economics of the Value Web

When you have determined the types of partners you will need and the roles they will play in your value web, you need to consider the economics of the relationship from your perspective as well as that of your partners. It is imperative to deliver value to your partners as well as your customers in order to have a mutually beneficial business relationship. Depending on the type of partners involved, money, knowledge or eyeball time (already a slightly outdated form of currency) will likely be exchanged. Before partnerships are put into place, all parties must set goals based on the desired result. You must agree on margins, discounts, fees, commissions, and terms of payment (for example, when money changes hands relative to the sale or exchange of services). In addition to the business factors, network protocols and architecture should be considered. These arrangements need to be negotiated and in place when the relationships starts.

To negotiate the amounts and terms, you need to consider what the return on your investment will be. That means you need to consider your costs to do business with the potential partner, compared to the expected return of revenue. This is a traditional return on investment metric. However, it is also appropriate to compare your costs to do business with the potential partner, with the expected value they provide to your customer (which you may not be able to quantify). This is probably a more important metric to use for evaluating and selecting value web partners.

As you evaluate current or future partners, you will likely find that multiple partners have varying revenue streams and varying returns on investment. Every few months, it is worthwhile to compare the returns on investment (in terms of revenue and customer value) and evaluate your partners' performance in the value web. Because the rules have changed, partnerships no longer are long-term relationships. If it's not working, you should either dissolve the partnership and move on to another who can fill the role and empty node, or find another way to add value to the Web. Building and maintaining successful value webs requires constant monitoring.

According to Andrew Krainin, Senior Vice President of Sameday.com, "Partners need to act as if they are a part of your company. They need to understand and care about what they are doing for you as a functional part of your operations. The lines are blurring between partners and customers and between partners and suppliers. The same level of business value should be shared among everyone in the business relationship."

Integrating the New with the Old

Not every company is a brand new dot.com entering a market for the first time. Some companies have been doing business the old-fashioned way for decades but must now become e-commerce "enabled." Indeed, they must adopt new models in order to survive. There are ways to create a virtual value web even if you have a functioning value chain in place.

Affiliate marketing partners can be added easily, and it is possible to experiment with different partners and measure the results over a period of a few months. Distribution partners may be more difficult, especially if there is potential for channel conflict. If the incumbent distribution partner has an effective Web presence, it's possible to continue to use the distributor—as long as the customer continues to perceive value. However, if the distribution partner is not efficient or is not delivering added quality, different distributors can be tested. For this to work consistently, you need to set quality goals and performance metrics for continuing partner qualification.

Online exchanges and marketplaces offer new ways for suppliers and vendors to participate in business to business e-commerce, for a much wider population—and with greater economic benefits for all involved. Many interim business and partnering models represent a step in this direction: a wider, community-based participation rather than one-to-one partnering. This seems to be the evolutionary path for business models and partnering.

Fulfillment or business infrastructure partnering can also be a way to e-volve into the e-commerce world—either by providing these services or by contracting with a partner who will provide them to you. The economics of the situation may result in outsourcing, enabling your own company to focus on your core competencies as well as ways to keep customer value at the forefront of your business.

There are ways to deliver value to your customer that are totally unrelated to the old value chain but that haven't even been created yet. One way to discover these value nodes is to revisit your customer: Who are they now, and where do you find them on the Web? Even though business models will continue to e-volve, they must all have a solid foundation and focus on the customer in order to succeed and be profitable.

Successful business models are those that are working and that can adapt and e-volve. Business models are never finished; they should be thought of as a continuum. As opportunities arise, and as business processes adapt and technology continues to advance, the models need to e-volve accordingly. This will continue to be true for click and mortar companies as well as for pure dot.coms, as we all discover and understand the potential created by the Internet. If you haven't started exploring current and future business models, or if you're moving too slow, watch out. Your competitors are right behind you, in the same race, so the time to move fast is now. Do it or disappear!

E-Volutionary Tactics

→ Classic value chains and supply chains are e-volving into value webs, where any entity can play the role of any node in the Web—buyer, seller, supplier, and customer.

→ Partnering has become a necessity for the success of new e-commerce business models.

→ Several types of business models and partnerships are emerging, with different purposes including marketing, distribution, supply chain and exchanges, fulfillment, and business infrastructure.

→ The customer still needs to be the focal point of any successful business model.

→ Value needs to be delivered to all participants in the value web.

→ Business models need to be adapted and changed regularly and consistently.

PART

II

Deploying E-Commerce

3 The Plan Is the Thing   47

4 Customer Touch Points   65

5 Content Will Always Be King   83

6 Instant Global Presense   99

7 Outsourcing Is Always an Option   119

The Plan Is the Thing

IN CHAPTER 1, "E-Commerce Thinking," we talked about how you must think outside of the box. When it comes to e-commerce planning, it requires a slap in the face! Put aside all your preconceived notions, and toss out all the old plans and processes. It's time to start over. Think of it as waking up today with the task of creating a brand new business—from scratch. That is how you need to approach the work of planning your holistic Internet-enabled entity. As my son would say, it's time to make a mess. ▶ ▶

What's different about
planning for a holistic
Internet-enabled
entity?

We will start now. To help re-orient you, the reader, and keep
you from straying into your old ways of thinking, I will not use
the word "e-commerce" in the remainder of this chapter.
Instead, I will refer to this as a *holistic Internet-enabled entity*,
as defined in Chapter 1. That is what you need to create.

Planning is the backbone for the creation of a holistic Internet-
enabled entity. However, this is no ordinary planning exercise.
Your existing business plan will not work for this purpose, even
if you just wrote it or updated it last week. It was not written
for a holistic Internet-enabled entity. Other plans that you may
have in place, such as marketing, operations, or IT plans will
not work either. Because they are discrete plans for specific functions, they are not holistic. To create and manage a holistic
Internet-enabled entity, planning requires you to rethink the
basics about your business and how you will implement and
deploy the massive changes required in people, processes, and
systems—because that's what is needed. Expect no less. This
represents a fundamental change in how you will do business.
One the example of this fundamental change is Egghead's clos-
ing of its retail stores to focus entirely on the online market,
which was a whole new business model.

Planning enables these massive changes. With a baseline plan in
place, it is much easier to experiment and to e-volve the business model, processes and organization to fit the internal and
external environments. Also, because of the need to change and
e-volve quickly in response to the dynamics of today's business
world, planning is even more critical. Companies used to develop a five-year vision. Today, any vision that lasts more than
18 months may be too long. Some would say that even 18
months is too long. "With the New E-Conomy, it's hard to
get a handle on more than a six-month window," says Doug
Nelson, President of the Seabright Group. "You build a great
plan and then three months later your competitor offers a
similar product for free...uh oh, back to the drawing board."
However, a vision might have certain components that, in fact,
last three years or more—through all the changes that must take
place in order to truly e-volve. But if the vision is hampering
evolution, change is necessary.

Brick and mortar companies aren't the only ones doing strategic planning. More and more dot.coms are discovering that planning is essential for survival, and the pressure is on from the investors of many dot.coms, requiring them to execute and pay more attention to their primary mission. Boo.com is one example of a failed dot.com that lacked planning from many perspectives, including a plan for how their customers would actually use their Web site. In contrast, a prime example of "planning as corporate culture" is HelloAsia. From the very beginning, this company spent several months engaged in a detailed planning process, instead of rushing to market by spending buckets of money on mass advertising. The CEO of the company believes that this will not only be the secret to their survival, but that it will lead to success in terms of meeting their key business objectives. [1]

Planning in the Business Context

Planning begins at the most fundamental level: defining (or redefining) your business. When faced with new opportunities or pressures, it is easy to lose sight of the company's core business. If you plan to continue the same type of business, write out a description of the business you *are* in. If this exercise is part of a new effort to transform your company, describe the business you *want to be* in. Either way, the planning process must be done in the business context of the holistic company. This business context should also include your competitors and strategic alliances.

In this early stage, the key question to ask is, "Why is Internet-enabling being pursued at all?" Sometimes, the reason is the company's very survival. Or maybe it represents a way to keep from being acquired, keeping the edge on the competition, a means of attracting new talent delivering greater customer satisfaction, or reaching the global market. Whatever the reason, it should be clearly articulated and referred to during the entire planning process.

---

1 *Fast Company*, June 2000, pages 148–152.

The Big Picture and the Vision

The Internet has opened up a whole new world of business possibilities. It provides opportunities to grow or expand a business, new ways to integrate products or services and the innovative technology at your disposal, as well as ideas for conducting business in ways that no one had thought of before. Company leaders need to decide which opportunities are attractive and then prioritize them in light of the company's core business and strategic business objectives. From this cloud of possibilities comes the vision.

The big picture and vision need to come from the top. The CEO must not only be willing to commit resources to a standalone initiative, but be prepared to implement the complete change the company needs in order to be transformed into a holistic Internet-enabled entity. It's important that the plan in fact *plans for change*.

What is your vision statement?

The CEO or other key executive needs to create a vision (mission statement or architectural framework) that articulates the holistic Internet-enabled direction of the company. Like all mission statements, this should be something that every employee can recite in a 30-second "elevator pitch." Creating the vision is a vital first part of the planning process, and it deserves the "right" attention from the "right" level of the organization. Then it needs to be shared with all. (See Figure 3.1.)

Can you identify the legacy people in your organization?

With the framework in place, the 12-month goals or strategies should be developed—and they should articulate the high-level actions that need to be taken by the entire organization. These goals or strategies will identify which existing systems, processes, and people will need to change. Planning moves from the vision to the goals or strategies to the detailed set of activities

Figure 3.1

The starting point is to consider which opportunities fit the company's business objective, and then to create a vision.

that will accomplish the vision and define the changes that need to be made to the legacy systems, legacy processes, and legacy people.

For any corporation there should be a maximum of five goals or strategies. These goals, together with the vision, are used to rally the organization. In 1999, Jack Welch stated that of General Electric's five corporate goals, goals 1, 2, 3 and 4 were about the Internet. Jack Welch (who, in my opinion, is probably the best living manager, with Alfred Sloan being the best all-time manager) makes a bold statement to his employees and the world when a conservative company like GE is putting such a high-level emphasis on incorporating the Internet into its business. (See Figure 3.2.) The high-level goals are rolled down through the various hierarchical layers of the company's infrastructure. It's important not to lose the connection to the higher-level goals as they are established and expanded throughout the organization.

The Measure of Success

How will you know if this transformation project is successful; how will it be measured? These measures should be both qualitative and quantitative. It is necessary to identify these measures of success at the very beginning of the planning process, and to share them throughout the organization. Every

Figure 3.2
www.ge.com
GE is putting a high-level emphasis on incorporating the Internet into its business.

employee should be compensated based on achieving one or more components of the goals being measured. Not only should internal employees be made aware of the metrics and how the company is doing against those metrics, but partners and customers should be made aware of them as well. In the New E-Conomy, metrics can be measured in real-time, rather than the quarterly or monthly measurements done in the Old Economy. Technology enables results to be communicated immediately to employees via pagers or email, which allows them to make immediate changes and adjustments. If the organization's employees and partners know how the company measures success, everyone can help the organization achieve its goals. In today's world of Internet time, it's important to give all parts of the corporate value web as much information as possible to help the company reach its goals.

> How can you tell the difference between a company that talks the talk and one that walks the walk? In the company that walks the walk, everyone in the company can recite the company's vision in a 30-second elevator pitch, and everyone can point to how they are compensated relative to the corporate metrics.

The metrics that are used should be similar to those used to measure basic business performance and process effectiveness. There should not be a special case or a new set of rules for a holistic Internet-enabled entity. When metrics are applied, the results are either favorable or unfavorable. Unfavorable results might indicate that the required changes to systems, processes, and people are not yet complete. Or maybe it's time to re-evaluate the metric itself and see whether it has outlasted its useful life. Metrics must make sense in the business context and must be a meaningful way to evaluate progress against established goals. Sometimes new or updated metrics need to be added in order to keep up momentum in the organization. Live metrics that are tied to compensation can also positively affect your corporate culture over time. (See Figure 3.3.)

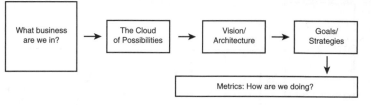

Figure 3.3

Metrics need to fit the business goals and vision.

The Roadmap

A roadmap identifies the various plans that must be developed and implemented in order to carry out the vision of the company. It defines the relationship among the plans, as well as when they need to be completed. It is like a master schedule of everything that needs to be done to create a holistic Internet-enabled entity. Each milestone on the roadmap will have a detailed plan that supports it. The traditional tools used in your company to manage complexity can be applied, such as project management systems. However, it is critical to deploy an interconnected or network-based system so everyone has access to the master schedule. (See Figure 3.4.)

After the metrics are in place, it's easy to create the series of projects (the roadmap) that's needed to meet the metric or satisfy a goal. Because they were created top-down, by default, each project also moves the organization one step closer to reaching its vision. (See Figure 3.5.)

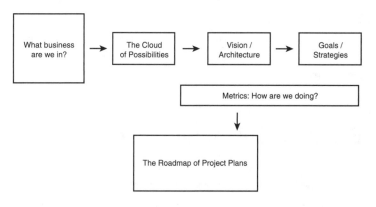

Figure 3.4

The roadmap specifies which plans need to be created and which will be continually measured against the goals.

Figure 3.5

The roadmap defines the milestones along the way, with a detailed plan for each milestone.

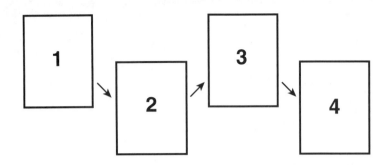

Keeping the Processes Moving

Which of your business processes needs to change?

While a new initiative is being developed and implemented, the company must continue to operate. Because of this situation, business processes cannot handle a major disruption or sudden changes. A transition phase is needed as each process is re-shaped to enable changes in operations.

An essential part of the planning is to identify the existing processes that need to change. Any business process that is re-engineered will require buy-in from the owner(s). The ideal situation is to have these owners directly involved in defining the changes that need to be made, because they know how best to do it with minimal disruption. As re-engineering takes place, it is important to focus on the reason for change. Is it to align more closely with customer needs? To increase efficiency? To save costs? To migrate the processes to a networked environment? In almost all cases, anything that can be done to change processes to improve customer interaction is desirable; that reason should be at the top of the list. Cisco and Dell, for example, have both changed processes around their changing customer service needs.

Ensuring Customer Value

This is the era of customer-centric commerce. Just as the customer should be at the center of the business model, so should the customer be at the center of the systems, processes, and people that must change and e-volve to implement the holistic Internet-enabled entity. Customer-centric commerce means that everyone in your company has a 360-degree view of your customer.

It is absolutely necessary to deliver value to the customer at all possible interaction points (see Chapter 4, "Customer Touch Points"). Therefore, your business processes need to be shaped accordingly. According to Brian Kellner, Development Manager for Zoho Corporation, it's necessary to personalize the customer experience first: "Once you understand the value from the customer's point of view, then you build the solution that provides that value—that should be the order in which you do things, not the other way around. This concept applies to the business processes, along with the systems and people required to implement the solution. It's an exercise in *planning value*." Using customer value as the foundation for your business processes is a necessity of doing business in the New E-Conomy. (See Figure 3.6.)

For each business process that is evaluated, several questions need to be addressed:

- ▲ Does the process get the right product or service to the right customer?
- ▲ Is the method of fulfillment appropriate from the customer's perspective?

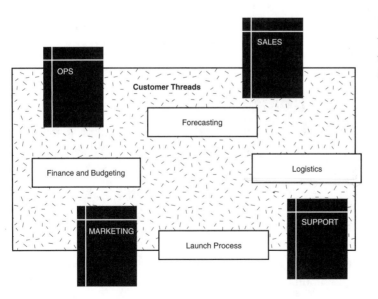

Figure 3.6

The customer thread should run through all processes and plans in the organization.

- ▲ Is the pricing appropriate for the customer?
- ▲ Do your costs make sense in terms of the customer's needs; are you spending more than is necessary to keep the customer satisfied?

To answer the questions, you must have an up-to-date description of your target customer. Sometimes you must revisit the customer's needs and value proposition by conducting some primary research in the form of surveys or other customer feedback.

Most large companies have many types of target customers, because they offer several product lines or several products in a series that are sold to different segments. It is important to understand what each customer segment wants; their needs and sophistication levels are often very different. As an example, one customer may be content to place all their orders through the Web, but another customer uses the Web for research and then prefers to speak with a salesperson when they are ready to buy. All processes (and, therefore, the plans) must take this into account. A single set of processes may need to serve several different customer "threads," which can become a thorny issue. It sometimes means that the systems or infrastructure need to be upgraded or changed in order to offer the choices your array of customers requires. Deploying new infrastructure that is built on customer relationship management also enables you to provide much more service to your customers online. Cisco has e-volved their processes in this way—according to personalized customer satisfaction—and with much success.

Stakeholders

Whether you are a new company or an existing company, you will have many stakeholders in your holistic Internet-enabled implementation, and everyone will have an opinion on the matter. Stakeholders are individuals or entities who have a vested interest in making changes or maintaining the status quo. After the vision/architecture and goals/strategies are set by key executives, those executives become sponsors, handing off the implementation to other key managers. In some situations, everyone may simultaneously be the sponsors and the implementers.

Whatever the organizational situation, the impact to all your stakeholders needs to be considered in your solution, because you need all of them to make it work successfully. All functional areas of a company should be involved: marketing, corporate communications, sales, information technology or MIS, finance, legal, manufacturing, logistics, purchasing, operations, key outside vendors, strategic partners, and customers. Each constituent's needs and influence must be taken into account when planning the solution. (See Figure 3.7.)

One of the ways to satisfy the stakeholders is to begin with a requirements framework. Each stakeholder should have an opportunity to define his part of the framework, as well as the constraints that apply. As prototypes of the Internet-enabled implementation are developed, stakeholders can continue to review the iterations to make sure the constraints are being met. It is tempting for stakeholders to try to resist change, but without change, it may not be possible to satisfy the goals/strategies that have been set. It is also tempting for stakeholders to insist on perfection. So a word of caution is in order: Make sure you have an understanding of what is absolutely required, what is "optional," and what would be nice to have. Focus on the must-have first.

Who are your
stakeholders?

Partner Involvement

In the majority of Internet-enabled companies, one or more key business partners are involved in the value chain already or will be an essential link in the new value chain. These existing or

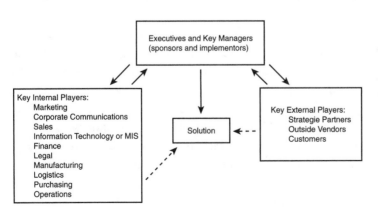

Figure 3.7

All stakeholders must be involved, but may work with different processes, and be involved at many different levels of the enterprise.

potential partners must not be forgotten in the planning process. If your partners have a supply chain (Web) or fulfillment relationship with your company, they must be involved in any re-engineering of the processes that serve those functions.

A key question to ask is this: Are you going to use any partners in delivering your Internet-enabled solution? If the answer is yes, they need to be involved. When the project grows, the process changes, and the requirements are defined, it's time to get them involved—before the detailed plans are put into place. Partners still need to be compatible with your overall business objectives and must have the required speed, expertise, core competencies, and philosophy regarding holistic Internet-enabled operations. If not, it's time to re-evaluate the relationship or evaluate other partner candidates.

Plan Creation and E-Volution

The purpose of planning is to document actions that will take place in the future. However, as conditions change, plans must change accordingly. The key is to figure out and document a reasonable baseline that people can understand so that when you do change it, the actions that must take place are clear, and the impact to everyone involved is also clear. Throughout the process, remember that all plans flow down from the vision and the corporate goals.

In the New E-Conomy, changes occur every day. You may have new competitors or existing ones whose latest announcements will affect your market position. Customers change and become more savvy, changing their expectations in how they want to deal with you. If you don't continually monitor customers' and your partners' interactions with customers, you may fall prey to not knowing who they are and how to satisfy them. When you launch new products, plans must change, and specific marketing and launch plans must be generated. HelloAsia would likely not have been able to survive their four simultaneous launches without their detailed baseline plans in place. And each time that you evaluate your plans against your metrics, changes may be required. With a well-defined set of metrics, it's easy to envision the project plans continually changing to reflect new situations regarding technology or people's capabilities—without necessarily affecting the metrics. Also, if your vision is being updated every few months, it will be essential to restart the planning process—from the beginning. That means realigning strategy, process, methodology, and deployment of an evolving business solution. It's all a part of success in the New E-Conomy.

Most companies that do a good job of planning agree that a "rolling" planning model is more effective. Rather than completing a plan, following it for a few months, and then starting a new one, the company evaluates the plan's performance and objectives and then makes changes on-the-fly. It is absolutely essential that you incorporate a change control or version control system into the planning process. Without it, you will likely have much confusion, especially among those responsible for implementing the plan.

Because of the compressed time cycle, New E-Conomy plans should be more abbreviated. The technology and business models are changing rapidly. It is difficult enough to find the time to think through the changes that need to be made, without having to compile a 50-page plan that documents every detail. Simple and concise plans serve the organization more effectively. Continually focusing on meeting the vision and satisfying the goals/metrics are the best ways to keep the company on track. Make sure that the appropriate feedback mechanisms, reward systems, and technology choices are in place to enable the flexibility required during a continuous planning process.

The Tactics of Planning

The skills of planning that we have all learned in business will indeed work well for a holistic Internet-enabled enterprise. The simplest plans are often the best, because they don't take long to develop or read, and everyone can quickly grasp the essentials. Plans that go on forever, whereby creation of the plan is the sole objective, are not the type that will help transform your company into a holistic Internet-enabled entity. The content of the plan stems from the vision/architecture, goals/strategies, and metrics, along with the continual changes in those requirements. It is in the tactical phase of planning (the detailed roadmap) that the changes to the systems, processes, and people are documented in detail.

Who needs to do the planning? A small cross-functional team of major stakeholders is best; three to six people is about right for the core group. A leader should be appointed who can coordinate the work, cost, schedule, resource allocation, and communication. An empowered, self-directed work group usually works best for this purpose (see Chapter 9 "Managing the E-Commerce Organization"). The separate group is vital to the success of this planning effort because that group may recommend ultimate restructuring, transformation, and potential elimination of the current functional lines in the entity.

The amount of lead time for planning depends on the roadmap that's established in the early phase. If a milestone is six months into the future or less, it is time to begin the planning process. For any milestone that is further out, it makes more sense to wait because conditions change so quickly. Of course, after the planning process begins, it never ends. It is a continuous process. In the words of General MacArthur, "The plan is nothing, but planning is everything."

You might go through a few iterations before you develop the prototype plan that will not only satisfy the customer requirements but will also function in accordance with normal business operations. Tweaking will always be needed; in fact it is desirable to experiment during the planning phase and to have flexible plans so that the holistic Internet-enabled entity can freely e-volve in response to external conditions.

The Objective: A Smooth, Empowered, Self-Running Entity

If the planning process is done right, the organization is able to run itself—smoothly. This means that all the people involved are committed to the vision, goals, strategies, and plans. They also understand the plans and are capable of executing them. This also requires that people *believe in* planning, because if people don't, it will be impossible for the organization to react quickly enough to changing conditions; essentially, you will be unable to e-volve. In the New E-Conomy, everything moves too quickly to do business any other way. (See Figure 3.8.)

A committed, empowered organization will be able to deliver customer value consistently and to e-volve the plan as customer needs change and as new processes are added, and to take advantage of the continuing stream of opportunities from the cloud of possibilities. It is the CEO's responsibility to create the environment for this to happen, including any painful decisions that need to be made so the organization can be transformed. These decisions affect the systems, processes, and people in every part of the company. The CEO must be able to develop the vision and gain the commitment of each and every participant in the value web to follow the vision, work toward the goals, measure progress using the established metrics, and change the plan as business circumstances dictate. And all this must be done with the prime objective of delivering value to the customer at every opportunity. That's what it takes to create, implement, and e-volve a holistic Internet-enabled entity.

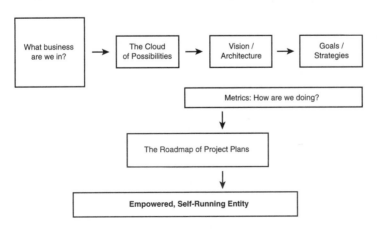

Figure 3.8

The ultimate goal is to have an empowered self-running entity.

E-Volutionary Tactics

→ Planning should be done with the goal of creating and implementing a holistic Internet-enabled entity.

→ Other common plans, such as business plans or specific functional plans, will not work for this purpose.

→ Assume that creation of the holistic Internet-enabled entity will require massive changes in legacy systems, legacy processes, and legacy people.

→ All planning must begin by considering the big picture of the business objectives and the opportunities that are available.

→ From the vision/architecture, a set of goals/strategies are created to harness the power of the company so it can reach its vision.

→ From the goals/strategies, metrics are created that enable the company to track its success at achieving its goals/strategies and that are used to compensate employees.

→ Using the goals/strategies and metrics, a series of projects are created; this is a called roadmap.

→ Metrics should measure success, be realistic, and be appropriate for the business goals.

→ The customer should remain the focus of all processes and plans that are developed and implemented.

→ Assigning goals/metrics into every employee's compensation and empowering employees with the necessary information is essential in the Internet age.

→ Proper planning leads to an empowered self-running entity that can be responsive to rapid changes in the external environment.

→ The CEO needs to establish the vision, gain commitment of all participants in the value chain/web, and create the proper environment for the holistic Internet-enabled entity.

4

Customer Touch Points

IN THE NEW E-CONOMY, the customer is at the center of commerce.

Some would argue that the customer has *always been* (or should have

always been) at the center of commerce, so why is e-commerce any

different? The situation is different because the Internet is the great

equalizer in the economic world of supply and demand. From the cus-

tomers' standpoint, it gives them a newfound power; if they don't like

the level of service they receive from one supplier of goods or servic-

es, they can quickly and easily find another—with the click of a mouse.

▶▶

Brand loyalty is starting to erode, even with more recently established businesses. Loyalty is being replaced by convenience, service level, selection, and added value; that is what customers prefer. This reality creates new worries for all types of companies—from the dot.coms to the established brick and mortar incumbents.

Brick and mortar companies who are migrating their business online are delaying the transition until they feel they can provide the same level of fulfillment and customer service in the online world that they provide in the physical world. Dot.coms need to make sure that the new infrastructure, products, and services they develop have the customer's best interests in mind. To do this successfully requires the ability to think through the marketing, selling, fulfillment, and customer support functions from a different point of view—that of the customer.

The Role of the Customer Is Changing

How much do you know about your customers?

Companies are studying customer behavior at a rate that is unprecedented in our economic history. Why? Because customers are changing at an unprecedented rate, and a lot of simple and affordable tools made possible by technology allow us to measure those changes.

Customers have taken on the level of sophistication inherent in the technology that created the Internet itself. They demand much more information about products and services, and it had better be current. They do more research and comparison shopping; this is true in B2B, B2C, and C2C marketplaces. Greater negotiating power results from greater knowledge. Customers want simplicity and ease of use if they are going to do business online with you. And in the area of service, they want choices in terms of how they can contact the company. Customers have regained control of the buying process. (See Figure 4.1.)

Customers have taken on different roles in the business transaction, according to Michael Tilson, Senior Vice-President of Technology and IS at Rainmaker. "The customer becomes an

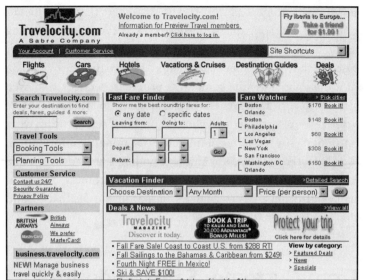

Figure 4.1
www.travelocity.com

With Travelocity, the customers act as their own travel agent.

active participant in the business. With Dell, the customer takes on the role of product designer. With Travelocity, the customers act as their own travel agent. It's important to provide a framework for the customers to succeed, but you don't want them to make mistakes, either."

Companies use a variety of means to study customers. Traditional methods include focus groups and direct surveys by phone or in person. Some companies refrain from focus groups because people aren't always truthful. Other companies try to limit feedback to a more select group of customers, working with them one-on-one. Online surveys or systems that provide interactive feedback through the Web are more recent, are simple to set up, and are relatively inexpensive. Sometimes a company will email a satisfaction survey immediately after a tech support case is completed. Some of the most efficient customer satisfaction surveys I've seen are those that provide immediate, real-time acknowledgment of the feedback. For instance, there is an online survey that displays three graphic "faces" to the user—happy, okay, or sad—after the user enters his or her selection. Surveys that make it entertaining and interesting for the user are likely to be used more.

When a company is in transition (and I would argue that all companies are or should be), it's important to talk to potential or future customers as well as past customers that were dissatisfied and left. Sometimes, this feedback is even more revealing and may point to critical areas in the company's processes or systems that need immediate change. Information provided on how customers use the company's products, services, and Web site is also desirable. Generally speaking, the methods that characterize true customer *behavior*, as opposed to capturing what customers *say*, will result in more meaningful information. Whatever the means, companies are finding a great deal of value in the information they gather about their customers. The companies also must make changes based on the feedback—and that is a lot more difficult to do.

From Customer Satisfaction to Customer Retention

Just a few short years ago, the ultimate goal of any business was to keep customers satisfied. If you made a quality product and delivered adequate service, that was enough. In the New E-Conomy, that is no longer good enough. You need to think about how to turn that satisfied customer into a lifetime customer. The new focus is on customer retention. It requires you to think about your customers as your business partners; they need to be active and involved participants in your business.

"The key factors in retention are trust, security, and service," says Mohit Mehrotra, Vice-President and General Manager of American Express Interactive Business Development. "Trust relates to brand loyalty, and if you're not the big player with brand recognition, you must work hard to gain that trust. Security and service are also intangibles, but it helps if the company can effectively demonstrate that changes are in the customer's best interest and back that with consistent, good service."

In the case of some products that have greater longevity, it can be argued that customer retention might not apply. That may be the case for one product, but how about other products or services that the company might be developing? Also, if a customer replaces or upgrades a product every two or three years, what can you do to support the customer until they are ready to upgrade? That situation presents an opportunity to provide improved levels of service that will keep the customer coming back to you.

Customer retention doesn't apply only to existing customers. Indeed, the targeting and selection of new customers or new market segments is part of the process as well. As companies identify new prospects, it is important to think about how future customers can become lifelong customers. It's like a two-way learning relationship between the company and your customers. The process begins with marketing to those new customers and carries through all the interactions thereafter. In all these interactions, however, it is still critical that customers are satisfied as well: You should not lose sight of customer satisfaction entirely. Customer retention is really the result of long-term continued satisfaction. This has been true throughout the Industrial Age, but now, in the Internet Age, there are more ways than ever to achieve customer retention because there are more ways to serve the customer.

Customer Relationship Management

One of the many catch phrases of the New E-Conomy is "Customer Relationship Management" (often abbreviated to "CRM"). It's a new term for an old practice: paying attention to the whole range of communications through which your customer can contact you, along with managing customer accounts and prospects. Referring to this practice as CRM adds a new dimension, however, and that is the idea of a continuous business relationship between the customer and the company—as well as the work that is required to manage it. The customer relationship requires managing the knowledge you have about the customer, the visibility you provide to them, and the interactions your company enables through your infrastructure.

The customer relationship has many phases. Brooks Fisher, Vice-President of Corporate Strategy and Marketing at Intuit, describes it this way: "Think about all the interactions involved in a business transaction. The customer relationship begins with the marketing messages that the customer hears or sees, followed by discussions with a sales representative or placement of an order—online or otherwise. Then, there may be installation or post-sale support of some type, and ultimately, retention. In all these interactions, the customer may deal with different people or processes of your company. They all need to contribute to building that customer relationship." Managing the relationship throughout the whole cycle requires an understanding of how the company performs during each of these phases.

Clyde Foster, CEO of eConvergent, believes that CRM is about managing the relationship and not the customer, because the customer can't be managed; they have the power and the choices. "It's critical to manage the business relationships so that the customers get a rich, consistent experience," he says. "This means the technology employed, the people involved, and the processes must be in place to deliver that consistency."

The Five Major Touch Points

A company has a certain number of opportunities to interact with its customers, and each interaction must be a positive, or at least a neutral, experience. There are five major classes of touch points, during which the company (or its representatives) communicates with the customer, and information, goods, or services change hands (see Figure 4.2). Each class of touch point represents one or more actual interfaces with the customer. The five classes are listed here:

- ▲ Generating demand
- ▲ Communicating product characteristics
- ▲ Conducting the transaction
- ▲ Fulfilling the order
- ▲ Post-sale customer service

During these touch points, the communications can take place using a variety of vehicles. These include telephone, in-person,

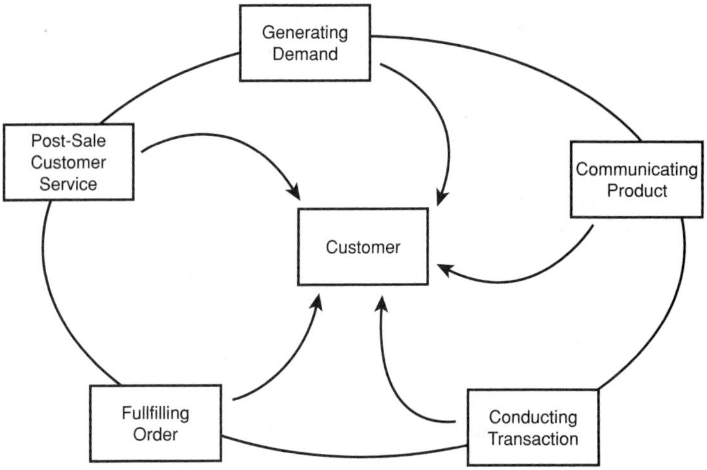

Figure 4.2
The five customer touch points.

Diagram boxes: Generating Demand, Post-Sale Customer Service, Communicating Product, Customer, Fullfilling Order, Conducting Transaction

fax, email, or Web. Most of these are "technology-enabled" touch points and are susceptible to depersonalization of the customer interaction. "It's important to have some human interface with customers, even with all of the tempting technology solutions available today," says Russ Cohn, Chairman of Brigade Corporation. "You also may be missing an opportunity to get live feedback from a customer if you give up all of the human interface." The "high-tech, high-touch" ratio is still an important consideration. Each vehicle may be managed by different people or organizations in the company—in other words, somewhere along the way, human beings are involved who serve as receivers of the communication sent by the customer. With five classes of touch points and five different communication vehicles, a vast number of interface points are possible, and all must be managed consistently no matter who is responsible—a computer, an individual inside or outside the company, or an outsourced service provider.

Stratifying Your Customer Base

In a holistic Internet-enabled entity, it's important to know your various customers and service them with the right corporate tools. You should also fire customers you can't service efficiently. Figure 4.3 illustrates this simple stratification.

Figure 4.3

Stratification of your customer base.

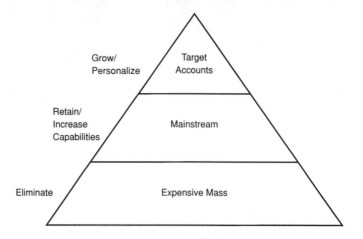

The target accounts are the 20% of your customers that represent 80% of the business. If your business model supports a direct sales force, these customers are the ones they service. Playing golf with these customers is more important than providing a Web-based interface. However, the tools built for the next tier (the mainstream) can certainly be offered to the target accounts. It is also possible to provide valuable content and applications online that are exclusive for this audience. Schwab has developed their Signature services to provide research reports, enhanced trading tools, and other benefits to the high-net-worth investor.

▲ The *mainstream* is the 60% of your clientele who represent the next 10–15% of your business. These are the customers for whom you build Internet-based tools. It's important to migrate these customers from the individual salesperson and telephone-based support to an Internet-based model. If they want to use the older methods, you need to give them the ability to pay for more personalized service. The tools built should be made available to the target accounts and also the partners that might take over the ownership of the customers who were "fired" from the expensive mass.

▲ The *expensive mass* is the 20% of your customers who represent the remaining 5–10% of your sales. Typically, the model used to service these customers produces a loss for you. You should fire them. It's the hardest thing in the world to fire a customer. You can make this less painful by finding a partner (potentially a channel partner) that is able to serve this class of customer more efficiently. If possible and appropriate, you can supply goods, information, and Web tools to the partner to better service these customers.

Do you need to fire the customers that you can't afford to service?

Individual and Personalized Interactions

Customers have high expectations not only that your company will be consistent in the way you treat them, but that you will always keep their best interests in mind. You must also anticipate what customers will want next. This should be easier after your market research has been completed; however, the most important thing to remember is that customers are human. They change their minds and behaviors from time to time. As humans, they behave as individuals and usually like to be treated that way. But how is that possible, especially in markets where you may have thousands or perhaps millions of customers? It requires a new perspective. Steve Larsen, Senior Vice-President of Net Perceptions, suggests "If you have 100,000 customers, you need to have 100,000 stores—at least in terms of your business philosophy. Each customer is a "free agent," and has a different set of behaviors, preferences, and decision patterns—and that is their "store." This philosophy also applies to B2B markets.

Technology can help personalize the experience even for individual customers who are part of large or small market segments. Techniques such as data mining and online interactive surveys powered by artificial intelligence (neural networks) can identify individual needs and make targeted product recommendations in real-time, online. Amazon.com was one of the first dot.coms to use this technique successfully, and this is one of the key ways Amazon builds customer retention (see Figure 4.4).

Figure 4.4
www.amazon.com

Collaborative filtering is one of the key ways that Amazon builds customer retention.

Who Interacts with the Customer?

How will your partners deal with your customers?

In the old economy, vertically integrated companies were able to contain and manage all business functions internally. In the New E-Conomy, there are many more opportunities to out-source, and in a lot of cases, it's an economic advantage to do so. But if you do, you still need to *own* all the touch points, no matter who personally interfaces with the customer. Your company needs to manage the entire end-to-end customer experience. This means that all the systems, processes, and people in the value chain deliver a consistent, valuable experience. It's like having a 360-degree view of your customer at the heart of your business.

E-Volving Your Business Processes Around Your Customer

Companies invent or change business processes as external or internal forces dictate. It is critical that business processes map to the five touch points, because it is through processes that you deliver service to your customer.

It is not easy to accomplish this in an existing organization. If your business processes change, systems and *people* must also change. This requires commitment and action from the CEO on down through the organization. This often means major changes in organizational structures that have been created to satisfy business needs of the Industrial Age. These structures need to be reinvented to better serve the customer, using the tools and capabilities now available in the Information Age.

It benefits the company when business processes become more customer-centric. Polaroid launched a B2B Web site that offers business and professional customers real-time imaging solutions—specific to their profession or need. This provided an accelerated way to reach customers, but more importantly, it improved marketing and sales processes (see Figure 4.5).

You also need to give your customers a choice as to which of your business processes they will use. Sometimes customers may prefer to keep using the old process, and in that case, you should provide a way for the customer to "opt out" of the new and (theoretically) improved process. It's all part of maintaining customer-centric processes. Peter Ostrow, CEO of Testmart, believes that it's important to give customers a choice so they can transition to the online environment at their own pace. He says, "You must give customers options...for instance, a new Web site

Do your business processes fit your customer?

Figure 4.5
www.polaroidwork.com
Polaroid's B2B Web site offering business and professional customers real-time imaging solutions.

that doesn't even list a phone number for contacting the company is a bad move. People's experiences aren't uniform, and they also need a way to provide feedback directly to the company—as well as contact a human once in a while. In B2B situations where there aren't that many customers, this is especially critical."

From Customer to Process to Business Model

In order to make sure that value is passed through all participants in the value Web and on to the customer, it is necessary to revisit the business model from time to time. It is especially important to do this as business processes e-volve.

Do you deliver value at each customer touch point?

There are several components to delivering value. The first component is that the experience must be positive. That means that the customer always gets what they expect, and sometimes more. It is possible to over-innovate; delivering more may actually decrease the perceived value! The second component is that the experience must be consistent: There should be no surprises. What the customer expects to happen in the way of response time and ease of use *does* indeed happen. Yahoo does an excellent job of delivering positive and consistent experiences to their customers. Their focus on this has contributed to their overall success and profitability.

Profitability of your company also plays a part in delivering value. If you build in processes and systems to maximize the experience for your customers, but you can't afford to sustain them for a very long time, you won't be in business very long. What you offer that delivers value must be balanced with high-level business goals, without overtaxing the company to support the new model.

If you are a brick and mortar company in the process of moving your business operations online, it is necessary to re-evaluate the value proposition for your existing customers. What happens when you migrate your operations? Will your customers go with you? Sometimes the value proposition can change drastically if you pressure the customer to interact with you online.

You need to offer existing customers choices, and you need to be consistent in how you continue to support those customers. Sometimes migrating operations to an online environment can result in tremendous cost savings for your company. What better way to bring your customers along with you than to pass some of that savings on to them, in the form of incentives, discounts, or rebates? An example is United Airlines (and others) who have provided frequent flier rewards for tickets booked directly online. It is important to remember that you are still in the same business; you are merely using a different mechanism to deliver your products and service to your customers. Williams-Sonoma has been successful at developing and maintaining both their retail and online environments with a comparable level of customer service and support.

Intuit discovered the need for choice with their existing customers. "With our QuickBooks product line, we provide annually updated income tax tables to our existing customers. Since most of our customers only upgrade their software every three years, we had to offer choices as to whether we mailed out diskettes or allowed people to download the tables from our Web site. We decided to keep the price points the same for both products because we didn't want to influence the customer's choice. Our customers were much happier with us as a result," said Brooks Fisher, Vice-President of Corporate Strategy and Marketing for Intuit.

Sometimes the exercise of delivering improved customer value can result in discovery of a new business model, as in the case of Tupperware. By making their products available to customers online, not only were they able to respond to customer demand, but they also found a way to credit each online sale to a local sales representative near the customer's geographic location. This way, the company was able to keep its main distribution channel going, as well as providing new incentives for the online business.

Delivering Value on an Individual Basis

Online markets vary in terms of how value is perceived. For high-bandwidth services such as entertainment and sports, you can add value only up to a point. You can offer the interactivity and entertainment features that customers want, but past that point, there are diminishing returns. However, in a low-bandwidth environment such as online financial services, customers expect basic transactions and easy, dependable usability. In that case, the impact of adding content or service can be huge, because customers regain control. They can make their own decisions and handle their own transactions. If you can also personalize the service you provide to your online customers, it's even better. Due to their emphasis on customer research and feedback, Intuit has been very successful in their online offerings as well as their traditional products. CDNOW.com also is successful at personalized, highly targeted marketing based on customer behavior (see Figure 4.6).

Figure 4.6
www.cdnow.com

CDNOW.com utilizes personalized, highly targeted marketing based on customer behavior.

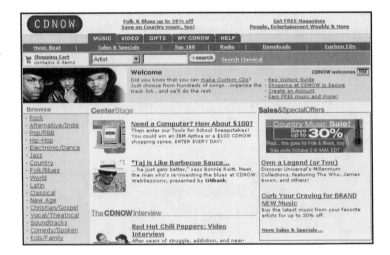

Many of the early companies who are successful in managing touch points are still servicing only one or two touch points at a time, but not all—at least not in real-time. They may be excellent at Web interactions, but they don't provide a convenient way to speak with a customer service person simultaneously. The companies that will survive and win will be those that are able to deliver the information, product, convenience, and level of service at every single touch point—all customized for the specific customer and relevant to that customer's needs. Companies need to be both proactive and reactive in managing these touch points. (See Figure 4.7.)

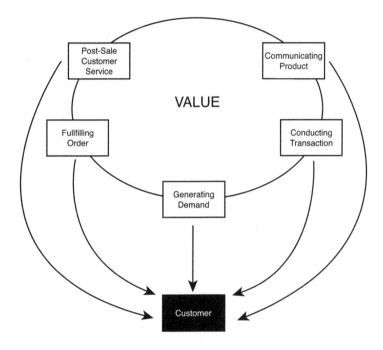

Figure 4.7

Provide value at every touch point.

E-Volutionary Tactics

→ Keeping the customer at the center of your business requires attention to customer touch points.

→ You must know your customer in detail and be able to anticipate your customers' needs.

→ Even if you outsource, you must still own the customer touch points.

→ Customers in the New E-Conomy are more informed and sophisticated and expect personalization—of information, products, and services.

→ You (or your partners) must deliver personalized value at each and every touch point.

→ You must fire the customers you can't afford to service.

→ As customers change, you must e-volve your systems, processes, and people in order to keep the customer at the center of your business.

5

Content Will Always Be King

IN E-COMMERCE, content plays an increasingly important role. In fact, it can be said that the line has blurred between content and commerce. Not every site is content-driven, but every site has content. The minute you set up a Web site, you are publishing content, whether or not that is your primary business. In the early days of e-commerce, there were content sites and commerce sites. "Content-only sites couldn't figure out how to do business, and commerce-only sites couldn't generate the right content to attract, convert, and retain customers," says Dylan Tweney, Writer and Consultant, Tweney Media. "Content is the primary

▶▶

way to effect loyalty, that is, keeping a potential customer at your site longer than your competitor's."

Today we are doing business a different way. It can be described as "contextual transactional commerce." Companies sell products in the context of what business they are in and the strategic objectives they have identified. Content serves to define and shape the context in which the e-commerce business transactions take place. Sometimes content is free, and sometimes it has a price. Says Sean Kaldor, Vice-President of E-Commerce, NetRatings, "Even if your content is free of charge in terms of dollars, people pay with their time to view ads—that is the 'currency' of content. You need to keep this in mind when you decide how content will serve your business and your customers." Content extends the business to the online environment and should be regarded as just another part of doing business. Companies need to decide if they will give content away or if they will charge for it. If you have free content, you need stickiness. If your business model enables you to charge for content and still keep customers interested, you must do it in a way that fits the value proposition of your customer.

What's included in content? The text, the images, and the way they are organized and presented on a Web site. Content conveys to the site visitor what your offerings are, and it forms the corporate face that you present to the online world. The business goals of content might include sales, promotion, education, entertainment, distribution, research, forums for feedback, and customer support. The opportunities are endless for ways to creatively use content to further any or all of these goals. (See Figure 5.1.)

Content Must Provide Value to the Customer

As you have learned in previous chapters, the customer's needs come first when you're developing Web site content. Because today's customers are better informed and very sophisticated, their expectations for content that "lives" on the average Web

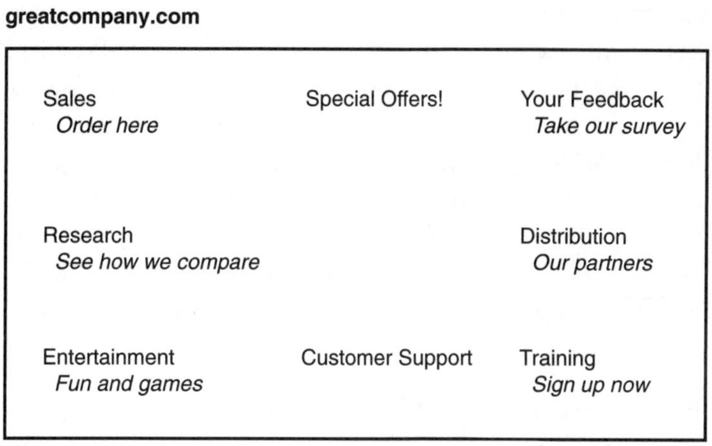

greatcompany.com

Figure 5.1
The possible uses of content.

Sales *Order here*	Special Offers!	Your Feedback *Take our survey*
Research *See how we compare*		Distribution *Our partners*
Entertainment *Fun and games*	Customer Support	Training *Sign up now*

site are very advanced. They expect you to anticipate their questions and post the prepared answers on your site. They want to see comparisons of your product versus other alternatives; if you don't provide some guidance, they will look elsewhere on the Web.

B2B enterprises face some tough challenges. Chemdex.com and e-STEEL.com are both online marketplaces that have been successful at combining an exchange environment with content that helps support both the buyers and the sellers. It is more complicated when you must serve multiple constituencies and you need to anticipate the information your "trading partners" will need to conduct transactions. Another B2B example is Xerox. Through a private network link, Xerox provides the capability for the customer to view copier usage throughout their company and be notified when there are problems so that maintenance or repair can be scheduled.

How do you determine what content is needed at your site? Once again, you need to have a clear and detailed understanding of your customer base and their behavior. You need to determine why existing or potential customers visit your site and how you might be able to serve them better with content. You can also take a look at your competitors' Web sites to see what content you like; you may decide to provide comparable content or entirely different content. Desired content may include news, product reviews, customer feedback, FAQs, or online

What do your customers think of your content?

community-generated chat. Sometimes even ads are desired by customers, according to Steve Larsen, Senior Vice-President, Net Perceptions. "Even in the print world, publications such as *Computer Shopper* or *Whole Earth Catalog* were purchased *because* of the ads. The ads were the content. Online, the ultimate situation is to have all ads become content—only show ads for topics and products that customers are genuinely interested in—on an individual basis. Recent technology advances are bringing this closer to reality every day." This is an example of contextual commerce.

It's very easy to get caught up in the creative process of generating content and lose sight of the customers' best interests. This is especially true for content that serves a marketing purpose (and any time you have any content at a Web site, you are automatically doing marketing). Adding a marketing spin to the content needs to be balanced with the true informational content. Customers these days are savvy enough to see right through any marketing hype. However, if you can begin to provide high-quality targeted information, people will come back to your site often; there is a lot of hype and "empty" content out there on the Web. Some companies that do a good job of providing value are Garden.com and CDNOW.com; both have a good balance of product information and educational or informative content, and both have very high site traffic (see Figure 5.2).

Figure 5.2
www.garden.com

Garden.com has a good balance of product information and educational content on their Web site.

Content also needs to further the business objective, and you need to determine how content will do that. Ask yourself these questions:

- ▲ Will you be expanding your sales or generating leads?
- ▲ Adding new geographic markets?
- ▲ Launching a new product line?
- ▲ Entering a new strategic partnership that will provide more products and services?

The answers to these questions will determine the types of content you need to develop. Studying your customers will help you develop the content so your customers will be attracted to it and will read it. Remember: Along with your business processes, content must be customer-centric.

The creation, management, and potential syndication of content should be regarded as a vital business process. Content is a marketing process, a sales process, a logistics process, and a customer service process—all at the same time.

- ▲ For content to be an effective marketing tool, it needs to carry the overall branding of the company, as well as convey the product-level messages you want your customers to receive.

- ▲ Content is often a non-human sales process and, as such, provides access, ease of use, and information the customer needs to order and purchase goods and services.

- ▲ Logistics come into play from two perspectives: You deliver needed information to the customers who will be making decisions, and you provide a way to deliver goods and services to the customers who place orders.

- ▲ Customer service is a very important aspect of content. Although you may have dedicated content for post-sale support or customer questions, all the content should convey the level of service and attention the company intends to give the customer. Remember that it takes five to six times more effort to acquire a new customer than to sell to your existing customer base.

All four of these content processes need to be organized so they are presented in the business context of what you are trying to accomplish and so they contribute to a holistic and compelling customer experience. Many Web sites focus on content creation but do not set up the right business processes to update or delete content to reflect the changing business offering. It is absolutely critical that you spend the time and energy to make content an organic part of your business. (See Figure 5.3.)

Organizing and Designing Content

For content to be effective for its target audience, it must be accessible and user friendly. If your customers can't find the content they need, or if accessing it is complicated, they will go elsewhere.

A good starting point is to consider these questions before you develop and organize your content:

▲ *Business objective:* What do you want to accomplish with your content?

Figure 5.3

The four content processes.

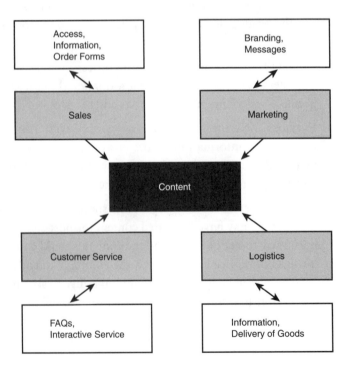

- ▲ *Audience:* Who are they and what are their needs?
- ▲ *Navigation and usability:* How sophisticated are your typical users?
- ▲ *Product or service:* What are your offerings at the site?
- ▲ *Value proposition:* What can you offer at the site that's of value to your customer?
- ▲ *Type of site:* How will the site deliver on its promise?

With these questions answered, you will have a much better idea of the high-level organization needed for your site.

The next thing to do is to identify and gather the content that will fit this high-level organizational scheme. Do you have existing content that you can repurpose online? If not, identify the new content that needs to be created, who will generate the content, and who will make sure it stays fresh. When the content is listed, create categories and subcategories that form a site architecture. Some of these categories include home page, content pages, navigation, search and result, help, company, contact info, job, and transaction pages. Whether you have a static or dynamic site, categories should be diagrammed into a hierarchy that will become the site map. Until the site map is in place, the content should not be generated. This will eliminate possible duplication of effort and ensure that the groups of content relate to one another in accordance with the overall architecture. It is also important that the site map itself be consistent with the navigation and usability requirements. If you post the site map for your site visitors to use as a guide to content, you don't want to make it so elaborate that it confuses them. (See Figures 5.4 and 5.5.)

For sites that aggregate content from many sources and also provide links, you will face a greater challenge to organize it all and keep it accessible. A company that does a good job of integrating content is ExciteClassifieds.com. For example, for a used-car listing, ExciteClassifieds.com would have an ad for a car, consumer reviews, and a link to blue-book values—three vital pieces of content with which to convert a site visitor into a customer.

Figure 5.4

Organize your information into a site map that will cover all the purposes of content.

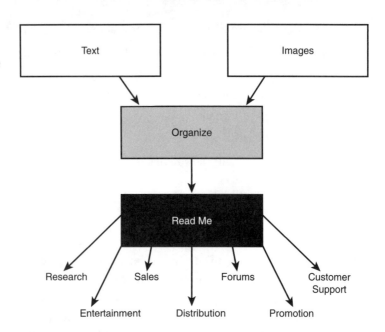

Figure 5.5

www.ecnow.com

ECnow.com's hierarchical site map.

Site "stickiness" is a prime objective (*stickiness* is the overall quality of a site that keeps visitors at your site and keeps them coming back). Stickiness is more than just navigation and interesting text or graphics; it's the way the content is organized, updated, and presented in the business context. Stickiness means that you are providing a valuable customer experience for all site visitors and a reason for them to come back frequently.

Valuable Content Is a Differentiator

Companies often monitor the content on competitors' sites to find out how often they change content and how it compares to their sites. It's tempting to copy what your competitors are doing with their site, especially if they have high site traffic. However, modeling your site or content too closely to a competitor's is not such a good idea, because if you do that, what is your differentiator? It is more important to focus on the content that has value for your customer and fits your company's culture, philosophy, and brand. Remember that your content represents your company's face to the online world, not your competitor's face. Web site content is a valuable part of every company's marketing department, as discussed in more detail in Chapter 10, "Ongoing Internet Marketing."

If you can create a unique way to present or organize content, you can generate a lot of site traffic. Lands' End became the first retailer to find a way for customers to "try on" clothes online— using 3D modeling based on customer measurements (see Figure 5.6). This is one example of how a single customer's needs can be matched with Web site content powered by a Web site tool. Unique content that also adds value (from the customer's perspective) can help keep customers coming back to your site.

Figure 5.6
www.landsend.com

Lands' End allows customers to virtually try on clothes.

Competitive Advantage Means Constantly E-Volving Content

If you are satisfied that your content is fresher, more targeted, and more valuable than your competitors' content, that is just the beginning. Your competitors merely set the benchmark. You must constantly update and find new ways to keep customers interested.

Content needs to be updated as often as possible—even daily if that makes sense in the business context. The rate at which content is added is not as important as getting the eyeball time for the new content. One way to do that is to use personalization; you can send an email notification to selected customers who would benefit from the specific content that was updated (Chapter 10 also discusses the topic of personalization). Amazon.com has been doing this successfully for their book business, and customers like it. The real challenge here is how the business process would support such an effort. It's one thing to deliver personalized messaging; it's quite another to put in place the content creation process to create these individualized messages. Your infrastructure and processes need to be in place first.

If you set up your site map and content properly in the beginning, it will be easier to update content. You should provide a way for content to be easily archived or deleted. Make sure you have style guidelines in place so that the content creators maintain consistency in their updates and new content. Keep an eye on competitors' content, but don't overuse buzzwords just to be trendy. Make sure you add value for your customer with every change or update.

Measuring the Effectiveness of Content

Because content lives on a Web site, it is very easy to measure traffic for each content page. But site visitor counts are only part of the picture. Depending on your goal, different measurements are called for. For example, to generate leads, you need more duration and interaction at the site. In that case, you need to measure site visitors, page views, click stream, time spent on the site, and the number of users who have signed up for either the "free" newsletter or the one-to-one marketing product reminder. If your goal is to generate sales, you need a snappy-fast interface with shorter site duration and a visible "Buy Now" button. In that situation, you need to measure site visitors, page views, click stream, conversion rates, and related metrics. (See Figure 5.7.)

The Web site should be designed so that the business goals drive the architecture of the content, which in turn should be organized by customer groupings (down to the personalized, individual level if possible). If this is set up properly before the content is posted, it is much easier to measure traffic to that area. Some key business measures to evaluate content include the following:

- ▲ Are leads increasing?
- ▲ How many catalog requests have occurred?
- ▲ Are sales increasing?
- ▲ Are there fewer calls to the customer service center?
- ▲ Are page views increasing?

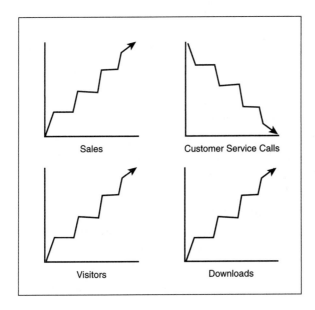

Figure 5.7

There are a number of ways to measure effectiveness of content. You must decide what makes sense for your business.

- ▲ Is the number of visitors increasing?
- ▲ Is the average length of stay on the site increasing?
- ▲ Are people using the interactive tools or downloading free information?
- ▲ How many software downloads have occurred?

Site logs for traffic analysis can help you fine-tune your site. Another important measure of content effectiveness is to get feedback from site visitors and customers. Interactive areas placed within the content can enable individualized feedback to be gathered. It is possible, however, to overdo this, which can lead to negative reactions from the customers and site visitors. According to Bill Daniel, Senior Vice-President of Products at Vignette, "It's better to try to use metadata to associate customer preferences on-the-fly, and then push information *choices* to the customer."

Who Creates Content?

There are many sources of content other than internally generated information. It's possible to use input from your business partners, from linked Web sites, from newsletter subscribers, and even from your customers in order to refine and e-volve your content. The premiere ECM e-zine, ECMgt.com, uses customer responses to generate content, and eBay allows their buyers and sellers to evaluate one another, resulting in a database of "ratings." These are examples of valuable content generated by users.

Your content does not have to be developed internally. Many companies provide tools and services to help you acquire or manage content. Syndication includes developing and acquiring content to other sources, and several companies do this as their primary business. iSyndicate.com is a company that makes it easy to acquire content. Vignette's tools, such as StoryServer and Syndication Server, help personalize product and deliver content, as well as measure performance. You can even outsource this function if you do not have enough internal resources to manage content. Throughout all of this, however, you must make sure the customer touch points are addressed—even if you use outside content.

You can also create new partnerships with content providers or act as a portal for content, but you need to make sure these methods still meet your business objectives. Whenever you link to or "rent" other people's content, it's important to remember that it is not your content, so it must add value to *your* site visitors and customers. If it doesn't add value, or if it distracts or causes people to leave your site, it might not be in your best interests. (See Figure 5.8.)

Whoever creates the content should also have the role of managing it. It's necessary to update it, and the creator of the content has much better knowledge of what needs to be changed and how to change it.

What other sources of content are available to you?

E-Volving Content in Context

The key to successful content management is to e-volve it for the right reasons and to keep the content in the context of your business when you do change or update it. Content that is developed in context can fulfill many business objectives. Content needs to be considered an asset of your company that affects many of your business processes and is central to your vision and strategies for the future. Content can help you strengthen

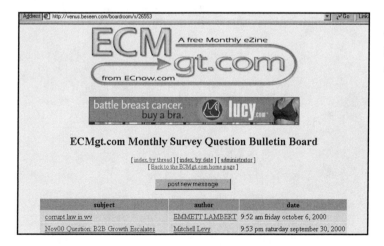

Figure 5.8
www.ecmgt.com
ECMgt.com's organic readers comments page.

your brand and corporate image, improve the quality of customer service, streamline your internal processes, and improve competitive advantage. It is also key to expanding your global reach, as addressed in the next chapter.

E-Volutionary Tactics

→ Content can't be separated from commerce.

→ Content must be developed and organized to fit the business context of the company.

→ Customers have a major influence on the type and amount of content on your Web site.

→ Valuable content is a strong differentiator.

→ There are many sources of content other than your company.

→ It's important to e-volve the content as often as possible to keep it fresh and to be consistent with other changes in the company's business model or processes.

→ Content needs to be the responsibility of all participants in the organization's value web who deal with customer touch points (described in Chapter 4).

Instant Global Presence

FASTEN YOUR SEAT BELT! It's time for your business to venture out to the rest of the world. I know what you're thinking… "But, we are already global. We have a Web site that can be accessed from anywhere, and we have international sales. What's the big deal?" The big deal is this: Being truly *global* means having to re-create and re-deploy your holistic Internet-enabled entity every time you venture into another geographic market. It is a *very* big deal, and you are in for a wild ride.

▶▶

Just because your Web site is accessible from anywhere in the world doesn't necessarily mean you are a global business.

The entire online world connected by the Internet breaks down boundaries of communications, culture, and business. The minute you establish a Web site, you are instantly global… or are you? Just because a Web site is accessible from anywhere in the world doesn't necessarily mean you are a global business. Customers need to be able to find you. You must be able to support multicultural business operations, and it must be part of your business vision and be understood by your entire organization. And you need to have the committed resources to support truly global business operations. (See Figure 6.1.)

What is your home country? Where do you want to go next?

Whether your company is based in the United States, Europe, Asia, or any other part of the world, you are probably thinking about extending your reach beyond where your company's headquarters reside. There are many factors involved in deciding where, when, and how you will globalize the operations of your holistic Internet-enabled entity, as this chapter addresses. Before you read on, however, think about the rest of the world as a new frontier—a global marketplace waiting for your business. When you venture into this new frontier, you must first build a new foundation for your business, which will require time, attention, and many resources. Before you venture out, think first about where you want to go next and *why*.

Figure 6.1

Global boundaries and barriers are disappearing.

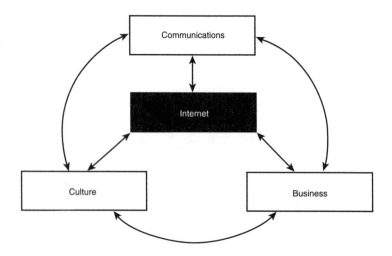

Being Global

Being global is a conscious decision that requires strategy, planning, and resources. "It means that you are doing business online without being restricted by the location of buyer and seller," according to Jorden Woods, Chairman and CTO of GlobalSight. It also requires an understanding of customers who reside in other cultures and who have different currencies, languages, and laws.

Being global means that your entire organization is involved in global operations, including marketing, sales, procurement, logistics, legal, customer service, fulfillment, IT, and accounting. All your front office and back office processes need to be ready to support global business. According to Mark Resch, President and CEO of CommerceNet, "You need to have business processes in place that will enable you to manage the *success* from having international business." (See Figure 6.2.)

When will you be truly global?

For a holistic Internet-enabled entity, there are tremendous advantages to being global. Expansion of market presence and

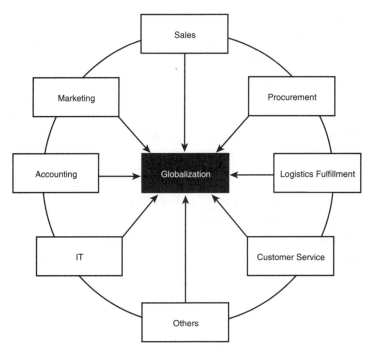

Figure 6.2

All of your processes and your organization need to be involved in globalization.

brand, increase in revenues, competitive advantage, improvement of communications, faster growth, and accessibility of new ideas for innovation are just some of them. Likewise, there are many ways to find opportunities—within your company, in the marketplace, from your partners, and on the Web. Two good sources on the Web for identifying market opportunities by region are emarketer.com and nua.ie.

The Case for Globalization

Does your company need to be global? Does only a part of your company need to be global? What are the benefits and the risks? The Internet economy has blurred or erased most of the traditional geographic boundaries, and some companies feel pressured to be global because of their competitors, but they may not be ready to develop and manage global operations. Globalization needs to be analyzed like any major business decision; you need to examine the benefits as well as the risks.

Some of the benefits include revenues, profits, growth in market share, building brands, and overall growth. For many large multinational companies, more than 40 percent of their revenues are derived from outside their home country. Some examples include Philips, which is 95% non-Netherlands; Toshiba, which is 40% non-Japanese, and Cisco, for which 50% of revenues are generated outside the U.S.[1] Beyond revenues and overall growth, companies might also see gains in technology, ideas, communications, and brand presence, all of which can be attained by maintaining operations and interacting with customers and partners in international locations.

The risks include strain on company resources, costs, legal hurdles, and fit with the company's vision and strategy. The way to minimize these risks or mitigate them is to develop your global strategy and plans so that your entire organization is aligned for

---

1 "Global E-Commerce: Taking Your Business Global on the Web." Course material from Jorden Woods and GlobalSight Corporation, 2000, used with permission.

global operations. Sometimes it is easier to approach the issue on an incremental basis in terms of implementation, but no matter how you roll out global programs, it will be necessary to think globally—from the beginning. This will entail building a new foundation for your business and evolving your business processes, systems, and people in order to function in a global world. Seeking new partnerships and outsourcing are other ways to convert the risks into benefits. (See Figure 6.3.)

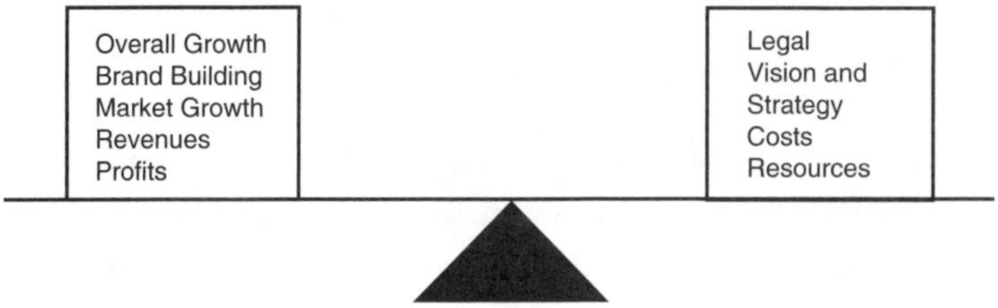

Overall Growth Brand Building Market Growth Revenues Profits		Legal Vision and Strategy Costs Resources

Figure 6.3

Globalization decisions involve weighing benefits and risks.

Your Vision Determines Your Global Presence

In Chapter 3, I described the importance of your vision. Revisit that vision statement; what did it say about the extent of global operations? Because globalization is a tremendous undertaking, it's imperative that you make it part of your vision or develop a new vision statement that captures your global objective. This vision statement also needs to be communicated and understood by your entire organization, because they *all* will be involved in the globalization process. You need everyone's help to build a new foundation.

If you don't have global operations now, what geographies will you serve in the future, and when? This is a key decision, because even if your short-term plans don't include a truly global presence until several months or years into the future, you must implement any online presence accordingly. For instance, if you need to *exclude* any geographies because you can't support business there, your Web site must be designed so that it is clear to site visitors and potential customers.

Thinking Globally

Before you can think globally, you must make several decisions regarding how you will address some of the hurdles of global e-commerce operations (see Figure 6.4). These include:

▲ *Legal issues:* trade boundaries and policies, contractual, marketing

▲ *Logistics:* shipping, customs, processes, and distances

▲ *Currency:* e-currency, exchange rates, transactions

▲ *Language/culture:* localization, tools

All these issues are a matter of choice. The important thing is that you are aware of some of the hurdles you will need to overcome, and then you can decide how you are going to address them in the context of your vision and your business operations.

Thinking globally means taking the time to understand how business is done in each country where you plan to operate. Maria-Luisa Rodriguez, co-founder and Director, e-co consulting, discovered that it's necessary to understand the mentality and the business practices. "When we formed our company, we decided that we would start with the French market, and yet none of the founders are French. We had a long learning curve to understand the planning cycles, communications, negotiation style, and sales practices in our marketplace." It pays to do your homework ahead of time regarding your target geographies, especially if your company has no previous experience there. Sometimes knowledge can be gained from established business partners who already operate in the area of interest.

Figure 6.4

Legal issues, logistics, currency, and language hurdles must be overcome for successful e-commerce operations.

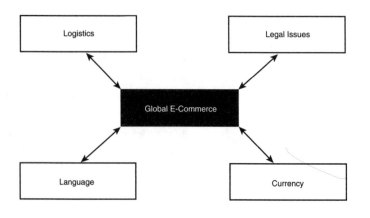

Legal Barriers

The number of legal barriers you have to overcome depends on the number of countries in which you can do business. Import/export laws and trade regulations vary by country, and they affect what you can do online, as well. Not only does the law apply between countries, but each country that you want to do business with has its own laws that may govern how you can market, advertise, and deliver goods and services. Planning has to be done on a country-by-country basis. Depending on the nature of your product or service, you may or may not be able to export to every country. If you already have established brick and mortar businesses within those countries, you are ahead of the game; however, even though you may have the logistics, legacy, and cultural barriers satisfied, you still need to look at the legal differences online. It will merely be a matter of extending your business online as another way to serve your existing customer base.

Some companies choose to ignore local laws and begin their business operations anyway. That may be a short-term solution, but doing so will create a longer-term issue of credibility that will limit your growth, especially if you plan to become a public company.

The European Union has many consumer protection laws that vary by country, which affect how you do business within those countries. These laws primarily serve the following functions:

- ▲ Regulate the way advertising and promotion can be done.
- ▲ Regulate the claims that cannot be made.
- ▲ Impose bans on certain types of ads altogether.

It's critical that you understand these laws in detail before you put expansion plans into place for these geographies—to avoid costly and lengthy litigation or to eliminate the need to rapidly pull out of a market.

Sometimes contractual issues need to be handled as well. Vendors or distributors in a foreign location may have exclusive import or export contracts with the local government, and you may have to use them instead of your own infrastructure or outsourced services. You might need to evaluate your current business partners to find out whether they can do business in the geographies you are targeting. If not, you will need to seek out those who can. Certain countries have different laws regarding validity of contracts. Chapter 11, "The Law Catches Up to E-Business," addresses some of the legal issues that affect international e-commerce.

Worldwide Logistics

Delivery of goods from your company to your global customers will still be affected by customs regulations and processes, and even in the most economically advanced countries, this can be a painfully slow process. Customs can add several days or even weeks to the delivery time of goods, and tracking a shipment's progress through the red tape can be a nightmare as well. Says Todd Elizalde, Director of E-Commerce, Cisco Systems, "Customs are a huge issue. Sometimes your ability to track shipments through the customs process is limited by each country. It can have a direct impact on customer satisfaction as well as the bottom line."

Also, in terms of shipping, you may need multiple carriers to get your goods to their destination. This adds complexity to the tracking process, as well as introducing potential delays to the delivery process. Another factor is speed of delivery. In some parts of Europe, for example, only one or two large-volume carriers do business, which may mean that demand might overload their capacity to deliver. Smaller, more localized carriers may not have express service, but they may be able to provide better (and often faster) service because of their established relationships with local customs offices. They also may be able to provide fulfillment and inventory services for you.

Online Currencies

You can decide how many currencies you will use in your online business. Most companies find that one or two are sufficient. From a financial point of view, deciding which ones to use is a matter of weighing credit risks by country, as well as currency fluctuations. From a marketing point of view, you need to determine where your highest-priority customers are located and which currencies they commonly use.

Once you decide which currencies you are going to use, you must be able to implement the corresponding payment and banking systems to support the transactions. Fluctuating exchange rates, the bureaucracy of banking systems, and varying levels of security are just some of the issues you need to address when dealing with multiple currencies. That's the back office side of things. Don't forget the front office side, however. Any and all price lists accessible online must reflect the multiple currencies as well.

Multilingual E-Commerce

Being successful online means that your customers can access information about your company's products and services, and that they are able to conduct information or financial transactions. Given this definition, it is advisable to plan your Web site content so that it is translatable into several languages. Luckily, many technology solutions available today can instantly provide translation; it's a matter of deciding which languages you will translate and then installing the tools on your site. Although business transactions in a B2B environment are still largely conducted in English and are not translated, for B2C enterprises, it is becoming more important. The problem with any translation tool in today's environment is that it will only translate 80–90% of the language. You will still need a human to review the results and customize the tools so that they make sense in the context of your business. It is critical that you learn more about your customers' preferences before you make a decision on what to translate. This should be part of your global market segmentation process.

Figure 6.5
world.altavista.com

Tools like Altavista's allow the user to translate an entire Web page into another language.

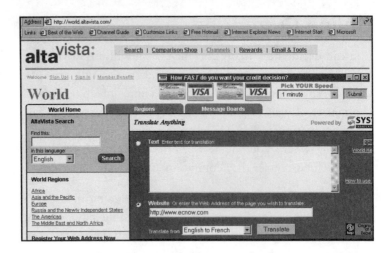

If you decide to do translation, differences in usage and dialect must be taken into consideration. For example, Canadian French is different than that used in the country of France. Even with English, there is U.K. English, American English, and Australian English. Which version do you choose? Once you decide upon the version, it is probably best to have the translation done in-country to capture local usage and nuances. Sometimes, the translation of "technospeak," or technical terms, can mean different conventions or acronyms in other countries. By using localized translators, this issue can be addressed at the same time.

Acting Locally

It is difficult to act locally without personal knowledge of a country's customs, culture, business practices, language, and laws. In order to act locally, it is necessary to not only become familiar with all these aspects, but to individualize or personalize Web content, transactions, and business operations.

It has become easier to translate Web content and Web user interfaces into multiple languages and to index them with search engines. In some cases, content needs to be arranged differently, as well. This is easier said than done, however. You must decide how best to serve your customers. (See Figure 6.6.)

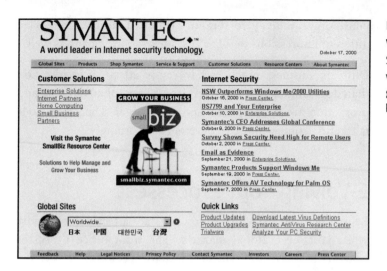

Figure 6.6
www.symantec.com
Symantec's site allows the visitor to quickly view the geographical info and language they want.

For example, is it better to create parallel Web sites that serve the disparate needs of customers, or to have one Web site enhanced with technology tools that help guide customers to the appropriate parts of the site? Creating parallel Web sites may be the simplest approach, but you must be prepared to support and maintain those sites, which requires additional resources. With one Web site, you can take advantage of available tools that can provide real-time DNS lookup to direct your customers to the right Web page. There are also integrated content management and delivery systems that provide content based on customer information. To make these decisions, you need to be very familiar with your customers and their level of comfort with technology, as well as their business practices. You also need to make sure your products will work in the countries you are targeting—before you go down the path of content development and deployment.

How can you best serve your global customers?

Arranging and customizing content, whether it resides on one or multiple Web sites, requires planning as well as familiarity with the culture and business practices. "The French are community-oriented, the U.K. is commerce-minded, and for Germany you'd probably need to address technical issues in detail and put the right infrastructure in place," advises Maria-Luisa Rodriguez, Director of e-co consulting. "The challenge is in addressing the individual needs by country without diluting your corporate image or brand." Different cultures may have different impressions of what customer service means as well.

Different business practices have more effect on localization than does language. In Germany, some types of advertising and promotion are unacceptable and even illegal. Therefore, your marketing content must be developed accordingly.

E-Volving Your Processes

Back office and front office processes are affected profoundly when you serve global markets. The front office processes (those that are customer-facing) need to be compatible with the multilingual content and must deliver a consistent experience in all transactions with global customers. All front office processes must interface seamlessly with back office processes to support the business operations, especially in the area of customer database information.

Your current business processes may be set up to do business online, but not to multiple geographies. So each process needs to be re-evaluated to make sure it is consistent with the geographies you intend to serve. When you are ready to e-volve your business processes, you'll find that the local business practices of each geography have a greater impact than culture does. To set up global marketing and bring customers to your site, you must address the cultural problem. However, if your operations don't support the various business practices of a region, that potential customer may not turn into an actual customer or eventual revenue.

Amazon.com ships books all over the world. They also have two localized Web sites: one that serves the United Kingdom and one that serves Germany. They set up those localized sites when they had the global operational processes ready to support them. However, all the books sold, even to those sites, are written in English. And they don't do targeted marketing for the localized sites. Are they truly global yet? (See Figure 6.7.)

Perhaps it requires more than just multilingual Web sites. Mark Resch, President and CEO of CommerceNet, suggests that

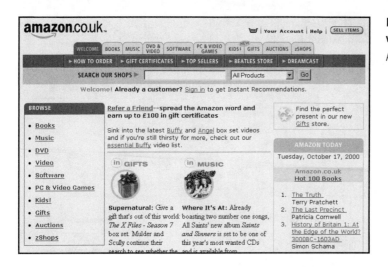

Figure 6.7
www.amazon.com.uk
Are they truly global yet?

these seven elements need to be in place for successful global e-commerce operations:

- ▲ A Web presence, so people are able to find you online
- ▲ Content that is understandable by each targeted geography
- ▲ Products that meet a need in the targeted markets
- ▲ The ability to take an order online
- ▲ System for accepting online payment
- ▲ Fulfillment of orders
- ▲ Support of the customer on an ongoing basis

Aligning your business processes for a global online business involves the same degree of thinking and planning that's required for offline or traditional brick and mortar businesses. "The additional challenge is that you need to put into place all of the processes involved in online operations, while conforming to the rules "on the ground," or in offline operations," says Jorden Woods, Chairman and CTO of GlobalSight. "The front office processes need to deliver relevant content, leveraging the speed of the Internet. The back office processes need to interface with all online transactions and still operate in the legal, regulatory, and business environment of each geographic region." (See Figures 6.8, 6.9, and 6.10.)

Figure 6.8

Web globalization is a complex process.

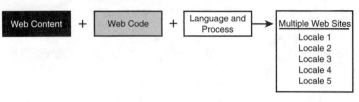

Figure 6.9

Many people and organizations are needed to meet the challenges of globalization.

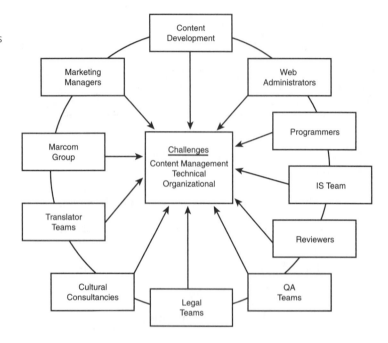

The Global Plan

As part of re-examining your vision statement, you have determined what you will do in terms of building your new foundation for global operations. But how do you go about implementing all of this? How will you manage this new operation? In the process of identifying your global business strategy, you may have identified new partners to help you reach and service your new customers. That's the approach used by Wine.com. According to Peter Sisson, Chief Strategy Officer, "We will not go live until we are sure we can deliver on our promises—and legally. In the wine industry, that means setting up sourcing and distribution agreements with localized partners in many different countries. The fact that we are on the Web doesn't remove this need."

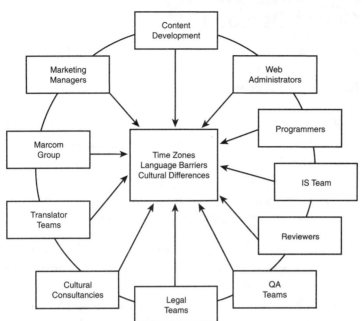

Figure 6.10

Everyone must overcome the barriers of world time, languages, and cultures.

If you decide to manage international partners from your centralized location, how will you ensure that these entities will be locally empowered to carry out your vision? "It's important to align all the players in the value chain for whatever you are delivering to the marketplace," says Maria-Luisa Rodriguez, Director of e-co consulting. "You need to satisfy demand at the right time, for the right person, under the right conditions. Partners need to understand their roles in the value chain and must perform—perfectly—to be successful." In-country partners and local offices must have a stake in the game and be committed to the international goals, and they need to constantly be reviewed and be replaced if necessary.

Once you know how your processes need to change, you will be able to develop or revise your detailed plans to implement the required changes. This means you must perform a complete analysis of all back office and front office processes, as well as deciding on the degree of personalization and localization required for each process. As you learned at the beginning of the chapter, globalization will profoundly change your business operations.

Do your business processes support global operations?

Global Operations in Action

A tremendous amount of coordination is required to deploy global operations successfully. Several different departments and functions need to communicate and share customer information or process transactions. If you are trying to develop or grow new markets, a consistent level of service must be provided that will help build and enhance customer relationships. Whether customer service is outsourced or managed internally, it needs to be consistent, constantly available, and responsive. If it is managed internally, you can streamline your processes by using your internal networks for communication. (See Figure 6.11.)

As you expand operations, you need to build your brand across multiple geographies—by providing localized content and personalized customer service. Your site needs to have flexible design and navigation that is expected by your global customers. And if you have any partners who provide any part of your business products and services, they need to be part of the coordinated efforts as well.

Sometimes it's necessary to establish localized, in-country service centers to support your customers. This can be done through partnering or outsourcing. Local partners who are accustomed to doing business in an area can provide more personalized and appropriate customer support. Outsourcing or partnering can

Figure 6.11

Much coordination of processes and people is needed among your global partners.

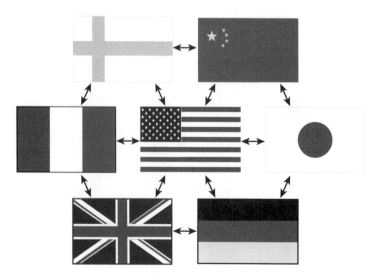

also be a faster way to set up international operations, eliminating the need for training or relocation of critical company resources.

Sometimes partnering between countries can create success. This is the model followed by Wstore.com and Mondus.com, who have both managed to become leaders in their markets in a foreign country. They were able to do this through effective partnering.

Dell Computer is another successful example of global operations. They implemented a global strategy that started from the top and was part of the company's vision from the beginning. They globalized their infrastructure to serve the extent of their global customers, including partners who could effectively handle logistics. They did their marketing with locally relevant content, and they made it easier for their customers to do business with them. Dell was also able to integrate it all and manage it effectively as their operations grew.

Options for E-Volving Your Global Operations

Now that you have deployed your global operations and you are receiving new revenues from those new markets, now what? You are not done. To stay in the game, you must be able to scale your operations within a geography or target new ones. Whenever you target new ones, remember that you will have to recreate and e-volve your company from top to bottom, from front office to back office, each time you expand your global reach.

In some situations, it might be desirable to stop operations or completely change your focus in a geography if it is not producing a reasonable return on investment. No matter what, there will be changes, and you will need to react quickly to changing conditions. There are several ways to e-volve your growing operations, including partnering, outsourcing, use of translation/localization vendors, and technology tools that can help you set up and service operations more quickly.

E-Volutionary Tactics

→ To be truly global, you must be committed to re-creating and redeploying your company for each geographic area that you target.

→ It's important for you to decide how global you want to be, consistent with your vision.

→ You must think globally, but act locally.

→ Acting locally requires individualization and personalization to your customers.

→ Understand that just because a Web site is accessible from anywhere in the world doesn't necessarily mean that you are a global business.

→ You must decide how you will overcome the four major hurdles you will face in laying out the plan (legal, logistics, currency, and language).

- Legal hurdles include trade boundaries, contractual issues, and local laws regarding advertising.

- Logistics hurdles include shipping, customs, and distance from your customer.

- Currency affects timing of transactions and exchange rates.

- Language can be a huge hurdle requiring localization, but several technology tools are available that can help.

Outsourcing Is Always an Option

IN THE NEW E-CONOMY, not only is partnering on the rise, so is the practice of outsourcing. New business models have been created that make it easier than ever to establish relationships with outsourcing vendors. Application Service Providers (ASPs), Commerce Service Providers (CSPs), and Business Solution Providers (BSPs) are some of the new forms that have e-volved, and businesses of all sizes are taking advantage of these services. Outsourcing saves companies money and time to market, in addition to freeing up time so they can focus on their core business. ▶▶

You Can Outsource Almost Anything

In the New E-Conomy, just about any corporate task or process can be outsourced. Every day, new companies are being started whose mission is to provide outsourced business services via the Internet. (See Figure 7.1.)

One of the first services to be outsourced was email and Web hosting/Internet access—by Internet service providers (ISPs). Shortly after, application hosting e-volved, providing a way to outsource IT functions such as internal or private networks and databases, which are provided by companies such as Exodus and Global Frontier. Individual applications followed— including accounting and payroll, human resources, and customer service and fulfillment. Some of the more recent applications are services that were routinely outsourced in the Old Economy but are now available via the Web by established outsourcers or new companies. The following list provides examples of services that can now be outsourced and a few companies who provide such services:

- ▲ Contract manufacturing (Flextronics, Solectron)
- ▲ Email hosting and management (Commtouch)
- ▲ Graphic design and collaboration (DGNonline)
- ▲ Marketing and sales (Digital River)
- ▲ Direct marketing (At Once)
- ▲ Employee benefits (eBenefits.com)

Figure 7.1

Many business processes can be provided through outsourcing.

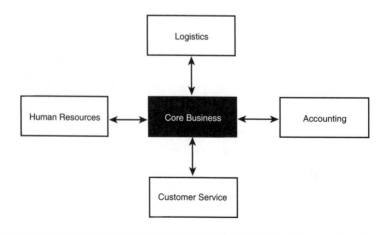

Many more applications are being introduced every day. Most of these applications are regarded as business overhead functions, and one of the basic rules of business is to find ways to reduce overhead expenses. If it makes economic sense for the business to outsource these functions, there will continue to be a market for outsourcing these services.

ASPs, BSPs, and Other Service Providers

Application Service Providers (ASPs) provide software applications that are hosted by these companies and are accessible via the Internet. These solutions are usually custom-built by the ASP. Business Service Providers (BSPs) are also sometimes called Business *Solution* Providers, and they are focused on entire suites of applications that perform multiple business processes on an outsourced basis, over the Internet. Some of the established companies providing ERP services are now providing these services on an outsourced basis and calling themselves BSPs. Another category, CSPs, are *Commerce* Service Providers, who provide hosted end-to-end e-commerce solutions—usually in data centers. Some of the functions of BSPs and CSPs overlap; the difference is in the number of applications that are hosted and whether they handle all the solutions required for a business or just one function of the business. (See Figure 7.2.)

There are probably many more TLAs (Three-Letter Acronyms) and combinations of alphabet soup yet to be defined, but there is no doubt this represents a significant trend in outsourcing. Here's a question attributed to Marc Andreessen, the inventor

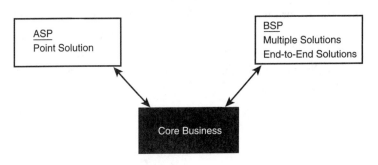

Figure 7.2

ASPs offer a point solution; BSPs offer multiple or end-to-end solutions.

of Mosaic and now chairman of Loudcloud: "Was the packaged software application business a fluke? If the network infrastructure had been in place for the last 10 years, would a Procter and Gamble, for instance, buy a packaged application for $250–500k, spend another $250k+ for hardware and an environment to run it, and hire ten people to support it? Most likely not." It is a question worth thinking about.

What is the future of all these (x)SPs? If the adoption rate is any indication, the future looks very bright. "Companies of all sizes are getting to the point where they don't want to buy and maintain software any more. The Internet is now the largest LAN in the world, and we are in the throes of a major transformation where software and applications are moving out of the corporate world and into the Internet cloud," says Rip Gerber, Chief Strategy Officer and Vice-President of Marketing, Commtouch.

Another part of the (x)SP future is forming partnerships and integrated packages to provide broader solution sets for companies. BSPs are already working with ASPs to bundle applications into suites, and the BSP can then centrally manage the suites. Also, we may see the re-emergence of Old Economy systems integrators to pull together several applications into unified frameworks—and then outsource the whole solution to a BSP or CSP.

"The most common strategy for ASPs is to focus on a single application solution for a single vertical market. The next evolutionary step is to attack multiple vertical markets at a time. This raises the issue of standardization on one business solution for a wider variety of users. Can one application be used in the same way in different industries, or will some level of customization be required? If there is customization to be done, that could slow the adoption rate," according to Alan Naumann, President and CEO of Calico Commerce. The momentum of ASPs and the rapid adoption rate will force the issue of commonality and standardization. Once that happens, this way of doing business will become the norm.

A Starting Point

To determine whether outsourcing is right for your company, take a look at your roadmap and plans (as described in Chapter 3, "The Plan Is the Thing"). Do a number of your business processes need to change? And are reorganizations needed in order for you to implement your vision? (See Figure 7.3.) If so, there might be an opportunity to use outsourcing to accomplish your objectives. Outsourcing can often speed up the change process and reduce costs as well. In most cases, outsourcing vendors offer the most current applications available and follow industry-based best practices, adding further value.

For example, if your vision specifies some deadline or milestone, such as "reposition ourselves as an Internet company by the end of the year," then outsourcing would certainly help speed you to your goal. Time sensitivity is associated with most visions and goals. One of Cisco's goals, for example, was to become a leader in selling products online, but it was a challenge to implement because of the number and complexity of Cisco's product lines. By outsourcing to Calico Commerce, not only were they able to accomplish this, but they were able to be the first in their industry to do so. They are now the recognized leader in their field.

> Can outsourcing help you accomplish your vision?

The other critical question to ask in the beginning is: What business are you in now, and what business do you want to be in? If you're not where you want to be, outsourcing can help get you there by allowing you to focus your energies on your core competencies.

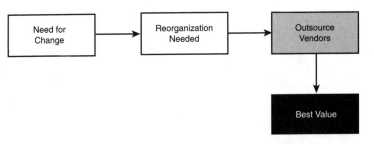

Figure 7.3

Revisit your roadmap and plans to identify outsourcing options.

Deciding What to Outsource

This is the tough decision, but the same tradeoffs apply in the New E-Conomy as they did in the Old Economy. It's a matter of balancing the financial, marketing, operational, and customer focus tradeoffs. You might want to think seriously about outsourcing mission-critical applications. It's important to focus on your core competencies and outsource the rest. Is your core business the implementation and integration of hardware or software technology? If not, outsource it. (I don't understand why companies want to spend a tremendous amount of resources investing in an MIS organization and infrastructure when they can use an outsourced provider with that core competency.) When making this decision, think about the processes you consider core competencies of your company that will help you accomplish your vision, and then outsource the rest. (See Figure 7.4.) Please remember, though, not to lose site of your customer touch points (see Chapter 4, "Customer Touch Points").

The basic approach to this decision should be to determine whether each process or function is a core competency—that has a critical relationship with the core business of the company.

Figure 7.4

A decision process for outsourcing.

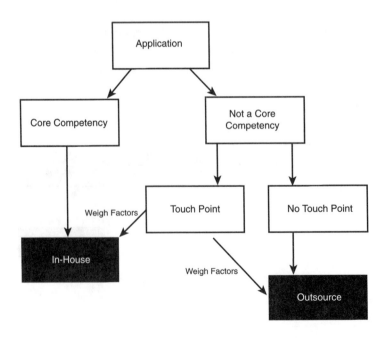

In other words, if you were to outsource that function, would you lose your competitive advantage or corporate image? Would it mean fundamental changes in the business you are in? If the answer is yes, keep it inside; if the answer is no, outsourcing is a possibility.

Which of your processes could be outsourced?

In addition to business processes, you also need to consider the organizational issues regarding outsourcing. If you are already resource-constrained, it's an easier decision to outsource. However, if you are displacing existing human resources, you need to examine the efficiency of your internal resources versus outsourcing. If you decide to outsource functions currently performed by internal staff, you will need to develop a plan for retraining and/or redeploying those resources.

Sometimes outsourcing processes creates conflict inside the organization—the "not invented here" syndrome. Management direction regarding the company's outsourcing strategy must come from the top and be understood by all employees. Those who resist this type of change need to understand the higher strategic objectives of the company and how it will benefit the entire company. Education and basic motivation can go a long way toward alleviating this problem. If employees still don't understand, they need to be let go. As a sign on Noah's Ark reputedly read:

Do your employees understand the reasons for outsourcing?

> *"The woodpeckers inside are often a bigger threat than the storm outside."*

Another key factor is the track record for that outsourced service. Is it mature enough, is it working, is it efficient, and is it economical? You may be ready to outsource a process, but the market may be too new or unproven to make it viable.

Some of these considerations and criteria are Old Economy rules that have been applied for decades; it's the "make versus buy" decision. However, in the New E-Conomy, technology has introduced some additional considerations such as processing speed, access, communication modes, and collaboration tools. These new criteria may provide more compelling reasons to outsource. Companies like Nike, Dell, and Sara Lee have already benefited from outsourcing some of their processes to support their transformation into the New E-Conomy.

In addition to these high-level criteria, several outsourcing vendors interviewed for this book list the following specific considerations that companies use when making the outsourcing decision:

- ▲ Time to market
- ▲ Total cost of ownership
- ▲ "Ilities": Scalability, reliability, availability
- ▲ Level of integration required (with internal processes)
- ▲ Security and privacy (network and encryption)
- ▲ Application's compatibility with corporate Web architecture
- ▲ Impact on customer experience
- ▲ Competitive advantage
- ▲ Impact on distribution channels
- ▲ Resource constraints
- ▲ Compatibility of software and systems

Control and Access: The Differentiating Factors

How much of the process, data, or task should be outsourced, and what should be kept in-house? This varies all over the map, and some outsourcers offer companies a choice in terms of the degree of control and access. Some outsourcing vendors control the applications and data offsite, merely providing access. Sometimes access is even limited to only certain individuals within your company that you designate. Other vendors act as "mid-sourcers": You host the applications, but they manage and control all processing remotely.

How much control do you need?

It is critical that for whatever level of control or access you implement, you must be comfortable with the outsourcing partner. Comfort level includes everything from business philosophy to trust to track record and references. You need to be satisfied that they have the proper security, privacy, and backup systems in place to fit your requirements, and you must be able to trust that they will implement all these procedures consistently.

Keeping Your Customer Touch Points Alive

Outsourcing can help you support your customer touch points, but you should not look to outsourcers as being responsible for managing them. If you choose to do outsource, you must manage the companies who are providing the services to make sure that consistent value and service is still delivered to your customers. Outsourcing will be transparent to the customer if it is implemented successfully. The companies that you form outsourcing relationships with should act as an extension of your company when it comes to customer interface. (See Figure 7.5.)

"It's important to carefully monitor your outsourcing partners and how they respond to customers—especially key customers. Do your partners just refer to a manual when responding to a customer, or do they proactively deal with each customer as an individual? You need to make sure that your partners consistently deliver the same experience you would," says Alan Naumann, President and CEO of Calico Commerce. Sometimes outsourcing can cause customer confusion, and it might be

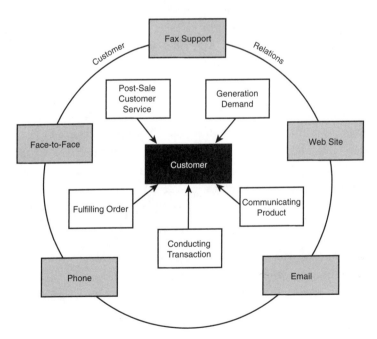

Figure 7.5

If you outsource customer-facing processes, make sure customer relationships are maintained.

necessary to make sure the look and feel of the outsourced interface are consistent with those of your company's interface. If this sort of relationship is implemented correctly, the fact that you are outsourcing should be transparent to the customer—whether you are outsourcing back office or front office systems. What counts is the consistency of the customer experience.

Outsourcing can introduce efficiencies and responsiveness that can actually increase customer satisfaction, according to Neil Gardner, Vice-President of Technical Operations at NaviSite. "If you use a world-class outsourcing partner, and they understand your business and customer service philosophy, it can improve your customer relationships."

Selecting Outsourcing Vendors

This is similar to the process for selecting any business partner (as described in Chapter 2, "Business Models for the E-Conomy"). Some of the key factors include credibility, track record, knowledge of your market and customer, and familiarity with the business operations for your industry. Some new criteria should be: Are they providing the best next-generation applications so that you can fully leverage the value of the technology? Do they continue to migrate to the next generation in a manner satisfying to their (and your) customers?

Do your outsourcing partner candidates understand your business?

"You should view outsourcing partners as companies who are helping you solve a business problem, not a technology problem," says Ashu Roy, CEO of eGain. "Your partners need to understand and operate from this business perspective." That means understanding your industry, market, vision, goals, and most importantly, your customers. It is also important that they be compatible with other key partners that you already have in your value chain.

Outsourcing is a very important decision that affects the infrastructure of a company, its productivity, customer relationships, and ultimately, the bottom line. Neil Gardner, Vice-President of Technical Operations at NaviSite, suggests these four sets of criteria for evaluating outsourcing candidates:

- ▲ *Viability:* How large is the candidate's company (financially), and how mature is the outsourcing application?

- ▲ *Service Level Agreements:* What are the terms, such as length of time, give and take, performance milestones, enforceability, and benefits to both sides?

- ▲ *Breadth of Service:* The broader the range of services offered, the more likely they are to grow with your company.

- ▲ *Quality:* Does the candidate have a methodology in place to manage problems and change?

One of the best ways to ensure that candidates will meet your selection criteria is to request and check references. This will give you an idea of what the partner will be like to work with, as well as the effort they make to understand their partners' businesses. Sometimes, there are metrics available for outsourcing partners as well. For example, Commtouch is the only email/messaging ASP to hire an outside firm to measure their customers' satisfaction levels—and they make it available to potential customers. Because of their focus on the quality of their own service, they have one of the lowest customer turnover rates in their industry.

Some of these criteria are fairly standard for selection of any type of business or strategic partner. However, for these new types of (x)SPs, there is also a technology component to consider. Do they have as part of their strategic vision a goal to develop and provide next-generation software applications so that you as a client can take advantage of the new value provided by these enhancements? This will be critical for your business if you are to stay current with the demands of your own internal processes as well as the needs of your customers. (See Figure 7.6.)

Managing Your Outsourcing Partners

Just because you have outsourced some of your business functions doesn't mean you are freed up from managing those partners. "It's important to remember *why* you are outsourcing.

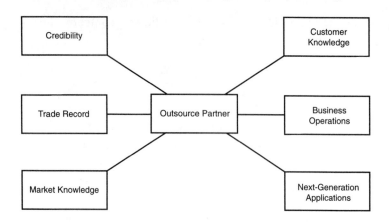

Figure 7.6

Outsourcing partner selection criteria.

You need to set expectations early on with your partners, and make sure that the terms of the business relationship are understood by both sides," says George Roman, CTO of DiCarta. "You must also define the performance metrics up front, and actually measure the results."

As in any partnering relationship, it's important to align the two organizations—in terms of business processes, culture, and vision. In most cases, your outsourcing partner has different business objectives than your own company. *How* to do that should be addressed early on in the outsourcing relationship. One of the ways to ensure this exchange is to assign someone from your own company to your outsourcing partner's company to act as liaison, or vice versa. Not only does this result in shared learning between the companies, but it makes it easier to implement any necessary changes when the need arises.

Consistent and frequent communication is necessary to sustaining any business relationship. It's critical to establish the mode of communications as well as the degree of structure used between the two companies. Highly structured communications such as regular project reviews may be desirable for your company, and if so, this should be made clear in any agreements that are put into place.

E-Volving the Outsourcing Plan

It's a good idea to evaluate your outsourcing relationships regularly to make sure they are still serving your business objectives and supporting your growth. If an outsourcing partner is not performing to your expectations, consider eliminating or replacing them. You should also build evaluation milestones into a service level agreement or service contract that you execute with outsourcing partners. (See Figure 7.7.)

After working with an outsourcing partner for a period of time, you may mutually discover new ways to outsource additional functions or services, or new ways to integrate processes to gain new efficiencies. Either way, your company will certainly benefit.

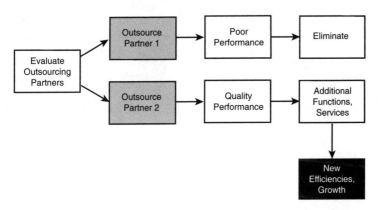

Figure 7.7

Keep e-volving your outsourcing plan and make changes when necessary.

E-Volutionary Tactics

→ Any business function in the holistic Internet-enabled entity can be outsourced.

→ The company's roadmap and set of plans is the starting point for identifying possible areas for outsourcing.

→ You need to decide what levels of control and access are right for your company.

→ Customer touch points must still be managed by you, even if some processes are outsourced.

→ When considering what to outsource, you need to evaluate financial, marketing, and technical factors.

→ Evaluating outsourcing partners is similar to evaluating any type of business partner.

→ You should put a service level agreement (SLA) in place with your outsourcing partner and establish a frequent communication schedule.

→ Be prepared to replace partners that don't live up to their SLAs or don't adequately deal with the customer touch points.

PART

Maintaining Momentum

8 New Expectations for Customer Service   137

9 Managing the E-Commerce Organization   155

10 Ongoing Internet Marketing   171

11 The Law Catches Up to E-Business   195

New Expectations for Customer Service

REMEMBER THOSE customer touch points from Chapter 4? Well, now it's time to implement the program to keep those touch points supported throughout your entire organization—now and into the future as your company e-volves. ►►

The Internet world is very impersonal. In the early days, people thought this might be a good thing; the Web would become self-service, and all companies would have to do was supply information at their Web sites and provide a way for people to buy their products or services online. However, as it turns out, because of this impersonal environment, it is even more critical that you find a way to provide superior and consistent service, including human support. Dave Deasy, e-Business Consultant and former COO for hpshopping.com, describes it this way: "The early adopters of the Internet and Web-based shopping were willing to accept lots of problems. However, when the mainstream consumers started shopping online, they were (and are) less capable of dealing with problems. For mainstreamers, it's a new shopping medium. You can't touch the product, drive home with it, take it back to a store, and in some cases, even figure out how to buy it. The companies who realize that the Web is a new *customer service* medium and act accordingly will be those who survive."

Customer service has been redefined in the New E-Conomy. It's not just a department or someone who answers the phone when a customer calls. It isn't provided by only those who are "customer-facing"—that is, the people in the organization who interact with customers. Rather, it has become the basic business philosophy that companies must follow if they want to stay in the game. It's as if the entire company becomes one department or functional organization that is called customer service. This philosophy needs to be present in the thinking and actions of all employees, regardless of their job descriptions. And everyone needs to be motivated and compensated based on customer service metrics. Business processes and infrastructure need to be designed to provide superior *integrated* customer service, no matter how or where the customer interface occurs. (See Figure 8.1.)

How do your customers want to be treated in the New E-Conomy?

How do customers want to be treated in the New E-Conomy? On a personal basis. Todd Elizalde, Director of E-Commerce at Cisco Systems, puts it this way: "It's as if the customers are saying: No matter how I contact you, I want you to know who I am, and treat me accordingly and consistently." Customers also

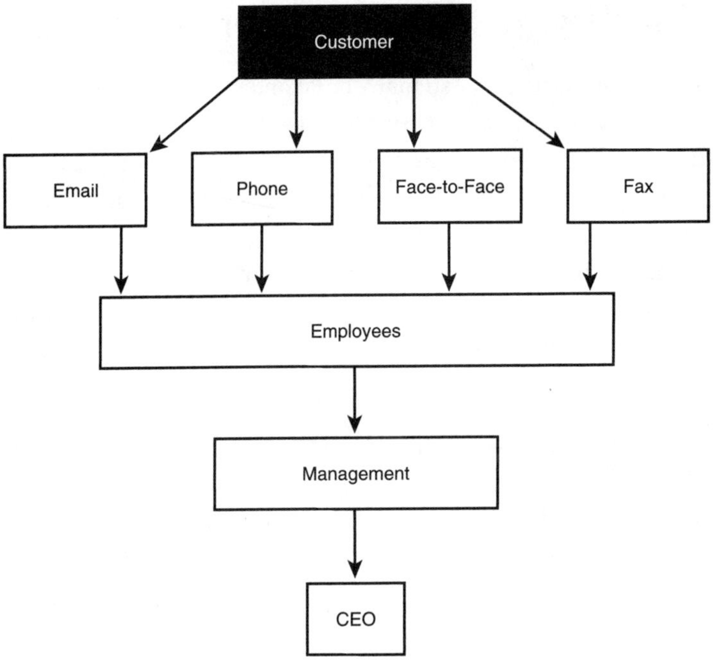

Figure 8.1

The customer should be at the top of your company's organization chart.

want more information than ever before, they want it fast, and they want it to be available on a 24 by 7 basis. If customers don't receive the level of service they seek, they are less forgiving and will move on with a click of the mouse.

Most people would say this has always been true. What's so different about customer service in an e-commerce environment? The basic philosophies about customers and the basic skills needed *are* the same; it's just that it all has to function in a more technical environment. Phone contact has to be coordinated and integrated with Web contact, and often in real-time. People who may be excellent at providing service over the phone may not be so effective at delivering the same level of service over the Web or email. For example, look at how customer service representatives provide online service at LandsEnd.com. Users can call up an online chat session with a representative from Lands' End, who can answer their questions using the text box and can even push particular Web pages to the user. The dynamics of servicing the customer here are very different than on the telephone; text interaction is different from voice interaction.

The Customer Service Organization

Why is it that corporations that talk about customer service being their highest priority pay their customer service representatives the lowest salaries in the company?

I find it interesting that so many companies talk about how they rank customer service as their highest priority, yet they pay their customer service representatives the lowest salaries in the company. There are a couple of different issues here. One is that *everyone's* job should be focused on customer service (see Figure 8.2). The other is that *everyone's* compensation needs to be tied to customer service metrics. (And while you're at it, please pay those people more who have the "customer service" title or job description!)

Educating all employees about customer service should be a top priority for all companies. There are a number of ways to do this. Some companies require that all employees do a rotational assignment in the customer service organization (which can be a real eye-opener for employees). Another way to approach this is to have each employee *use* all aspects of the company's online business as if he or she were a customer—and to resolve any problems *without* using internal resources. These are experiential methods of training employees to think and act "customer service."

Figure 8.2

Every department should be called "customer service."

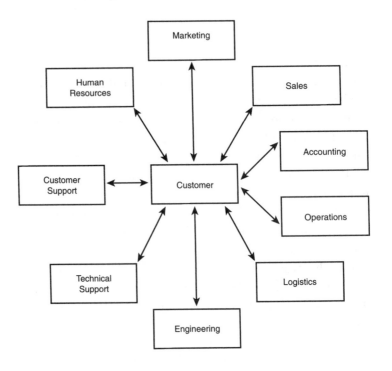

Other areas of training for customer service people or all employees include very basic people skills. "The most important thing to teach employees about interacting with customers is that they are people—just like your friends or your neighbors. It's critical to put a *face* on the customer," says Norm Hullinger, Vice-President of Sales and Operations for Egghead.com. "In our business, there are usually a lot of technical questions that come up, and lots of things can go wrong. We make sure that our customer service people are trained to keep up with it all. And we have re-assigned people as necessary so that we have the best match of their skills with our service goals. This has resulted in high customer satisfaction levels for us."

If there is a separate customer service organization in the company, at what level should it fit into the hierarchy? Some suggest that it should report to the CEO or a Vice-President of Operations or Marketing. Another possibility is to create a position such as "CCO" (Chief Customer service Officer) or "CCEO" (Chief Customer Experience Officer). Some would argue that the CCEO and the CEO should be the same person. One of the reasons to elevate the customer service organization is visibility, especially in the area of performance against metrics. This high-level visibility keeps customer service at the top of the priority list during strategic planning and decision-making—especially when decisions need to be made to improve company performance.

Where does customer service fit into your organization?

In addition to visibility, the people in the customer service organization need to have the budget and authority to solve problems for customers in real-time. If a customer service representative puts a customer on hold while he or she attempts to resolve an issue or check with someone higher in the organization for an answer, that customer likely will not appreciate the delay. It's a good way to lose customers.

There is a very long list of skills that are desirable for people who interface directly with customers on a regular basis. Most of these skills can be learned, but some relate to basic personality types and natural "people skills." Personalities can't really be changed; it's important that you understand this and allocate resources accordingly. Indeed, a lot of people who work in technical support centers have excellent analytical and technical skills for solving problems, but have few if any people skills. Sometimes it's better to assign employees who have good people skills and then train them on the technical information they need to solve problems. This can greatly improve customer experiences.

Sometimes, customers have different experiences dealing with the various customer service organizations within the same company. The important thing is to remember that consistency across the entire customer experience is key, and you might have to assign or reassign your people resources accordingly to achieve that. Regardless of whether hundreds or thousands of customers have had ecstatically positive experiences with your company, just one unhappy customer can tell a multitude of online friends and colleagues, and word spreads quickly on the Web. Ultimately, this will have an impact on your future business.

Some of the people skills that are important include empathy, ability to listen, patience, conflict management, influencing skills, and the power to negotiate. It's important that customer-facing employees preserve their objectivity and do not take things personally—which is often very difficult. If possible, try to find people who are enthusiastic and have a positive attitude; almost everything else can be accomplished through training.

The degree of technical training needed for customer-facing employees depends on the technical complexity of your products and services. Whatever level of training is required, it is critical to make sure that these people are trained before new products are launched.

Another area of technical training is how to use customer relationship management technologies or other tools that you have added to your infrastructure. People need to know how to use these tools efficiently when they are dealing with a customer in real-time.

Metrics

You won't know how well you're doing until you measure it—with your customers. You must first develop valid metrics from the customer's point of view. There are a couple of ways to do this. Barbara Jones, Director of Customer Service for Cisco Systems, suggests talking to customer service professionals to find out more about why customers contact the company (in other words, what questions they have), as well as *how* customers are contacting them (email, phone, and so on). "The other side to that," Barbara says, "is to work directly with customers. You can set up formal Customer Advisory Boards, or use third parties to gather relevant metrics for you."

Whatever you decide to measure, it should be representative of the whole customer contact experience, according to Dave Deasy, e-Business Consultant. "This includes the initial Web site visit, browsing, shopping, purchase, delivery, receipt of product, use of product, and post-sale support. If breakdown occurs anywhere in the process, it will be regarded as inferior customer service. You must have a clear goal and metric for each step of the experience. For instance, how quickly phone calls or emails are answered, resolution rates, sales conversion rates, referrals, and repeat purchases are metrics that cover many stages of the whole experience." Other useful metrics include the number of returns and refunds.

How do you measure customer satisfaction?

After you have identified the metrics you want to use, you can decide which ones you will keep over a period of time. You don't want to change them too often, because then it's too difficult to look at patterns over a period of time; you need to look at some history in order to find out if improvements are being made.

It's also important to benchmark your customer service results with other companies in your industry. Lisa Sharples, Chief Marketing Officer for Garden.com, believes that benchmarking helps you identify opportunities to create new models for customer service. "When we set out to develop our business model, we looked at our industry to find out what customers expected from ordering gardening products by mail. I sit on the executive board of an industry group, the Mail Order Gardening Association. By working together, we found ways to improve delivery times and personalize products and service for customers across the industry with our online model. In setting up our online operations, we also benchmarked ourselves against retailers in other vertical markets. We intend to keep doing this to make sure we are serving our customers' best interests."

Incentives

One of the best ways to improve customer service is to tie all employees' compensation to customer satisfaction goals. This is a policy that Cisco Systems uses. Says Barbara Jones, Director of Customer Service at Cisco, "If you decide to implement this policy on a company-wide basis, you need to make sure that all the metrics are in place and that you do indeed use those metrics when it's performance evaluation time. The other critical factor is training; all employees need to not only understand how they are being measured, but how customer service is delivered by the company. They need to put this into practice every day." At Cisco, 30 percent of every employee's bonus is based on customer service metrics.

Compensation incentives such as these not only help reinforce the company vision, but also improve attitudes of all people, including those who have minimal or no direct customer interface. Departments such as finance, accounting, manufacturing, and engineering are often left out when it comes to customer service. But if they can be trained to think about what is in the best interest of the customer, they will be more productive and be able to figure out how they can contribute to customer satisfaction, if indirectly. Actually, the newly organized holistic Internet-enabled entity may not have separate functions of finance, accounting, manufacturing, engineering, and so on, but these functions may be integrated into a hybrid of the existing infrastructure organized around customer satisfaction. This concept will be addressed in more detail in the next chapter.

Amazon.com's customer service employees often receive awards for solving difficult customer problems. Incentives don't always have to be monetary to affect employee performance.

The Role of Partners

If your partners are customer-facing, you need to make sure the customer experience they are delivering is consistent with yours. But how do you do that if you can't tie their compensation to it, like you can for your own employees? Well, you can incentivize them as part of your business relationship, and even formalize it contractually. It is in their best interest to provide superior customer service also, but they may have different strategies and incentives in place than your company does. It's important that your partners understand your philosophy regarding customer service, as well as the metrics used to evaluate performance and progress against goals. If there are breakdowns in the process due to their actions, it will reflect on your company. (See Figure 8.3.)

One way to do this is to make sure that you have written service level agreements between you and your partners that include customer service metrics. After these agreements are in place, it's important that you diligently follow them and evaluate the metrics from time to time. If results are not favorable, you need to make changes and make sure they're understood by the partner. This sometimes means you need to fire your partners if customer service results don't improve. Your customers often don't make the distinction between whether a service or product is coming from your company or a partner.

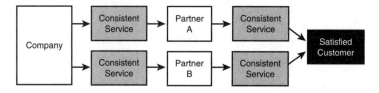

Figure 8.3

Consistent levels of customer service need to flow through your partners and to your customer.

Revisiting the Plan

Your e-commerce (business) plan should contain some description of your customer service goals and metrics. If it doesn't, you need to revisit it and figure out how customer service relates to your vision, and also how that will flow down to the roadmap of plans you have in place (as discussed in Chapter 3). It's never too early to think about customer service. WebVan established customer satisfaction goals at the outset and, from the very beginning, built in a "problem notification system." WebVan guarantees a 30-minute delivery window, and if they are running late, they will notify the customer immediately to work out a solution on the spot. This is just one example of how you can work a customer satisfaction goal into an operating process.

Do your plans address customer service?

Amazon.com also chose customer service as one of its corporate objectives—during the planning stages. Founder Jeff Bezos decided that the key to their success would be to compete on outstanding customer service instead of lowest price. During a panel discussion at CommerceNet in October '96, Jeff Bezos talked about his market strategy (this was before Amazon went public and went on to be a household name). At the time, everyone argued that there was no way Amazon could break into the book industry. Jeff talked about his two overarching concepts: 1) To deliver excellent customer service, and 2) to deliver this excellent customer service in an industry that had a lot of content but wasn't efficiently run. The result: His strategy seemed to work—at least in terms of customer relationship metrics.

With ongoing plans, it is important to use your current and historical metrics to identify and make changes to legacy systems, processes, and people that might be needed to improve customer service. It's also critical that you use customer service metrics when developing and allocating budgets. Items that have a higher customer service impact should have higher budget priority.

Service Level Agreements and Customer Stratification

Service levels need to be developed in accordance with your company's customer stratification scheme (see Chapter 4, "Customer Touch Points" and in particular, Figure 4.3). Your highest-priority customers should receive the most attention and the best possible customer service. "You must match the value of each individual customer with the resources that you allocate to that customer," according to Ashu Roy, CEO and Chairman of eGain. "That requires an understanding of what matters to your highest-priority customers, and treating them according to how they expect to be treated."

That doesn't mean, however, that you have license to treat other, less economically important customers in a rude or unprofessional manner. You never know when a lesser customer might become a key customer; people change jobs and network with one another all the time, and corporate reputations can easily be damaged. This means that if you know a customer does a huge amount of business with you, they can expect more time from your corresponding customer service resources; in effect, they pay for that extra time with their business.

E-Volving the Processes for Customer Service

Whatever your current business model, you need to decide how you will deliver customer service. The big issue becomes this: Which processes will be available to customers online? Some of the possibilities include providing product information, basic marketing, sales, ordering, training, fulfillment, technical support, non-technical post-sales support, order tracking, and accounting. It's important to remember that for every process you implement online, you must have corresponding customer service resources assigned, and that can have a huge impact on your budget and plans. You need to carefully plan this before you offer these processes online.

Some companies decide they will offer only a few processes online and continue the rest offline or in the brick and mortar environment. The most common ones are product information and basic marketing, with a way for customers to contact the company for further information or to ask questions. An example is the click and mortar strategy for customer service used by Barnes and Noble, where you can buy in one place (Web) and pick up or return in another (physical presence). When you take the step of selling products and services online, a whole host of other processes goes with it, such as ordering, fulfillment, tracking, and post-sales support. Selling online means a different set of expectations for customers. Moving these processes online means that you will likely be saving some costs, and customers want a cut. They will want online incentives or discounts, as well as a higher level of customer service.

The Universal Customer Database

How much more satisfied would your customers be if you had a single customer database?

With all the different communication channels that customers can use to contact you, it is imperative that you have a single customer database that is accessible to everyone. With the way systems are cobbled together at the majority of the Global 2000 companies today, a single customer database is unattainable without a complete overhaul of the legacy infrastructure. The database should have customer profile information that is easy to understand and is easily accessed. This database should also be made available to channel partners so they can serve your customers as efficiently as you can. (See Figure 8.4.) "Garden.com, along with many other companies, is adopting multi-channel business practices. A key requirement is to have a centralized customer profile database," says Lisa Sharples, Chief Marketing Officer for Garden.com.

Every department, whether or not it is customer-facing, needs to have access to the database so the employees can do their jobs efficiently and serve customers better. In addition to being accessible, the database must be *accurate* and current. It is important that you give a customer the impression that you know

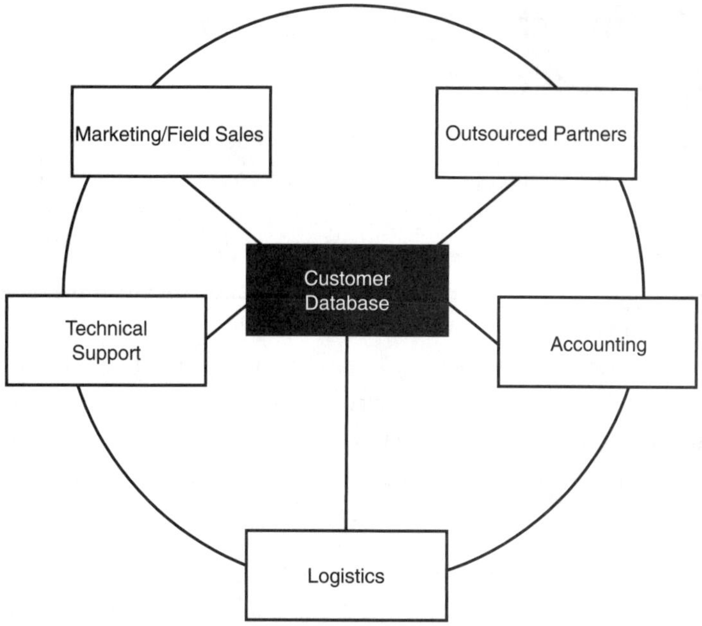

Figure 8.4

A single customer database should be accessible to everyone with a need to know.

who he or she is during any interaction, whether it occurs in real-time via the Web or the phone or via email. "Customer support people should be able to say, 'I can help you' rather than 'I can transfer you.' That's why a lot of companies are revamping their databases that were formerly organized by product line. They're now organizing around the customer and making the database accessible to everyone. It takes the right technology tools integrated together to create the proper infrastructure, but the result is a pampered customer instead of a customer on hold," says Jim Sterne, President of Target Marketing of Santa Barbara. There should be an area in each database record for customer feedback, complaints, case resolution, and the like, so that the customer service history for each customer is also recorded. If this information is accessible during the next contact with that customer, it gives the customer service representative another opportunity to find out whether the former problem was resolved to the customer's satisfaction. By tying all your profile databases into one, you can provide metrics to front-line people on the potential lifetime value of that customer.

Is your customer database up to date and accessible by those who need it?

An Infrastructure Made for Customer Interfaces

Everything needs to work from the customer's perspective—and consistently! Critical factors include response time to customer contacts, availability, degree of downtime, accuracy of information provided (pre- or post-sale), and degree of integration between Internet/voice interactions whether they're provided with internal or outsourced resources. No matter which business processes you decide to make available online or offline, the infrastructure changes must be there to support them. The infrastructure also needs to link with partners and suppliers to serve customers well throughout the entire customer contact cycle.

According to Dave Deasy, e-Business Consultant, interactive, live assistance will be required for some customers. "High-volume or high-priority customers demand live assistance—throughout the customer contact cycle. As the price of the product or service goes up, so does the level of service that should be provided. This means providing that service via Web, email, phone, and often via several media simultaneously. Your infrastructure needs to support *integrated* real-time customer service." Live assistance online (such as that used by Lands' End) is a very hot trend these days.

How do you go about deciding what infrastructure changes to make? You need to take a look at what your customers want, as well as what your competitors have been doing. Revisit your most recent metrics. Hopefully, you have collected data on how customers contact you, as well as how they would *like* to contact you. This should be a starting point. Also look at customers' suggestions for improvement. Is your Web site slow or inoperable? Are you responsive enough? Are your databases accurate and tied to CRM systems? Are you delivering when you say you will deliver? These might be areas where infrastructure updates will be required. (See Figure 8.5.)

Luckily, there are many technology tools that you can implement or outsource to update your infrastructure for enhanced

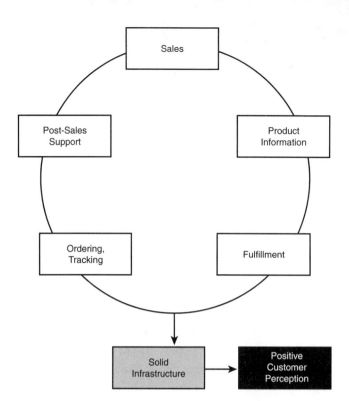

Sales

Post-Sales
Support

Product
Information

Ordering,
Tracking

Fulfillment

Solid
Infrastructure

Positive
Customer
Perception

Figure 8.5

Your customer's view of your company should be an infrastructure built for exceptional customer service.

customer service. Web collaboration tools, integrating email with customer chat sessions, and voice over IP are just some of the ways to augment your customer service systems. One note of caution is in order, however. Don't just throw technology at the problem without looking at the underlying reason for the change or the benefits to the customer. If you implement new technology solutions, it is absolutely essential that you follow up with customers, employees, and partners, obtain feedback, and add new metrics to the big picture.

Don't forget the company intranet. The internal infrastructure also needs to be there and serve the employees' needs, offering access to critical customer information, such as manufacturing, logistics, training, accounting, and sales. "At Egghead, we use our intranet to give all employees daily updates on what is happening with sales and our customers. Each newsletter has a new customer service message in it as well," says Norm Hullinger, Vice-President of Sales and Operations, Egghead.com.

Maintaining Service Levels As You Grow

If you are a brick and mortar company, take an objective look at your offline customer satisfaction levels. If your reputation is stellar in this area, you should make every effort to extend these same levels of service to your online operations—at least in terms of your philosophy and relative importance to the company. However, it's crucial to remember that the technology and infrastructure changes you make can support the new environment; don't assume that your good reputation is all you need. Many companies have been able to maintain or build on their good reputations online, such as Lands' End, The Gap, Hallmark, Cisco, and Dell. They have invested the time and effort required to operate in this new environment effectively.

E-volving your customer service processes means using metrics effectively, taking them seriously, and making the changes necessary to effect improvement. "hpshopping.com was successful because we took the metrics seriously," says Dave Deasy, former COO of hpshopping.com. "We put a closed-loop customer monitoring system in place, and we analyzed the feedback, reported on it, followed up with customers and then took all the information back into our planning process. The result was a customer referral rate of greater than 97% for the next two years after we made the changes."

It's important to make the commitment to maintain and change the customer service systems and processes as your business grows. When your customers become accustomed to certain service levels, the bar only gets higher in terms of expectations. For you to be responsive to your customers, it's important that you keep a constant eye on your metrics. If your resources are limited to make the required changes, outsourcing might be a good solution. Many companies have been created to provide this service on an ASP or other basis that might be a good short-term or long-term solution.

E-Volutionary Tactics

→ Create a "CCEO" (Chief Customer Experience Officer) who is part of the executive management staff.

→ Your entire company must function as a customer service organization.

→ All functions need to be redefined to incorporate customer service into their goals, and you need to increase the salary levels of those closest to your customers.

→ In order to e-volve people and processes to fit changing customer expectations, you must have realistic metrics in place and use them on a regular basis.

→ Customer service incentives should be provided for all employees and should be tied to compensation.

→ Your customer service levels should be consistent with the customer stratification of your market.

→ Partners need to provide the same consistent customer service as your company or be replaced with partners that can.

→ All appropriate business processes should serve customer service goals.

→ A common customer database should be universally accessible across your organization.

Managing the E-Commerce Organization

THE ORGANIZATIONAL STRUCTURE of corporations is e-volving in the

New E-Conomy. There is a multitude of new business models, and

there are just as many ways to set up and manage companies. You may

decide to start a new division of your company now to focus on your

e-commerce opportunities and then transition the rest of the organi-

zation later. Another option is to transform the whole company all at

once. And if your company is a dot.com, you must decide on the opti-

mum organizational infrastructure from the beginning and then grow

▶▶

your organization by hiring according to the skills that will maintain the chosen structure.

Organizational size is also shifting in the Internet Age. Large companies are becoming smaller and more entrepreneurial in an effort to be closer to the customer and more responsive. Small companies and startups are trying to grow. Merger and acquisition activity will likely continue at its current pace, resulting in larger, combined companies and the elimination of some smaller ones. Regardless of the size of your organization, the people issues remain, and organizational structure choices still need to be made. Some companies choose to keep the hierarchical structures that have been used in business for decades but modify them to allow for more self-directed and cross-functional teams who work on specific projects or customer groups. Other companies adopt whole new organizational schemes that have not been conventionally used.

In the New E-Conomy, employees are changing, too. People change employers more frequently than ever before, and their stay at any one company may be shorter. Loyalty to employers has changed a great deal, and gone are the days when people work for a single employer for a decade or more. Startups and dot.coms often lure employees away from large, established companies by offering stock options and a more entrepreneurial environment. Along with more traditional needs of employees such as challenging work, opportunity to make an impact, and career growth, it presents a challenge to companies to keep up with the e-volving mix of needs. As a result of these trends, companies need to reconfigure compensation schemes and job descriptions to fit the changing motivations of today's workforce.

Employee communications have changed significantly because of Internet technology. With company intranets and the use of email, it is much faster for management to communicate with all employees and for employees and teams to communicate with one another. This makes it much easier to assemble virtual teams and keep the momentum going. Brainstorming becomes "page storming," and intranets enable company-wide collaboration. Employees also have greater access to management to communicate ideas and feedback. An example of this

---

was the Kinko's employee who created a calendar product at a local retail location and sent an email about it to an executive at the corporate headquarters. All Kinko's locations now offer the service.

People and organizations need to e-volve to enable the smooth operation of an Internet-enabled entity. This chapter focuses on the issues, choices, and options you will be facing in the transition.

A Blueprint for Organizational Alignment

E-volving your company into a holistic, Internet-enabled entity includes six key actions:

▲ From the top down, your vision should drive the organizational structure.

▲ Your goals need to be aligned with your customers, consistent with your customer stratification, and the organization must be able to function to meet those goals.

▲ Be flexible and creative with the organizational structure (such as separate groups, divisions, or a flattened hierarchy).

▲ Empower people and involve them in realigning processes to fit the goals.

▲ Get rid of legacy people who cannot or will not change.

▲ Be aggressive and committed to making the transition happen; set an example and give people an incentive.

There is a lot of thinking to be done, decisions to be made, and changes to implement. The whole process deserves the attention of the best and brightest from your management team (and outside parties with unique sets of inputs) to not only develop the strategy, but also implement the action plan across the organization. The best ideas may come from the bottom of your organization. However, commitment to making a change starts at the top.

Aligning with Your Vision

Does your vision fit
your organization?

It's time to revisit your vision statement. Can it be accomplished by the organization you have in place today? You may need to make some changes at the highest levels of your organization. If your organization is very large, it may take quite a long time to make company-wide changes. It might make sense to create a wholly owned subsidiary or separate division to realize your vision and then transition the rest of the company. Says Narry Singh, Vice-President of Global Trading, Rapt. Inc., "If you're an established company and not a new dot.com, there are a number of organizational models you can pursue. One is the 'dot.corp,' a spin-out from a larger company (such as US Steel and eSteel). Another is the 'dot.div,' a wholly owned subsidiary (like Kmart and Bluelight.com). A lot will depend on your highest-level business objectives, over the long haul, along with your target market. How best can you serve and grow your customer base?"

A lot of factors come into play in making these decisions. According to Atul Vashistha, CEO of neoIT, "You need to think seriously about whether you want to form a separate company or integrate your EC operations with your existing company. Some of the concerns include brand and whether it extends to the Internet environment, your market segmentation plan, and especially the management strengths—are you really built for speed and flexibility? Addressing these issues will help you decide which way to go, but either way, it is a tremendous challenge." It's a matter of looking at your "new" business objectives alongside your existing business, and assessing whether there is still a match in terms of your organization.

Other considerations are company culture, costs, core competencies, and partnerships. How fast can your organization make the changes necessary to be successful, and how much of a budget do you have to accomplish this? What makes sense in terms of your core competencies? Does it make sense to work more closely with partners at this time or to outsource? These are the tough high-level decisions you need to make.

Organizational Structures for the Internet-Enabled Entity

Organizational structures are maps of reporting relationships among employees. In the Industrial Age, organizational structures were very hierarchical; with the CEO at the top and many, many layers of management down the "pyramid" to the lowliest employees at the bottom. Some companies are still very hierarchical and continue to function that way now, at the beginning of the Internet Age. Others are experimenting with a more "flattened hierarchy" that reduces the number of layers of management. Another structure is to use a truly horizontal structure, where employees work together in virtual groups, coming together for specific projects for set amounts of time. (This is sometimes referred to as the "virtual corporation," which became popular in the early 1990s.) Regardless of what your structure looks like now, be prepared to take another critical look at it to see if it still serves your business purpose.

What does your organizational structure look like?

If you examine your vision statement and decide some reorganization is part of your plan, how do you organize in the New E-Conomy—around customers, product lines, markets, technology, processes, or function? (See Figure 9.1.)

Organizing your company by technology or products, or anything else besides customers, will not be effective in the Internet Age. In Chapter 8, "New Expectations for Customer Service," I described how the whole company needs to be aligned with customers—that everyone's job is customer service. I believe

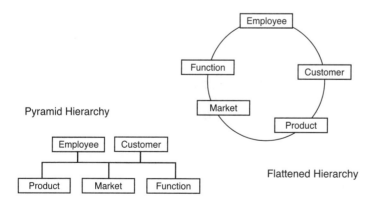

Figure 9.1

You can reorganize your company by customer, product line, market, or function.

that the best organizational structure is one that puts the customer at the center of the company. It requires reorganizing people, departments, and functions consistent with your customers' needs. If you choose any other area as an organizational focal point, it will be close to impossible to e-volve quickly enough in tomorrow's business environment. One of the biggest challenges management will face will be meeting new customer demands by integrating new business models and new technology into existing business processes. Even if you have a traditional hierarchical organization that is divided by department or function, it is still possible to use a classic "matrix" arrangement. A matrix arrangement enables people to have a functional "home," such as engineering or marketing, that allows them to keep up their skills in these areas along with others in their department. However, project teams are built with people from these functional groups who serve on the team from the beginning to the end of a project, and while they are on it, they may report to a team or project leader; that is their project "home." This type of hybrid arrangement will also work in the New E-Conomy.

This customer-centric organizational scheme is not just focused on improving customer satisfaction. Rather, your customer stratification scheme (as discussed in Chapter 4, "Customer Touch Points") should be the basis for your new organization. (See Figure 9.2.)

According to Atul Vashistha, CEO of neoIT, "There are many examples of companies who have been able to transform their companies into the Internet Age by reorganizing by market segments, such as EasyJet. They had a difficult time selling

Figure 9.2

The customer-centric organization.

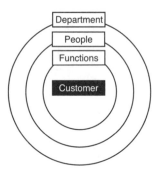

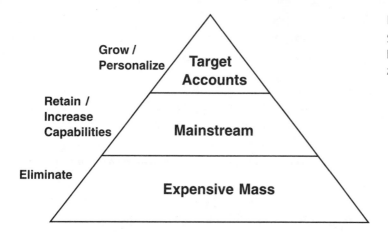

Figure 9.3
Stratification of your customer base should dictate your organizational structure.

Grow / Personalize — **Target Accounts**

Retain / Increase Capabilities — **Mainstream**

Eliminate — **Expensive Mass**

tickets, so they analyzed their customers' psychographic profiles to define a new market segment. They reorganized the company accordingly, and were able to move 70 percent of their business online in two years." Other companies have been able to transform their companies as well, such as Charles Schwab's transition to eSchwab, a real "click and mortar" example. They created whole business units around their redefined target market, and the job functions were realigned accordingly. Likewise, Dell set up their company initially around their discrete market segments such as SOHO, large business, and consumers.

What are your key market segments, and are they served by your current organization?

Your most important customers and market segment need to receive the most attention from your employees. How can you organize your company to make that happen? One way to do it is to create key account teams, consisting of people from cross-functional areas such as development, marketing, sales, customer support, and logistics. These teams are empowered to make decisions about how best to serve the key customers and to take whatever action is necessary to keep those customers happy and turn them into "lifetime customers." "An organizational structure is nothing more than a communications structure," says Ben Horowitz, President and CEO of Loudcloud. "Each time you create a new mission for the company, you may need to change the communications structure. If you are reorganizing by customer or market segment, you first need to find everyone in the company who has an interface to that customer, and where the communication path is internally. Then you can reorganize the people accordingly. That way, you can be assured that the customer relationship can continue, and you have a built-in customer-centric organization."

Participation in these key account teams may be full-time and static, or it may be more virtual, with people rotating in and out of the teams to gain experience and skills. Whichever mode is used will still serve the customer, as long as the service and attention given to the customer is consistent. You need to integrate a 360-degree view of the customer across all functions of the company, including the access necessary for employees to accomplish this. For other customers within your stratification team, similar teams can be formed; the only difference might be the amount of time and attention each customer receives as his or her level of importance decreases.

Transitioning to a New Structure

Moving an existing organization into an entirely new structure or set of reporting relationships is a challenge. Company reorganizations are always painful to some degree. Often, people who have never worked together find themselves on the same team. New managers and job descriptions are unsettling to people and can drastically affect career paths. Personality conflicts and inconsistent communications can make matters worse.

Is your current organizational culture the right environment for change?

The company culture and management philosophy has a big effect on the reorganization process and how people react to it. In companies that encourage open communications and consensus management, it may be easier for employees because they are informed about what is going on and may even be involved in making the decisions about what needs to be changed. UPS is one of those companies that was able to make widespread changes relatively quickly because of the long-established "open" leadership style, according to Alan Amling, Director of E-Commerce Marketing at UPS. Not all companies have this philosophy, however, as they tend to be more autocratic. In that environment, it will be more difficult to obtain commitment because people might feel threatened or left out of the decision process.

Because of the need to make changes more quickly in the New E-Conomy, an open leadership and communication style will likely be more effective; not only do you want to communicate what changes need to be made, but by involving employees in the process, you will get ideas on how to make it happen—more quickly. "Enron was able to move their business to the Internet in just seven months without organizational upheaval. The employees saw the Internet as a tool to make their existing business better, and they came up with ways to deliver their services in a whole new way," says Atul Vashistha.

All employees should be skilled in using email communication, collaborative tools or groupware, and electronic document workflow.

People and Processes

To e-volve the company into a holistic, Internet-enabled entity, legacy processes and legacy people must change to fit the new vision. The question becomes this: Is it easier to change the processes first and then the people, or vice versa? (See Figure 9.4.) If you make the organizational changes first, you can enlist the people in getting the processes changed for the better, with more commitment and teambuilding. If you make the process changes first, it is easier to determine which people changes must be made. "I think that form follows function," says Atul Vashistha. "If you first re-align your processes by customer need, and then figure out how your employees can support them, your new organizational structure will become obvious. That's not to say, however, that you shouldn't involve employees in making the changes. You must give people a chance and keep them involved. It may take some experimenting until people feel comfortable in new roles. It's important to encourage employees to speak up and be proactive during the change process."

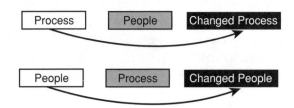

Figure 9.4
Do you change processes or people first?

Legacy People

In any organization, there are always a few individuals who resist change. There are many reasons for this—complacency, job security, conflict with personal goals and desires, politics, and work styles. A "legacy person" is an individual who refuses to make the organizational and behavioral changes necessary to accomplish the company's vision, and in the process, can make other people miserable who *are* willing to change. This may not be a lower-level employee; often senior managers or executives become legacy people as well.

Do you have legacy people in your organization?

What do you do with legacy people? They should be given a chance to communicate concerns to management because they do carry with them important knowledge, or "intellectual assets" of the company. After their concerns are addressed and they have had a chance to be heard, they have an opportunity to get on board and participate in the change. If they refuse or are unable to transition with your company, you need to transition them *out* of the company. There is just too much at stake. (See Figure 9.5.)

Transforming People

When transforming your organization, after the legacy people are gone, some transformation of the remaining people may also be necessary. It is critical that employees fully understand the changes taking place, as well as the impact on their job functions and how they relate to their fellow workers. How do you transform a person? Through training and motivation. However, you can't begin to train people and motivate them until you know what makes them tick, and that gets back to the basics of people management 101. The only difference in today's economy is that employees have less patience; if an employer does not meet their needs, they will move on to a different company. It's truly a seller's market right now, and in general, there is less loyalty. However, every individual has a different mix of what

Figure 9.5

If legacy people resist change, get rid of legacy people.

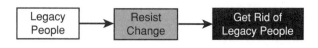

they look for in their job/career—money, challenge, learning, fun, good coworkers, risk-taking, responsibility, advancement, equity, being on the bleeding edge of technology, fame, job security. It's up to the company to understand what those motivators are and find ways to keep employees happy and contributing.

Generally speaking, most employees want to do a good job, want to feel that they are contributing and are valued, and want to be paid accordingly. If your company does not provide this environment or do these things for employees, maybe your human resource philosophy and processes need to be redesigned.

It is important to hold all-employee communication sessions when undergoing major organizational changes. This is one way to get everyone on the same page and help foster greater levels of commitment to the company's vision and necessary changes. Training can help, depending on what type of training is conducted. If the training is designed so that employees learn new skills or new ways of communicating they can use anywhere, they will view the experience with more value than if they are "force-fed" company dogma and processes without having a chance to participate.

One of the secrets to Charles Schwab's success was to focus attention and resources on team building and management commitment. They also learned that it was important to focus on individual personalities and culture rather than job skills of people; those factors will determine whether your teams will be functional or dysfunctional. It's important to understand that all employees must 'morph', in other words, undergo some change, in order to transform the organization. It takes time and work to build well-functioning teams—it's a matter of making an investment in the company's most precious resource—people.

Self-Directed Work Groups

One of the ways to create a positive environment for employees is to put into place a system of self-directed work groups, whose mission it is to solve business problems. Organized teamwork has been used in companies for years, with varying success and popularity. However, in the New E-Conomy and the speed at which business moves, teaming has become a necessity for productivity and communications.

"Self-directed" means that the team members are free to appoint a leader, set goals, allocate work, apply metrics, report results, and communicate in a way that works for the team. The team typically defines its charter and its deadlines and governs itself with no participation or oversight from management. In some cases, teams are given a specific charter high-level metrics to meet; however, the metrics or charter by its definition shouldn't inhibit thinking outside the box. Working in this manner empowers the team with decision-making authority, responsibility, and involvement. Although there is always a team member or two that don't do their share, most team members enjoy the experience, perform well, feel creative, and do great work.

Collaborative Management

Once the new structure is in place, management styles may need to change as well. If a more horizontal structure is put into place, with teams or empowered groups, then middle managers or team leaders need to act more like facilitators than supervisors. It is collaborative management that is needed. "Open leadership styles work much better in today's economy," claims Love Goel, CEO of Personify. "It's important to share thought processes and get people involved. Teaming the seasoned executives with the younger managers helps enable the learning to take place on both sides, and helps the company move forward toward its goals much faster." Mentoring has been used successfully in companies for many years to train and motivate employees and help them grow their careers. It's also a valuable method of increasing the amount of collaboration within an organization to keep it more open and flexible.

If significant reorganization is done in a company, job descriptions and duties may change considerably. It may be necessary for people to participate in cross-functional training to gain the skills they need for a more horizontal organizational environment. Often, it is advisable for employees to seek external training through continuing education programs offered by local universities or even to seek additional formalized degree programs. Most companies offer reimbursement of expenses for such programs, and this should be encouraged.

Walking and Talking the Vision

In order to e-volve, it may be necessary to implement many organizational changes. It is critical for top management of the company to continue to communicate and reinforce the vision of the company. Commitment to the vision needs to be demonstrated by action, essentially, leading by example. Any issues in the transition phase need to be dealt with, and employees should be encouraged to raise concerns that may hinder the company in accomplishing the vision. It's also critical to share business successes with employees and give rewards (monetary or non-monetary) to celebrate the accomplishment of milestones and maintaining the momentum. All of this should be done in an open communications environment.

Everyone in the newly structured organization should still be able to recite the 30-second elevator pitch that captures the vision for the company. In addition, every employee should be empowered to interface with the customer, and thus, everyone becomes a marketing professional as well—with every customer interaction.

Are you prepared to demonstrate your commitment to your vision?

E-Volutionary Tactics

→ Organizational changes will be driven by your vision.

→ At the highest level, spin-outs, subsidiaries, and cross-functional reorganization are some of the changes that may work to accomplish your vision.

→ Keeping up with the New E-Conomy requires a nimble and flexible organization.

→ Self-directed work groups are one of the best ways to manage people.

→ Internet-enabled communications should be leveraged to increase and improve collaboration and communication within the company.

→ Legacy people can stall the progress of the entire organization.

→ New organizational structures should be customer-centric, in accordance with your customer stratification scheme.

→ Collaborative management is one of the successful ways to manage the new organization.

→ Mentoring can help increase the level of collaboration within the organization.

→ Motivation results from empowering teams to serve the customer and make decisions.

→ If organizational structures aren't working, they need to be changed.

→ Training and re-training may be necessary to e-volve the organization, both inside the organization and externally through continuing education.

Ongoing Internet Marketing

INTERNET MARKETING has become a whole new type of marketing

unto itself. It is e-volving every day, and countless books have been

written on the subject, trying to capture what works and what doesn't

work in terms of using the Internet to find, attract, obtain, and retain

customers.   ▶▶

In my e-commerce consulting practice, I have spent more than one thousand man-hours examining the market techniques and approaches that work most effectively. The ECnow.com Web page (**www.ecnow.com/Internet_Marketing**) contains a representation of that effort; it is constantly updated to reflect best practices. The information available there in total practically represents an entire degree in marketing principles. This is an example of how you can make information available for free that benefits the industry as a whole. It is my way of making a contribution, consistent with my belief that what goes around, comes around. A sample of the main pages is included at the conclusion of this chapter. This chapter does not contain a lot of specific examples, because the Web page contains more current examples of the principles I address in this chapter. I urge you to visit the ECnow.com Web page often to stay current with my findings and recommendations in this area. One of the success factors for Internet marketing is keeping up with trends.

New Ways to Market and New Buzzwords

You've probably heard many new phrases that describe the new marketing, such as viral marketing, permission marketing, and personalization. What do they mean? Are they fundamentally different from the way we have been marketing from the beginning of time? Take a look at some of these strategies in detail.

Viral marketing is a new way of describing word-of-mouth referrals—a very old concept. The only difference is, word-of-mouth now travels over the Internet and via email, a much more widespread and ubiquitous medium with the capability of reaching Web communities (groups of Web users with common interests). Unlike other types of marketing, this is something that you can't directly control or implement as part of your marketing plan. The only way to impact what people say about you and your company is to develop and maintain exemplary customer service with every customer no matter how he or she contacts you. If you do that, viral marketing will essentially do part of your marketing job for you. Many people will copy and paste URLs into the body of an email document, making the "viral infection" that much faster. As an example, AllAdvantage signed up two million members in just 120 days using viral marketing. Many firms use cash or spot rewards for members who contribute new members. You can encourage viral marketing by supplying good information and building a cadre of evangelists. (See Figure 10.1.)

Permission marketing refers to online surveys, newsletters, and other types of online communication in which Web users agree to be contacted online via email, in exchange for incentives, such as give-aways, contests, or discounts on goods and services. Web users can "opt-in" to these communication channels that are set up and managed by you or third parties. You may find many ways to use permission marketing for your company, from conducting market research, to special promotions, to advertising campaigns. Permission marketing is similar to more conventional types of market research, such as focus groups or surveys where incentives are given.

Although some people believe that personalization and mass customization are synonyms, they are not. *Personalization* refers to the practice of individualizing your marketing content and programs for one customer at a time, based on that customer's unique profile. This marketing technique has also been used for a while, especially by companies who sell high-priced products; they often have few customers, but long sales cycles, and they must develop one customer at a time. Mass *customization* is when companies custom-tailor their delivered products to fit the individual customer's needs. Dell Computer Corporation uses both techniques. Using the Dell Web site to order a customized computer is an example of mass customization. Personalization (or personalized direct marketing) occurs

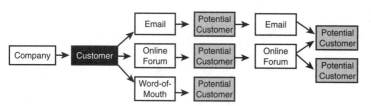

Figure 10.1

Viral marketing leverages the power of the online community.

when Dell sends you an email two years after owning your computer, stating that you can upgrade your "outdated" computer to the latest model. (See Figure 10.2.)

Figure 10.2

Personalized, one-to-one marketing can be done on a mass scale via the Internet.

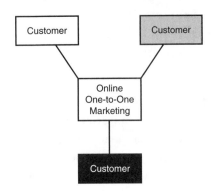

No Field of Dreams Here

Some companies believe that when their Web site goes live, their marketing is complete. All they have to do is build it, and the customers will come. No, the field of dreams concept does not apply to Internet marketing. (See Figure 10.3.)

The process of marketing your company, your products, and services begins with your customers. Who are they? What do they want, and how can you deliver it to them better than anyone else? You must know your customer better than your

Figure 10.3

Internet marketing is not like a field of dreams.

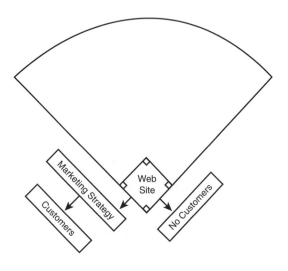

competitors do, and you must be able to build your customer relationships one customer at a time. After that, it takes just as much effort to maintain those relationships and earn lifetime customers, as you learned in Chapter 4, "Customer Touch Points."

Your Web site by itself is just a passive marketing device; it requires other "offline" types of communication between your company and customers to fully develop and maintain the customer relationships. That is not to say that your Web site doesn't play a significant role—it certainly does. Your Web site leverages search engines, can provide opt-in newsletters, and offer member sign-up promotions that are Web-based. It is a significant distribution channel, advertising platform, selling tool, customer service medium, and one or more customer touch points. Your Web site can help you do your marketing, but it requires much attention, feeding, and maintenance for maximum contribution. Let's look at some of the ways to do that.

The Basics of Internet Marketing

When it comes to Internet marketing, you must know the characteristics of your customer and entice them to learn more about your product or service. You must ensure that your customer has a positive experience so they will keep coming back for more.

If you are just beginning to build your Web site or have just finished the first version of it, here are some of the things you need to do to optimize the site's marketing effectiveness. (But before you begin, you must have a very clear understanding of what your competitors are doing before you build your site!)

▲ Decide on the primary goal for your Web site: Is it marketing communications, sales, leads, investor information, market research, or something else?

▲ Communicate these goals to the entire company and continually monitor your progress.

▲ Make sure the site is easy to use and navigate, *for your expected clientele.*

- ▲ Test-drive the site with your expected clientele.

- ▲ If you are implementing a shopping/sales capability, make sure the customer can place an order with no more than 1–2 clicks.

- ▲ If you are requesting personal information, include a trust/privacy statement.

- ▲ Use an auto-responder whenever possible.

- ▲ Provide a number of ways for the customer to interact with your company, such as by Web form, email, fax, and 800 numbers.

- ▲ You can never build in too many types of customer support.

What is your Web identity?

You may go through several iterations of your Web site before you are ready to deploy it. In building a Web site, you have to build 30% of it, get feedback, build another 30%, get feedback, build another 30%, get feedback, eliminate 20%, build another 30%, and so on. Otherwise, you will spend all your money building the wrong site. After you build it, however, your job is just beginning. Your Web site is becoming your marketing and advertising face to the world—in other words, the Web identity for your company. Expect to spend much time and effort maintaining and e-volving that identity. Don't forget that you can (and probably should) outsource your Web site design and hosting if it's not a core competency. Chapter 7, "Outsourcing Is Always an Option," addresses the issue of out-sourcing.

The first fundamentals you need to apply relate to your Web identity and how to leverage it for marketing purposes. Those seven fundamentals are listed here:

- ▲ Have a great URL.

- ▲ Design for ease of use.

- ▲ Give away something of value.

- ▲ Provide valuable content.

- ▲ Put your URL everywhere.

- ▲ Use signature tags on email.

- ▲ Submit the site to appropriate search engines.

If you are not doing at least these seven things with your Web identity, you have a business problem. The following sections address some creative ways to implement these seven fundamentals. (See Figure 10.4.)

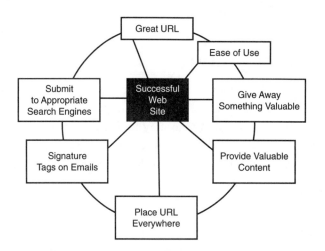

Figure 10.4

The basics that every Web site should adhere to..

A Memorable URL

It's a good idea to do a trademark search and Web search before you settle on a domain name. Try to incorporate as many keywords as you can into your domain name—words that relate to your company name, your core business, and your brand. With the race for dot.com domain names, the pickings are slim, but other extensions such as dot "net" and dot "cc" provide opportunities to do that. (Refer to the pages from my Web site at the end of this chapter for domain registration resources.)

Domain names are gradually becoming longer, instead of short abbreviations or acronyms, and the longer names might even be easier to remember than the shortened versions. The more you can do with your domain name will increase the likelihood that customers and prospects can find you online. It's much easier than relying on your relative positioning on search engines, which can change daily. Multiple domain names and "Web site fronts" can get you multiple listings with search engines as well.

Does your URL represent your company?

You also need to think about product names and other slogans that are part of your company. Those domain names should be registered as well; they provide another way for customers to find you. You can easily link those domain names to your main Web site URL.

Site Navigation

Test your Web content on different browsers and platforms before launching it. This is particularly important for marketing impact. Your company's logo may look great on one browser, but anemic on another. You may need to make changes to Web design, graphics, and colors in order to optimize your site for marketing purposes.

You should have your Web site evaluated for usability. There are several books on this subject if you want to do this yourself, or you can use one of the many companies out there who can do it for you. Some of the evaluations that need to be done include the following:

▲ If you sell online and use a shopping cart, do customers abandon their carts because the process is too slow or cumbersome?

▲ Does your site map make it easy for people to find the content they are looking for?

▲ Is the download time of your homepage fast enough for the average dial-up user?

▲ Do you provide a way for customers to contact you by other means, such as telephone or email, if they have questions?

Have you navigated your own Web site lately?

Many, many other measures of usability will also impact your marketing effectiveness. It's important to remember that from a marketing perspective, you need to use your Web site to first attract customers. In order to do that, the customer must be able to quickly grasp what your company is about and what you have to offer. Anything you can do in the way of usability to attract the customer's attention quickly will make you more successful at turning that prospect into a real customer.

Give Away Something of Value

If you give away something of value to site visitors, there is more reason for them to return. You can find working examples of this principle at these two pages: **http://ecnow.com/Internet_Marketing.htm** and **http://ecnow.com/resources.htm**. Your "freebie" can be anything from articles and information, to merchandise, to frequent flyer miles or gift certificates. Giving away free stuff works in both B2C and B2B environments; the only difference might be what you give away. In the B2B world, free stuff might include articles, books, studies, discounts, and gift certificates—all of which might be related in some way to the company's products or services. However, it is important to make sure that the customer or prospect views the give-away as valuable to *them*. Although it will cost you to provide these items, you will receive multiple returns on your investment from increased Web traffic and, ultimately, new customers.

Content and Related Content

Content is the heart of every Web site. You need content to deliver information about your business, your products, and your services. In Chapter 5, "Content Will Always Be King," I discussed the role of content in more detail, such as value, context, updates, and metrics. Those principles will make your marketing more effective. You also need complementary content that might be located elsewhere (and that is linked) to add even more value to your Web site—as long as it relates to the context of your business.

Besides the obvious ways of creating and adding content, you can explore these other avenues:

- ▲ Acquiring content through syndication (**www.isyndicate.com**)
- ▲ Joining affiliate programs
- ▲ Asking partners in your value web to share content

Chapter 5 also contains information on syndication and content sharing.

The Omnipresent URL

How are you using your URL?

On business stationery, your URL should be as much a requirement as your phone number. Every piece of stationery that has your company name should also carry your URL. And when you refer to your company in marketing materials or when the trade press editors write about your company, add the dot.com extension ("yourcompany.com" instead of "your company"). Even employees should be encouraged to refer to their employer using the dot.com designation; it is all part of "walking the talk."

Signature Tags

Email systems have those great little features now where you can add any kind of marketing message or contact information automatically to a signature line. Imagine if every person in your company used the marketing message of the week in their signature every time they sent an email message to someone else. Now that's powerful! Someone in your marketing organization should be designated to create and distribute a continuing stream of marketing messages and news that people can attach to their emails.

The Search Engine Game

Are your search keywords the right ones?

Search engine optimization is both an art and a science. The three or four keywords you should optimize in the search engines should come directly out of your vision statement. Although I have compiled many tips and teach a course/tutorial on Internet Marketing (including search engine optimization), the single most important suggestion I can give is that you go to Danny Sullivan's site: **http://www.searchenginewatch.com** (see Figure 10.5).

The rest of the techniques discussed on the Internet Marketing page of ECnow.com are listed here:

- ▲ Find and fuel evangelists (viral marketing).
- ▲ Establish a "free" online newsletter.

Figure 10.5

Comprehensive, up-to-date information on search engines; a must read.

▲ Optimize your site and positioning in the search engines.

▲ Establish an affiliate program.

▲ Use email marketing.

▲ Pay for Internet advertising.

▲ Publish articles and/or find ways to be mentioned in news stories.

▲ Use online press releases.

▲ Run an auction.

▲ Run contests and give away prizes.

▲ Determine online communities to participate in.

▲ Actively monitor and participate in online community.

▲ Establish and lead an online forum/community.

▲ Give away online coupons.

▲ Conduct surveys.

▲ Participate in a charitable Web site.

▲ Create links in Internet malls/portals.

▲ Participate in paid-for and free banner advertising.

▲ Establish a reciprocal Web linking program.

▲ Place paid-for and free classified ads.

▲ Host classified ads.

- ▲ Use email auto-responders.
- ▲ Create your own search engine.
- ▲ Apply for and win awards.
- ▲ Create a free-for-all page.

Online Newsletters and Magazines

In almost every industry, traditional trade journals and magazines provide articles or information on issues of interest. Your company can do the same thing—online. It may be a matter of moving your print version of an existing magazine online, or you might want to create a brand new one. Inviting your customers and partners to contribute content is a great way to build an online community for your company. Another possibility is to create a portal environment for your company, which provides community, content, and commerce—all from your Web site.

Online newsletters can live on the company's Web site or can be sent directly to recipients via email. If you have an email distribution list already, it's appropriate to let the list participants know you are starting a newsletter that they can opt into. If you are just starting out and don't have a database yet, offer a free first issue at your Web site, and include a place for people to sign up for additional issues with their email address. In addition, you should put all issues online because that provides more content for your customers and can help with search engine optimization.

If you were already sending out print versions of company magazines or newsletters, moving them online saves considerably on mailing expenses. It also has other benefits: Email by nature is a two-way communication channel, and paper mail is not. You have a means for automatic feedback directly from your customers if you choose to exploit it, and you should. It's important, however, to make sure that marketing communications guidelines for printed materials are also applied to the content you place online, for the sake of consistency.

Direct Marketing Online

Direct mail has moved from bulk mailing through the postal service to the online version: email. It's important to collect email addresses at every opportunity. In a recent Forrester Research study, consumers were asked what types of "direct marketing" email messages they would like to receive from companies. Here is the breakout:

- ▲ Coupons and gift certificates (67%)
- ▲ Free samples (65%)
- ▲ Notification of sales and special promotions (59%)
- ▲ Product updates and news (43%)
- ▲ Basic company information (16%)

As you build an email database for your company, you can leverage this in many ways to do marketing. The important thing is to know your customers and what they want to receive. It is also wise to give persons on your email list an opportunity to "opt-in" and certainly a way to "opt-out."

Is your email database leveraged?

Branding and the Web Site

Any brand or image that your company has should be reflected in your Web site. In essence, in the online world, your Web site and the customer experience you provide there *is* your brand. A common misconception is that your customers will always enter your site from the top—your home page. With search engine optimization, the customer can enter your site from any location. Although consistent navigation should be on all pages so that one can visit the site and get a good feel from any page, you should not underestimate the power of your home page. "Think about your homepage like you would a TV ad—the 30-second awareness factor applies to the Web world, too. Your Web site needs to be a brief, snappy, and visual representation of your company and your brand. After those 30 seconds, the Web user may move on. Your brand is not just your company logo, either. It's the whole experience of the site," according to Christina Cheney, President and CEO, Simmedia.com.

This means your messages have to be consistent throughout your Web site, as well as being consistent with your "offline" presence in the marketplace. Internet marketing offers a new opportunity to create an online brand; Amazon.com is a good example of that. However, if your existing company already has some brand recognition, you need to either strengthen it with your online presence or rebrand your company entirely. Whatever you decide to do about online branding must be consistent with your vision and goals for your company, otherwise you are risk confusing the marketplace. Online branding should include more than just logos and colors consistent with your company's identity. Branding extends to include the values your company's name and reputation embodies, and this can be manifested in the online experience your customers have.

Market Research

Your Web site is a business asset. You need to think about how you can leverage your site to gather information about your customers and to obtain direct customer feedback to enhance your planning and strategy efforts. If you do surveys directly from your Web site, you need to offer incentives, such as cash, merchandise, or other freebies in exchange for information. Third-party companies can provide this service for your customers—through a link from your Web site. Participants in the third-party service then receive their incentive directly from that company. Whatever incentives you provide either directly or indirectly are a mere pittance compared to what it might cost to gather such data using more conventional means.

Christina Cheney, President and CEO of Simmedia.com encourages her clients to use the Web for formal beta programs: "Every phase of a beta testing program can be created and implemented from the company's Web site. You can sign up beta customers and partners, deliver the product to be tested (and if it's software, it can be downloaded directly), receive real-time beta feedback, and communicate the results to the growing customer base. It's almost like building a Web community related to the new product you are developing. The payoff is that you have a built-in market when you're ready to launch."

Conventional Marketing and Internet Marketing

Many companies are using a combination of techniques: They use traditional marketing (such as direct mail or advertising) to drive people to the company Web site (where they implement different techniques). It requires a portfolio of marketing techniques to be successful in the online world, and you cannot rely on Web marketing alone. In a recent study done by ActivMedia Research, they found a different marketing mix emerging, at least among retailers. These were the most commonly used marketing techniques at the time:

- Search engine positioning (66%)
- Email (54%)
- Print brochures and collateral (42%)
- Print catalogs (40%)
- Trade shows (37%)

The shift toward online marketing techniques is evident. More conventional techniques will not go away entirely; indeed, they will help supplement what is done online. According to Eric Ward, President of The Ward Group (**www.thewardgroup.com**), "Today there is a danger of 'URL overload.' It's tough to remember all the URLs. The more a company can do with conventional techniques to get people to the Web site, the better. For instance, many people listen to the radio while surfing the Web; what an opportunity to have a radio ad directing a customer to a Web site in real-time. That's how companies need to think about marketing mix today."

What is your mix of conventional and Internet marketing?

Everyone Is a Marketer

By now, everyone in your organization can recite the corporate vision and is aligned with the customer. That means everyone is in a position to market to the customer. But what skills do people need to do successful marketing?

Product marketing skills are those closest to the development of the product itself. Such skills include the ability to create demos and samples of the product for customer use, the understanding of multilevel positioning of the product, performing complex usability analysis, and using innovation to "Web-ify" products. Another important skill is to focus more on graphics and design than on techno-jargon and excessive verbiage.

The "marcom people," or marketing communications department, may need to update their skills as well. The URL of the company needs to be viewed as a product and asset of the company and treated accordingly in marketing literature and promotional materials. Today's marcom must understand multimedia delivery channels and content that works accordingly. "Companies need to leverage the multimedia aspects of the Web," says Eric Ward, President of The Ward Group. "NoBrainerBlinds, for example, put together a video demonstration of how to install their Venetian blinds, and it's downloadable from their Web site. What they have done is make it easier for their customer to not only buy but also use their product—directly from the company Web site."

Locating and understanding the target audience is key, along with creating a unique identity for the company. A new skill is creating online "affinity" and loyalty programs linked to the Web site. This is not something people learn in an academic setting; instead it comes from the experience of understanding your customers and how they interact with your company and the Web.

The face of public relations has changed in the online world. The most unique aspect of public relations today is that companies are not totally reliant on the press for a channel to the customer. Today, they can effectively enter into a dialogue directly with the customer online via email or the Web, bypassing the press. However, if you choose to work with the traditional press, there is still a need to develop stories that are unique and newsworthy; that has always been true. Today, there are many more online media, creating additional new forums for public relations. Almost every print medium has an online equivalent these days; that's the good news. The bad news is, it will become more difficult to differentiate your company because developing an e-commerce transition success story isn't necessarily news anymore; every company needs to do this. The P.R. skills needed today are to find ways to develop new angles and stories by leveraging value web partners and other affiliates who can contribute uniqueness to your public relations programs.

New advertising approaches are needed today. Banner advertising and other types of Web advertising are relatively new, and it requires new knowledge of how to make these new techniques work. In addition, it is necessary to use offline advertising to drive customers to the Web site. That means traditional and online advertising need to be integrated in order to produce the desired impact. It includes everything from consistency of message, to brand and image, to quality of content, incentives, and search engine optimization. Today's advertising is far more complicated as a result.

Channel marketing skills are becoming more important today due to increased partnering. You must be able to identify and recruit the right online marketing partners and develop programs that will benefit both entities. It is also important that you understand the potential for channel conflict and develop measures to prevent it.

Is everyone in your company a marketer?

Your Holistic Marketing Strategy

This chapter has given you a lot of things to think about regarding marketing and the many ways you can leverage the Internet. Your strategies for market research, marketing communications, advertising, public relations, selling, fulfillment, distribution, and customer support are all key pieces of your Internet marketing plan. You need a portfolio of both online and offline marketing techniques that will be effective for your unique situation. You also need to evolve that portfolio as new ways of marketing are discovered and as your business conditions change.

More than ever, marketing is central to the business operations of every company in the New E-Conomy. Says Christina Cheney, President and CEO of Simmedia.com, "Marketing has become more like business development. It is now more of a strategic function and ties your company to the entire online community." You have more creative ways to market, through the powerful medium of the Internet. In Chapter 4, you learned that your customer needs to be at the center of your holistic Internet-enabled entity. Only through your marketing efforts will your customer *stay* at the center of your business. It's time to stop thinking of marketing as just another department in the company. In a truly holistic Internet-enabled entity, marketing is everyone's job. It is the foundation for e-volving your company.

Figure 10.6

Over 1,000 person-hours of time is captured and available for you at no cost. Enjoy.

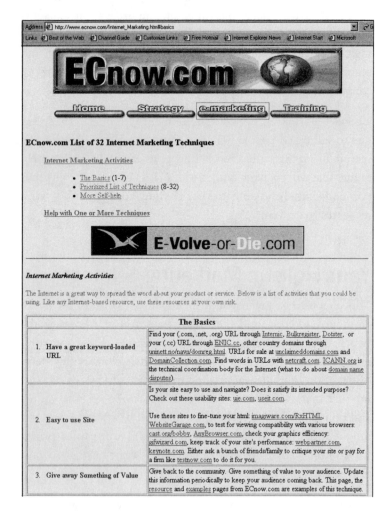

4. Satisfy Users Content Needs with External Resources	Let your audience quickly find what they need. Valuable content, good navigation and easily accessible contact/feedback mechanisms. *Add value to your site, by using some of the "free" tools on the Internet . For example, if you're a U.S. public company, point to the Edgar database (e.g. Intel). If you want people to visit you, use Mapblast to give directions (e.g. ECnow.com). Check out how a customer used Vicinity's services (Closest Tower Records to ECnow.com).* In the language of your user world.Altavista.com, Freetranslation.com, Globalsight.com, Ilanguage.com, Uniscape.com, US-Style.com
5. Put your URL Everywhere	All pieces of corporate literature should contain your URL: business cards, ads, letterhead, e-mail, etc.
6. Use a Signature Tag on your E-mail	A short description of your product or service should be automatically attached to the bottom of every e-mail. All employees should be encouraged to use it. Target your tag to the group receiving your e-mail. Here's an example from ECnow.com.
7. Submit Site at Search Engines, Directories, Announcement Spots, etc.	Make sure people can find your site in Yahoo and the top 7 search engines. Also submit to other locations. Check out: uran.net/imall/S&D_A-L.html, Beaucoup.com, Search.com, Successassured-com/netresources.html for other places to submit to. Look at Yahoo's list and Tucows list of search engine submission tools (also look at positioner.com, exploit.com). Check your listings manually with positionagent.com or learn the tricks of checking the major engines from searchenginewatch.com. Learn everything you wanted to know about search engines from searchengines.net.
Prioritized List of Techniques	
8. Find and Fuel Evangelists (Viral Marketing)	Whether it's an internal employee or an excited partner, empower your evangelists with the tools they can use to help market you in the on-line world. Essentially, find the best way to get word of mouth excitement about your product or service. Viral marketing story by ZDNet.com. Alladvantage.com, for example, grow to over 250,000 members in it's first 21 days at 2,000,000 members in 120 days by getting evangelists to push their concept of paying users to surf the net.
9. Establish a "free" On-line Newsletter	Package content that is of value and distribute it on a periodic basis. You can build trust and spread the word. Also a good way to gather e-mail addresses that you can market to. Announce everywhere you can, don't miss announcing at new-lists, and using these sets of resources: Australian Electronic Journals, eZine AdSource, EzineZ, eZineZ helpful list, E-Zine-List, eZine Search, InfoJump, ListCity, ListsNet Directory, Low Bandwidth, New Ezine Directory, The Etext Archive, The E-Zine Web Ring, PromoteFree, Poor Richard's eZine Registration Help, Zine-World. When you have over 10,000 subscribers, think about joining the Penn Media Network Opt-in e-zine vendors: eGroups.com, eZinemail.com, Infoads.com, ListBot, MeMail.com, Revnet, Topica.
10. Optimize Your Site & Positioning in the Search Engines	If your potential customer types in the key word or key phrase that describes your services, you want to make sure that your site is within the first two pages that show up. Click on examples (includes the methodology used) that ECnow.com has helped optimize ([Digitivity], [CGDC]), or (Crisislink). Learn more about search engines through searchenginewatch and search engine showdown. Brainstorm key phrases with Goto's searchable database and SearchTerms.com. Check out: Websiteresults.com, Yahoo's list.
11. Establish an Affiliate Program	Allow other sites to sell your products or distribute your value-added content. *Lists containing affiliate programs:* Adbility, revenue.linkexchange.com, refer-it.com, associateprograms.com, sitecash.com, associate-it.com, clicktrade.com, commission-junction.com, associatecash.com, www.clickquick.com, cashpile.com, linkshare.com, 2-tier.com, 4Yoursite, affiliatematch.com. *Running your own program:* associateprograms.com, befree.com, clicktrade.com, linkshare.com.
12. E-mail Marketing	You should be collecting e-mail addresses at every opportunity. E-mail people with info they've asked for. Annuncio.com, Bluemartini.com, Clickaction.com, Hallmark.com, Lifeminders.com, MarketFirst are interesting services that might be used.
13. Paid-for Internet Advertising	There's a myriad of paid-for Internet advertising opportunities. Clickz.com's Media Buying or Internet.com's Ad Resources for good starting points of on-line advertising resources.

14.	Publish Articles and/or get mentioned in News Stories	Write and publish articles of value. Include your URL in your bio. Contact news people who write about your area of expertise. Here's two lists of contacts: PR Newswire Links, PressAccess.com.
15.	Online Press Releases	Write and distribute press releases pointing back to your site. Check out Internet Newsbureau.com, PRweb.com, ProfNet.org/press.html, or Webcom/impulse/resource.html, Urlwire.com, Webwire.com.
16.	Run an Auction	Partner with a software company to run an auction at your site ebay.com, bid.com, moai.com, opensite.com, amazon.com. Check out Tucows for Auction Tools or auction portal sites Auctionrover.com, Auctionbeagle.com, Internetauctionlist.com.
17.	Run Contests, Give-aways	Contests and give-aways are great ways to generate traffic. Just look at iWon.com. Here's a site to help you run your contest: Faircontest.com. Check out these sites to help you advertise: Contestguide.com, Contestworld.com, Huronline.com.
18.	Determine On-line Communities to Participate in	Use these services to find: user groups deja.com, mailing lists liszt.com or paml, and discussion groups forumone.com of interest. Also available for general searches of all areas reference.com.
19.	Actively Monitor and Participate in On-line Community	Either manually or via on-line services, actively monitor and participate in user groups, mailing lists and discussion groups. Here are some services that can do this for you cyveillance.com, ewatch.com, Webpartner.com.
20.	Establish and Lead an On-line Forum / Community	If you can find the time, leading an on-line forum or running an on-line community is a great way to establish an affinity group and build credibility. Create a bulletin board in 10 minutes with beseen.com. Try anexa.com, eGroups.com, myfamily.com, clubs.yahoo.com for a host of on-line community services. Sign up for this e-zine to read about on-line communities: OnlineCommunityReport.com.
21.	Give Away On-line Coupons	Here are coupon companies that could help: Brightstreet.com, Cosmiccoupons.com, Coolsavings.com, Coupons.com, HotCoupons.com, RebatePlace.com, Valupage.com.
22.	Conduct Surveys	Check out Yahoo's or the University of North Carolina's list or try Addaform.com, SurveyBuilder.com, Zoomerang.com,
23.	Participate in a Charitable Web Site	As an example, go to the Hunger Site at the UN, click a button and somewhere in the world a hungry person gets a meal to eat, at no cost to you TheHungerSite.com (paid by the sponsors). Also try: igive.com, schoolpop.com.
24.	Links in Internet Malls / Portals	Posting links in high-traffic malls / portals is a trend some are trying. Use your best judgment, some are great, some are a waste of money. Absolutely put a link in Yahoo (#7).
25.	Participate in Paid-for and Free Banner Advertising	The best sites for paid-for banner advertising are those with traffic. Try any of the search engine companies that offer targeted advertising. For free banner exchange programs, check out: linkexchange.com, SmartClicks.com, trafficx.com, cyberlinkexchange.uswww.com, bannerswap.com, or click here for a list of banner exchange networks. Bannerworkz can create your banner. See bannertips.com for tons of banner information. Paid for services include Doubleclick & Flycast.
26.	Establish a Reciprocal Web Linking Program	Approach appropriate sites in your industry and closely aligned industries to link to your site. Create a link2us page to make it easy. Check out ecnow.com/link2us.htm. Joining or starting a Webring.com, (great write-up on Web Rings) might work for your site. Getting links to sites in the top100 is a great goal!
27.	Place Paid-for and Free Classified Ads	Place fee-based classified ads: uran.net/mall/Fee_Sites, or for free: uran.net/mall/FREE_Sites. Here's a list of low-cost physical world classified ads.
28.	Host Classified Ads	Host classified ads at your site classifieds2000.com.
29.	Use E-mail Autoresponders	If you have key information that you want to share, consider using an autoresponder. This is a good way to gather e-mail addresses for future marketing. Can be used for: Promotional Material, Product/Service Information, Training/Hiring Help, Article/White Paper Distribution. Check out: Apexmail.com, Biz-E-Bot.com, Databack Systems, E-Mail AutoReponder, RSVP Mail Processer
30.	Create your own Search Engine	Check out jayde.com, searchbuilders.com..
31.	Apply for and Win Awards	If you have a site worth talking about, apply for, win, and post your awards. Check out: market-tek.com/awardsite.html, focusa.com/awardsites/introduction.htm.

32. Create a free-for-all page	Write-up on free-for-all pages: upws.com/web/booklist/ffaguide.html Sites to submit to free-for-all pages: FFAnet.com, Linksrx.com, Linkomatic.com, MySubmitter.com, Submitad.com, URLomatic.a2zsol.com. Locations to download software for your own free-for-all page: FreeForAlls.com, Linksrx.com Linkomatic.com. Services that will host free-for-all pages for you: DGlinks.com, FFAnet.com, Link-me-up.com.

More self-help
Promotional tutorials and more: promotionworld.com, adbility.com, PrivateSites.com/warriors

Help with One or More Techniques

To create your own Internet Marketing Program, contact Mitchell Levy at (408) 257-3000 or send an e-mail to Mitchell.Levy@ecnow.com.

E-Volutionary Tactics

→ Internet marketing is not like a field of dreams; it requires a lot of work to create and maintain effective content for marketing.

→ Your Web identity needs to be leveraged wherever and whenever possible.

→ Viral marketing is today's term for word-of-mouth marketing, and it's a very powerful force.

→ Establish a newsletter or some form of opt-in communication with your customer.

→ Content needs to be updated constantly, and it must remain consistent with the company's brand.

→ Your home page is your company's brand and image to the world.

→ Personalized marketing needs to be accomplished through your Web site.

→ Content from third parties and affiliates will enhance your marketing efforts.

→ Everyone in your company needs to think and act like a marketer.

→ Be prepared to experiment and implement a wide variety of marketing methods.

11

The Law Catches Up to E-Business

NEARLY EVERY DAY in the business news, we read about yet another

legal issue related to e-commerce and the Internet. Many headlines

and precedent-setting cases appear, regarding privacy, security, trade

policies, intellectual property, electronic signatures, and taxation. All of

these issues have the potential to affect your business, and in particu-

lar, your e-volution into the New E-Conomy.   ▶ ▶

This chapter addresses the hot legal issues you need to be aware of as you set out on the path. This chapter is not meant to be a comprehensive or detailed discussion of Internet law; entire books and countless other resources are available for that purpose. Also, I am not a lawyer. However, I do have the good business sense to know when to seek legal advice and counsel—and that's what I did for this chapter. I talked with five experts who contributed the content and the quotations.

Do we need new laws that govern how we will do e-commerce?

The issues are addressed from the United States' perspective only, as it would be impossible to represent the worldwide bodies of law, with all their differences, in just one chapter. I chose the United States perspective because our experts practice in the United States. Those experts are:

- ▲ **Kaye Caldwell, Public Policy Director at CommerceNet.** CommerceNet is a non-profit organization that has partners worldwide to create value through innovation in electronic commerce.

- ▲ **Leo Clarke, Principal of TechRisk.Law.** Founded in 1996, TechRisk.Law specializes in legal counsel and consulting on risk management for information technology companies. They specialize in intellectual property issues.

- ▲ **Mark Grossman, Chair of the Computer and E-Commerce Law Group at Becker and Poliakoff.** Mark is also a nationally syndicated columnist who writes a column called "TechLaw" for the Miami Herald and other newspapers. His is a weekly column focusing on Internet and tech law issues.

- ▲ **David Steer, Spokesperson for TrustE.** TrustE is a privacy advocacy group, consisting of a coalition of enlightened companies and individuals who advocate electronic privacy. TrustE also functions as a third-party oversight body for privacy issues.

- ▲ **Carol Wu, Counsel and Manager of Legal Affairs for meVC.** meVC is a venture capital management and investment firm that focuses on private companies.

I hope that when you are faced with working out legal issues for your Internet-enabled entity, you will find experts who have the same high caliber of expertise these five individuals possess.

The Status of the Statutes

Do we need new laws that govern how we do e-commerce? Most practitioners believe it's much easier and faster to apply existing laws. In addition, technology is changing much too quickly to get new legislation in place that covers every last detail and situation that could be encountered. "The Internet has created the need for some new laws, especially in the privacy area," says Mark Grossman. "What's really needed, however, is *clarification* of existing laws. The basic question is: Is the appropriate 'intent' present in the existing law that can extend to an online situation?" Carol Wu agrees that clarification is important. "Much of existing law was passed long before the technology was in place, and clarification will help tremendously. If that is not possible, the next level is to amend the existing laws. The third option (and the least desirable) is developing new legislation; however, this may be a long process and technology continues to change in the meantime."

Some new laws are in the process of being enacted, such as COPPA (Children's Online Privacy Protection Act). This law prohibits data collection from children under the age of 13. It's a very focused law that places mandates on specific sites. "This new law is a step in the right direction," according to David Steer. "However, it is too new and we have no track record yet to see if it is working. It will take a long time for that to happen, and the amendment and change process takes a very long time if it's not working. In the meantime, we need to do a better job of enforcing existing laws or re-interpreting them, such as section 5 of the FTC Act, which gives the FTC the ability to take action against companies who engage in unfair and deceptive practices." (See Figure 11.1.)

Efforts have been made to expand the existing UCC (Uniform Commercial Code) to include online business. The proposed statute is Uniform Computer Information Transactions Act (UCITA), and among other things, it governs click-wrap and other types of online agreements. So far, only two states have adopted it. "This act enables companies to shift the risk to the customer, so it's a good thing for companies, but it's widely viewed as anti-consumer. It's an example of trying to do too much with new statutes," says Leo Clarke.

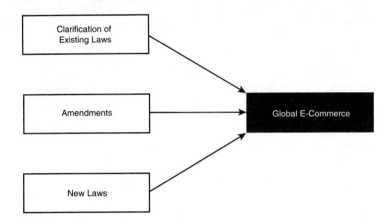

Figure 11.1

Laws need to e-volve to keep up with e-commerce; here is what's needed.

The wheels of government seem to move much more slowly than the wheels of the economy, and this is just one example. Most of the experts agreed that government recognizes the inadequacy of current law to apply to these new issues. At the very least, government is starting the process to address these issues and is beginning to work with businesses and industry in general to develop solutions that will not inhibit the growth of the economy.

Non-U.S. governments are in some cases further behind than the United States. Says Kaye Caldwell, "Certainly in some countries there needs to be additional protection against security crimes such as hacking and viruses. Essentially, these crimes harm the international digital infrastructure and all who use it. That means entirely new laws must be established, in a lot of cases." The example of the suspected hacker in the Philippines who created the "love bug" virus in 2000 is a case in point. He was ultimately released as a free man because there were no laws in place by which the government could prosecute him.

Regulatory and Enforcement Issues

Whatever happens with regard to clarification or modification of existing laws, someone clearly needs to enforce them. In the United States, regulation and enforcement can be handled at many levels, including federal, state, county, or municipal. Literally several thousand jurisdictions have regulatory and enforcement authority. Whether we will we see more or less regulation of the Internet and e-commerce is subject to debate.

Almost everyone expects that we are going to have more regulation and not less. According to Carol Wu, "I think we are going to see more regulation at both the federal and international level now that governments are beginning to fully understand the issues. In fact, international regulation is already starting to happen, such as the World Intellectual Property Organization (WIPO). There are 170 member nations who are developing uniform ways to enforce laws against piracy of intellectual property. Different parts of the world vary in terms of how strict they are." In the United States, the government is still coming up to speed on some of the issues. Says David Steer, "The U.S. Government does want to regulate these issues, despite what they say. They want to figure out a way to regulate e-commerce without inhibiting growth and the health of the economy. They will get more involved in the next couple of years, and by then, both government and industry should have a better understanding of what needs to be done."

Some people believe that self-regulation is much more practical and effective than getting the government involved. Contract law extended to online business is a way to strengthen the law and set precedents for corporations to govern themselves. "Purchasing networks and online exchanges are governed by contracts among the participants," says Leo Clarke. "These contracts also have provisions for resolving disputes among the parties before they make their way into the court system. This model can work very well in e-commerce, because the penalties for not being in compliance with the contracts are financial and immediate—*but* they are handled privately between the parties." (See Figure 11.2.)

In addition, hybrids might emerge, such as third-party oversight programs or organizations that are not regulated by the government but help corporations police themselves. "In the privacy area, TrustE is one example of an oversight program that will give companies an alternative," according to David Steer. "If the government recognizes these third-party programs, there will be a 'safe harbor' provision for companies to voluntarily

Figure 11.2

Regulation and enforcement by multiple government agencies or through self-regulation is the current tradeoff.

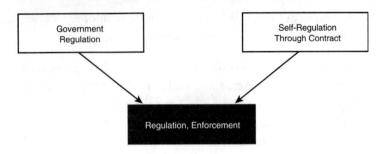

join these programs in lieu of direct government regulation. This would be an effective solution for all concerned and perhaps a better use of everyone's resources."

Global Differences

Currently, there is no international governing body for electronic commerce between countries. There likely will not be, because it is very difficult to do this on a worldwide basis, especially when it comes to enforcement. Leo Clarke believes that companies engaging in international e-commerce will develop private "treaties" of their own. "Contracts that govern business-to-business relationships in a consensual fashion are essentially like a treaty between the organizations. These contracts specify not only the terms and conditions, but also how disputes will be resolved. Microsoft and Dell are two examples of companies who do this. It's a good model and it seems to work quite well for the companies involved. I think that basic contract law can go a long way to regulate international e-commerce—privately."

Privacy

At the dawn of the Internet Age, online privacy was mainly a public relations issue. Now, after some high-profile legal cases (such as Double Click) involving collection of consumer information without permission, it has also become a significant legal issue in electronic commerce. According to David Steer, the privacy issue at its most fundamental level is about trust. "The number one fear that people have about doing business online is the feeling that Big Brother (the government) is watching, and also that Little Brother (a corporation) is watching, too. This issue has been with us, even before e-commerce; in some ways, our lives have always been an open book. It's just that now with the Internet we are able to see for the first time the data gathering and dissemination process that was always going on in the background. It heightens the trust issue. It's difficult for your company to build trust with your customers unless you are aware of this and respect their right to privacy. Everyone who uses your Web site should be given an 'opt-in' before any personal information can be transferred."

> With the Internet, we are able to see for the first time the data gathering and dissemination process that was always going on in the background.

What's at stake here is more than just customer satisfaction. "There are substantial risks in violating customers' privacy that a CEO should take very seriously," according to David Steer. "The first is your reputation in your marketplace; word spreads quickly among your customer base. Second is violation of law, enforcement, and the ultimate possibility of shutting down your company. And third is the bottom line: Ill will, litigation, and media publicity can decrease your bottom line and your company's valuation."

Privacy issues will only get worse as Global Positioning System (GPS) devices are incorporated into more and more consumer devices. There is certainly a benefit in having your car, cell phone, Palm pilot, kid monitor, etc. tell where you or the location of the object you're monitoring. But I have a serious concern about what companies will do with that information.

Intellectual Property

Intellectual property issues in the Internet Age have increased because of the high level of data interchange within and between companies and their customers. Because of email and intranets, it's become easy for company-sensitive information to fall into the wrong hands. In most cases, companies prefer to maintain control over their own intellectual property, and they would rather the government didn't get involved. However, when it comes to enforcement and dispute resolution, it becomes a legal issue—sometimes going all the way to the Supreme Court (in the United States).

Another intellectual property issue is copyright or trademark infringement. This has always been an issue, but the Internet creates a new twist on how intellectual property is controlled and delivered. This raises all sorts of control issues, such as, can you link to someone else's Web site without infringing on someone else's copyright? Companies are using quick-wrap agreements and boilerplate contracts to protect themselves and to manage the risk. With higher levels of copyright infringement or piracy (such as the Napster-RIA case) making their way into the courts, case law precedents will be set for future disputes. (See Figure 11.3.)

Contract Law

Companies have been quite creative in how they use contract law online. "Click-wrap agreements—where users designate acceptance with a mouse click—are very commonly used online contracts today," says Mark Grossman. "We will see a lot more innovative ways to do contracts online, especially with electronic signature legislation." Boilerplate contracts that contain the proper contractual provisions can protect your company and shift the risk away from your company. Courts are also willing to enforce standard contracts in situations where there are disputes. "I think that in the future, contractual relationships and privatization will be very common and eventually may replace reliance on case law," predicts Leo Clarke. "It's the best way for companies to manage risk."

Figure 11.3

Control of intellectual property remains an issue for the owners and creators of intellectual property because of the Internet.

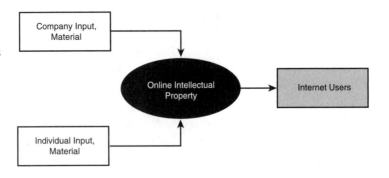

International Trade Policies

"International treaties that are in place already govern commerce between countries, and they in fact will also apply to e-commerce business relationships," according to Mark Grossman. "E-commerce does not necessarily call for new treaties; it's just another channel for doing business. Enforcement of existing treaties will continue to be done by the existing international bodies." It is important, however, to be aware of the existing laws to make sure that your company is not inadvertently doing something related to your e-commerce efforts that would violate those laws. When in doubt, check with your resident expert.

Taxation

It would be nice for the Internet and e-commerce transactions to remain tax-free. However, governments simply can't afford the revenue loss. "Collection of taxes will level the playing field; there really shouldn't be an unfair advantage for e-commerce companies. Brick and mortar companies have collected taxes before the Internet, and that shouldn't change now. The only difference with e-commerce is that it will be a lot more complex for states to figure out how to collect the taxes, begging the question of whether we need a more federal framework for taxation," says Mark Grossman. Sales taxes have always been assessed according to where the company's physical assets are located, but it's difficult to identify where transactions are taking place in cyberspace.

The Desire for a Holistic Internet-Enabled World

As e-commerce pervades everywhere, it is clear that the world is getting smaller. As the great equalizer, the adoption of the Internet into everything we do will allow the "true" laws of supply and demand to prevail. Arbitrary inefficiencies put into the marketplace by individual companies, industries, cities, regions, or countries will eventually need to be eliminated and replaced, if appropriate, with more efficient ways to achieve the goals for which they were originally put into place.

In terms of g-commerce (oops, I mean global commerce, no really, I mean commerce), we need to figure out how countries across the world will do business with one another. Specifically, I'm referring to international trade policies and taxation. So, for a second, let's forget about the rules that exist today and think about what an efficient system might look like if we started over with the Internet and global business in mind. Without spending a lot of time on economic and taxation theory, let me propose a solution that should be considered for adoption.

First, income tax is a problem. We should have a Value Added (VAT) tax instead. Corporate and individual earnings and savings are good for the economy. So, why tax them? Doesn't that defeat the purpose? Instead, let's tax when companies and individuals spend money. You should be able to earn all you want without taxes. In order to earn, you need to spend. When you spend, you are then assessed a use "VAT" tax.

Second, let's say we had a standard global VAT. This VAT, let's just say at 20 percent, would be used for the basic services any government provides. Now for the powerful argument: Because the Internet will be available in every household in the world, let's let the people vote for the incremental services they want. If free medical care is desired, let's add 10 percent to the VAT. If a high-end education system is desired, let's add another one percent. If a strong police force/military presence is desired, let's add another one percent.

Simple, but amazing. The power of the town hall concept put into action. Every country could provide the level of services its populace is interested in. Yes, there are many arguments and apparent holes in this suggestion, but it's certainly something to think about. To create a holistic Internet-enabled world, dramatic changes need to be made to the operations of the world economy.

What All This Means for Your Business Today

All these legal issues have the potential to affect your business in many ways. Depending on how you handle online privacy and security, it can affect your customers' attitudes about doing business with you. Are you gathering data about your customers without their knowledge or permission? This could have a huge impact on your brand, your customer satisfaction, and the bottom line. Your corporate Web site needs to have a privacy statement prominently displayed.

Do you have suitable protection in place for your intellectual property, as well as your partners' intellectual property? Inadvertently, information can easily fall into the hands of your competitors. Prevention is a lot easier and less expensive than litigation.

Is your company in compliance with trade policies and other international regulations that govern your industry? If not, you could incur substantial penalties. Do you have contracts set up with your international partners that contain avenues for dispute resolution? Using comprehensive and customized contracts can avoid expensive litigation.

Does your company collect the appropriate taxes online as it would in the brick and mortar world? Does your accounting system handle it in real time? It may take states and municipalities longer to catch up with you, but compliance is cheaper than fines and penalties.

Much work is being done by various legislatures. You and your company can get involved by helping educate people in your industry and your markets, as well as by lobbying for reform of these legal issues. Your company's board of directors can help in this regard as well.

Designating someone in your company to stay current with Internet law is the best approach to keeping your business moving forward. There may even be a need to formalize this position in the company. Some companies, such as Microsoft, AOL, and Excite At Home, have hired Chief Privacy Officers (CPOs) to look after these legal issues for the company.

What does your privacy policy state?

Staying Current

In the United States, some high-profile legal cases have been in the news recently, such as Napster versus the Recording Industry of America over copyrighted music. Decisions may be made by local courts and then appealed to any of the eleven different circuit courts, and so on up to the Supreme Court. Any one of the lower courts may issue a different decision than another circuit court. What does this mean for companies when a local or lower court issues a decision? "CEOs of companies shouldn't spend a lot of time worrying about these lower court decisions," says Leo Clarke. "When it goes to higher courts, or there is legislation passed that addresses the issue, then it could affect your company. It's best to be aware of the issues at a high level, and also have good legal counsel who has current training in Internet law."

• NOTE •
If you're in Silicon Valley, Carol Wu and Lori Hefner teach a course titled "E-Commerce Public Policy and the Law" at the premiere San Jose State University Professional Development E-Commerce Management (SJSU-PD ECM) program. For updates on course times and availability of online curricula, go to http://ecmtraining.com/sjsu.

CEOs need to be aware of what's happening with legal issues that will affect the company's evolution into an Internet-enabled company. Many resources can be used to stay current—from a high-level strategic perspective. Here are some of the resources suggested by our team of experts:

- ▲ General business publications such as *Business Week*, *Forbes*, *Fast Company*, *Industry Standard*, *Business 2.0*, *Red Herring*, and *The Wall Street Journal* contain news articles relating to hot legal issues.

- ▲ Weekly columns in print or online, such as *TechLaw* (by Mark Grossman) or online newsletters.

- ▲ Legal and other Web sites focused on these issues, such as **www.truste.org**, **www.ftc.gov**, and **www.doc.gov**. (the latter two government sites also have information on children's privacy issues and international privacy issues).

- ▲ Web sites that focus on public policy issues, such as these two, sponsored by CommerceNet:

    www.commerce.net/research/research.html
    www.commerce.net/resources/work/appc.html

- ▲ Seminars on Internet law for non-lawyers in your local area.

E-Volutionary Tactics

→ Create the position or assign the responsibility of Chief Privacy Officer (CPO) within your organization.

→ Seek out legal experts who specialize in Internet law.

→ Several e-volving legal issues could affect your business, including privacy, security, intellectual property, international trade policies, electronic signatures, copyright, and taxation.

→ Domestic and foreign governments are deciding how existing laws will be applied and enforced on a country-by-country basis.

→ Additional laws might be developed to cover Internet and e-commerce issues; however, most existing laws can be applied to these issues already.

→ It pays to keep up with business publications to remain current with Internet legal issues; many specialized online newsletters and resources are available.

E-Volving the Future

12 Shifting Markets   211

13 A View from the Real World   225

14 Change Is Constant, Change Is Good   245

Shifting Markets

THE NEW E-CONOMY that started with the Internet Age has stirred up

market dynamics forever. Keeping up with the changes, ideas, and

opportunities requires an open mind and the ability to move quickly. It

requires experimentation and flexibility in the workforce and ever-

changing technology infrastructure to keep it running. It is the new

rhythm of the New E-Conomy.   ▶▶

One of the most difficult challenges facing executives today is figuring out how to manage the Internet-enabled future. How do you decide on the right opportunities for your company? What will be the next trend for online marketplaces? How can new markets be developed in this age of the empowered customer? These are some of the key questions that should be considered on a continuing basis as the future unfolds. It is essential that you keep current with what is happening in many arenas: technology, creative business models, partnering, demand and supply, competitive intelligence, and changing customer behavior. If you are armed with the latest knowledge, it will be easier for you to make the decisions required to e-volve your company.

The Internet Is Here to Stay

The Internet isn't just a fad anymore (as many people initially believed), and it can't be ignored. Companies that don't embrace the Internet and view it as an essential part of their business will not survive for long. The Internet has impacted everything! In the process, it has created new opportunities, and it will continue to do so into the foreseeable future. "Brick and mortar companies are becoming aware that the Internet is not a fad. It is a digital sales channel and a business platform that won't go away. Companies who don't address it will pay; the Internet permeates everything you do in business," says Mark Walsh, Chairman and Chief Strategy Officer of VerticalNet. Your company needs to be able to keep up with changing opportunities and to recognize that the Internet is an extension of your business.

The proliferation of the Internet has allowed visionaries to change the way people work, learn, play, and invest (see Figure 12.1). Shouldn't your company be among the visionaries who create and actively participate in this new future?

Some visionaries and analysts believe that the Internet present and future is similar to the gold rush. The prospector's tools are Web sites, the motherload is the Internet worldwide market, and everyone is looking for the gold of online revenues. Like in the gold rush, some will make money selling tools and supplies

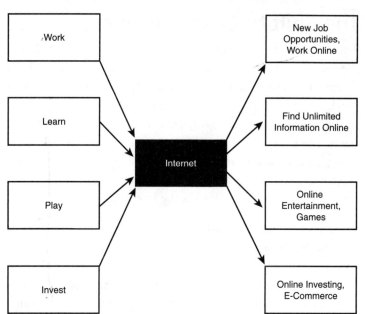

Figure 12.1

The Internet enables new ways
to work, learn, play, and invest.

to the prospectors, some will find gold, and some will come away empty-handed and ready to move on to the next big thing. The question is, has the gold rush ended already, or is it just beginning? "We are just getting started with the gold rush; we are only beginning to scratch the surface," according to David Perry, President and CEO of Ventro. "The future opportunities that the Internet will enable as it becomes part of mainstream business will make today's successes pale by comparison." The Internet will permeate everything. There will be many places to seek the gold and many ways to prospect for it. The challenge will be deciding when and how to prospect.

"The meshing of the Old Economy and New E-Conomy companies and resulting business opportunities will create the real gold rush," says Donald Davis, Director of Worldwide Business Development, Ricoh-Silicon Valley. "You will have the best of the capabilities of both types of companies, such as a company with an established retail presence and widely recognized brand, combining forces with a newer company who leverages online technology and uses a different business model. The alliance between Amazon.com and Toys 'R' Us is a good example of this trend, and many others will follow." Companies who can prospect together and combine their resources may increase their chances of success.

The Shift to Customer Focus

The worldwide Internet marketplace is being created and shaped by customers—down to the level of the individual. To figure out where to tap into this marketplace, you must have a much better and updated understanding of basic customer buying behavior—especially with regard to the Internet environment. The Internet has given the customer the power of choice, along with new and apparently limitless access to goods and services. Corporations are now scrambling to gain or regain the attention of their customers via the Internet.

Do you build collaborative relationships with your customers?

The basics of customer value and value propositions still apply. "Customers have always looked for value in business relationships. But there is a new opportunity for the marketplace to facilitate and strengthen existing customer relationships through these new ways of conducting business. Electronic commerce enables communication and collaboration between all participants in the marketplace that just wasn't possible before," says David Perry, President and CEO of Ventro. With the technology and the infrastructure of the Internet, it becomes easier and faster to communicate with customers and to understand what is valuable to them, as well as how their needs are changing by analyzing customer behavior and buying patterns.

New Products and Services

Because of customer demand, as well as advances in technology, most companies will shift the mix of products and services they offer to their customers. For most, far more services will be available than ever before, some that generate revenue and some that are offered solely for the purpose of boosting customer satisfaction.

The Internet has facilitated the creation of completely new businesses, including markets for new types of services. They include search services, online agents, portals, e-hubs, payment mechanisms, reminder services, Web page monitoring, and broker/referral services (see Figure 12.2). These are new types of businesses enabled by the Internet and the related infrastructure. Does your company have a core competency that could be delivered online?

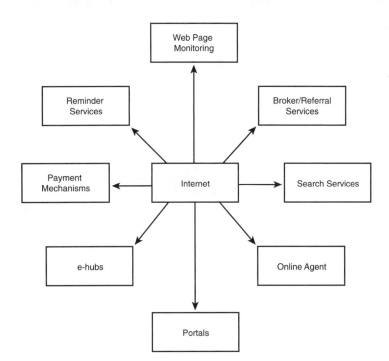

New Types of Markets

Because of the community nature of the Internet, new market models have e-volved. Online marketplaces and buying exchanges exemplify how markets are becoming larger. At the same time, smaller and smaller niche markets are developing as online versions of existing markets that are more targeted and personalized. The good news is that there are more choices than ever for your company. However, the bad news is that you may be faced with developing and maintaining new types·of segmented markets simultaneously. (See Figure 12.3.)

Finding New Opportunities

Will your company be a market creator or a market follower in the New E-Conomy? To be a market creator, you must be one step ahead of the game. You must think of new ways to deliver your goods and services, new ways to find and retain customers, and new partners to join your team—essentially, new ways to run your core business. That doesn't mean you need to

Figure 12.3

Some markets will be community based and others will be
niche markets.

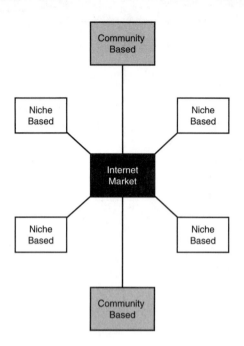

commission a multi-million dollar consulting study to find these
opportunities. A little creative thinking and a willingness to take
some risks are really what are needed.

Within your own organization are many talented employees
with ideas you can tap into, and those employees may be further motivated and enthused with the prospect of finding new
opportunities for the company. For example, when a service
representative at one of Kinko's retail stores discovered that
their copiers could be used to create personalized calendars for
customers, he telephoned a senior executive at Kinko's headquarters who not only listened, but implemented the idea at all
locations. This is an example of a business environment that encourages and empowers employees to submit ideas and then follows through with executive action.

One of the best places to start is to talk to your customers. They
are a formidable force in shaping new markets, and they have
greater expectations in terms of the total customer experience.
As you communicate with customers (both existing and
prospective customers), you may discover new ways to deliver
existing goods or services, as well as ideas for entirely new
goods and services. Of course, customers have always been the

Figure 12.4

In order to find new opportunities, be prepared to constantly examine your business operations.

best source for new product ideas, but in the New E-Conomy, they play a greater and more powerful role. You need them on your side from the beginning in order to be successful.

Another way to identify opportunities is to re-evaluate your business model and partner relationships. Are there ways to reach new customers and markets by reconfiguring your business model—by eliminating partners or acquiring new ones? Another possibility is to provide new services in the value web that did not exist before. Sometimes multiple services that were provided by one entity can be "unbundled" and instead shared among several companies. "We have seen several phases of evolution as companies move their businesses online. The first was to automate content—about their products and services. The second was to automate transactions—that enabled buying and selling. The next phase was to automate the processes on the front end and back end. The next phase will be what I call 'trading intelligence'—where companies automate the decision-making (qualitative and quantitative) and optimize all processes. This will be done at the highest level, the market level of the company. That's where the opportunities of the future will be," states Narry Singh, Vice-President of Global Trading, Rapt Inc.

Where will you find your next business opportunity?

It is also essential to stay current with changes in Internet-related and other technologies that enhance the use of the Internet. Changing your company's infrastructure by updating your technology may enable you to find new markets you can serve, new partners you can work with, and new products and services you can deliver.

The Role of Experimentation

Success is nice, but failure is better. I know this sounds very strange. But although wild success is best, it is through failure that a company learns how to run their business more effectively. The business models and markets of the Internet Age are so new, there is not a lot of history to learn from. Therefore, companies need to be bold and take risks in order to find the right path for the company's core competencies.

The other requirement for successful experimentation is the ability to analyze what you've learned and to change for the next attempt. It is absolutely important that you start the next experiment right away—speed is critical in the New E-Conomy. Many companies have found that time is the most important constraint here and that by experimenting with Internet-enabled applications, they can get something out quickly, knowing that not all of these efforts will be a success. Sometimes these experiments can turn into a delivered solution that is further modified based on customer feedback. (See Figure 12.5.)

Figure 12.5

Managed experimentation is the name of the game.

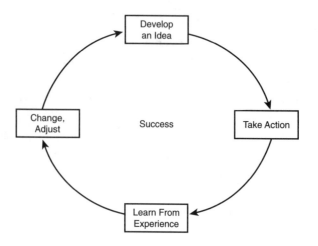

You must learn from the experiments and make changes. "Many companies use the Internet to enter new vertical market segments. They start with one and then move to another as soon as sales are achieved. However, if they fail to evaluate the results of each vertical market before starting with the next one, it defeats the purpose and is likely to result in confusion in the marketplace—especially among customers. It is vital to do the experiments, but you must take the time to evaluate what you've learned and be committed to make the necessary changes," says Donald Davis, Director of Worldwide Business Development, Ricoh-Silicon Valley. Experimentation needs to be made part of the company's core business processes, and everyone in the company needs to be aware of the importance of it and its relationship to the company's vision and goals. Employees need to be prepared to make changes based on what happens with these experiments.

Does your company believe in experimentation?

Market Development

Brand new online markets are developed every day. Not only are startups and new companies doing this, established brick and mortar companies are finding ways to develop new markets for their products and services as well.

Most new markets are driven by customer demand for new ways to buy goods and services. According to Donald Davis, Director of Worldwide Business Development, Ricoh-Silicon Valley, "The Internet plays a key role in market development, and it happens in three phases. First, you can use the Internet to do your research, to identify your markets and customers, and understand their needs and expectations. Second, you can use the Internet (through email) to make the initial contact with customers, which is the first step in developing a business relationship. And third, you can use the Internet to build and sustain your customer relationships over time. The exciting part is that you can do this on a global basis—instantly." Developing markets in the future will be a matter of building relationships, one customer at a time.

The technology power of the Internet makes it much faster and easier to use than ever before. However, it is also important to make sure that you have the back-end systems in place to support the new opportunities. Oracle and I2 were able to quickly develop and introduce their online offerings, but their companies were focused on how to not only deliver the solutions, but also support them. You can be the first to enter or create a new market, but without the customer-centric infrastructure in place, you won't be able to sustain your position in that market. It will quickly become another experiment and "lesson learned."

Partnering and Collaboration

The worldwide Internet marketplace will continue to move so fast that only the nimble will survive. That will mean more partnering and greater collaboration among companies to divide up the market pie. Expect to see collaboration between competitors, as well as "David and Goliath" combinations of dot.coms working with brick and mortar companies to share knowledge, infrastructure, and resources. "There will be greater outsourcing of key functions across boundaries of time and distance," predicts David Perry, President and CEO of Ventro. "Companies may contract out the engineering function to a vendor in India, or find the optimal manufacturing solution in China, allowing them to focus their efforts and resources on the core competencies of the business."

Companies may need to partner for different reasons than they did in the Old Economy. According to Narry Singh, Vice-President of Global Trading, Rapt Inc., "It's no longer about the core competencies of partners or what their companies do. It's more about their affiliation and who they know. Who do they collaborate with, and who can they influence? That makes a real difference, especially in terms of entering new markets."

The Future of Branding

Does the power of an established brand help create new opportunities in the New E-Conomy? The jury is still out on the relative importance of branding as a high-level strategy. Some people think that old brands will fade and new brands will take their places. Today, customer loyalty may be tied to the brand or tied to the company, based on the level of customer service, and that will continue to be an important differentiator. But first, customers need to exercise their newfound power and comparison-shop. Word of mouth now spreads online, through discussions, emails, and referrals. After they are through, branding may have some impact on the buying decision. "Most companies are still stuck in the mode where they wish the customers knew nothing, and they could market to their heart's content, just like they've always done. However, the Internet allows customers to be smarter about how they buy and what they buy, and branding won't help until they have all the information they need. The winning brands of tomorrow will be those companies who understand this and educate their customers," says Mark Walsh, Chairman and Chief Strategy Officer of VerticalNet.

Old Economy brands and New E-Conomy brands can limit a company's ability to enter new market segments. It's common to protect the assets of a strong brand presence. However, it's like the old adage: Be careful what you wish for; it may come true. If you place too much emphasis on a brand (especially if it's associated with specific types of products and services), customers may not be as ready to buy from your company when you enter new markets.

Metrics for Dynamic Markets

There seems to be a gradual return to the basics of business metrics. In this era of highly dynamic markets, the best measures of success will be revenue levels and profitability. That is the only way to sustain a business long-term, whether it is online or offline. After all, even gold prospectors must eat now and then....

"There is a return to reality now in the New E-Conomy. Investors are demanding real and proven business models, and companies need to show profits," says Mark Walsh, Chairman and Chief Strategy Officer, VerticalNet. Old and new companies alike need to balance the opportunities presented by the shifting markets of the future, with basic business metrics that ensure the company's survival and growth.

Non-financial measures are also important to measure success. "Companies should evaluate things such as number of mistakes made and lessons learned, how many key employees were retained, what new ideas were generated, which assumptions are no longer true. These measures are also very important, because they will determine whether a company is truly able to change and evolve in response to new opportunities," says Narry Singh, Vice-President of Global Trading, Rapt Inc.

No More Dinosaurs

Throughout the evolution of business, we have moved from the Agricultural Age to the Industrial Age, and now we are entering the Internet Age. As these transitions have taken place in the past, markets have gone through tremendous upheaval, and in the process, companies often get lost in the dust because they can't see the opportunities or move fast enough to take advantage of them. Also, companies can focus on the technology instead of the customer needs satisfied by that technology. Don't let your company become a dinosaur, fading in the shadows of your competitors and the newly formed companies rushing in to occupy new market niches. Re-examine your vision, figure out how to leverage technology, focus on the customer, and keep an open mind (UPS did this successfully; see Appendix A, "Case Studies".) That is how you will survive and e-volve.

This chapter presented some of the important trends related to shifting markets that you need to consider when e-volving your company's future. In the next chapter, people from the trenches—from the real world of creating and e-volving e-commerce—take out their crystal balls and predict other changes that may be in store for the next few years.

E-Volutionary Tactics

→ The Internet will not be going away any time soon.

→ The gold rush has not even started yet; there will be many more opportunities in the future.

→ New markets will be developed in response to changing customer demands.

→ There will be opportunities to change the mix of products and services that companies offer.

→ Expect to fail in order to learn and keep e-volving.

→ There will be a need for more experimentation and shorter experiments.

→ You will see more emphasis on distributing information and content, and less emphasis on selling products and services.

→ In general, more collaboration and partnering will be needed among companies to take advantage of opportunities quickly.

→ Dot.coms and brick and mortar companies can learn a lot from one another.

→ Revenue and profitability will continue to be important measures of success in shifting markets.

→ Focus on the customer's need that is being satisfied with the technology, not the technology itself.

A View from the Real World

ANY NEW BUSINESS PHILOSOPHY or set of principles should be test-

ed in the real world in order to validate what is real, what is feasible,

what works, and what doesn't work. I surveyed people online and

talked to several executives who are deeply involved in e-commerce

implementation about what they have learned so far and, more

importantly, what changes we can expect in the next few years. This

chapter focuses on what they said. The online survey was sent to the

readership of ECMgt.com, my online e-zine that explores the trends in

▶▶

e-commerce management on a monthly basis. The executives quoted here were also interviewed for other chapters in this book. (See Figure 13.1.)

As I evaluated the responses to the survey, ten general topic areas and trends emerged. All quotes and predictions are grouped by these ten categories, beginning with a look at the new economic environment and ending with ideas about e-volving the company for growth.

Ten Trends from the Real World:

What changes do you think will happen in e-commerce in the next few years?

1. The More Things Change, the More They Stay the Same
2. The Hybrid E-Conomy
3. Everything and Everyone is Connected
4. Customers Rule
5. Better, Faster, and Maybe Cheaper
6. Business Models and Value Webs
7. New Standards and Rules Create Opportunity
8. E-Volving End-to-End Infrastructure
9. The New Face of Marketing
10. New Dimensions for Growth and Evolution

Figure 13.1
www.ecmgt.com

A number of executives were surveyed for this chapter. The ECMgt.com readership was also polled for comments.

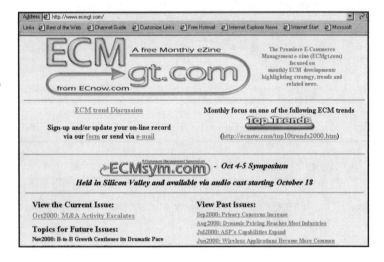

1. The More Things Change, the More They Stay the Same

The tried and true basics of business will be back—to remind us of the old-fashioned principles that still seem to work, even in this new Internet-enabled world. Profitability, revenues, and proven processes will be key.

Peter Sisson, Chief Strategy Officer, wine.com

"The new e-commerce brands will grow more slowly because the investment community has no patience for losses. The emphasis will be on profitability, which means we will see fewer expensive ads."

Sean Kaldor, Vice-President of E-Commerce, NetRatings Inc.

"E-commerce business operations will mature, and overall methods will solidify around a few key processes."

Gwen Hanna, Vice-President of People, Homebid.com

"New e-business companies are becoming more humble as they begin to realize that some of the basic rules and principles of business (such as profitability) applies to them, just as it does to the 'brick and mortar' companies. Based on these trends, what I humbly predict in the future is a mutual admiration between the 'click and close' companies and the 'brick and mortar' companies, where each will learn to respect and leverage their approaches to business."

Brian Kellner, Development Manager, Zoho Corporation

"Successful companies in the future will be real businesses. The Web does not mean gold."

Russ Cohn, CEO, Brigade Corporation

"The 'e' will disappear from e-commerce. It will just be commerce, and if companies don't understand that, they won't survive."

Sean Kaldor, Vice-President of E-Commerce, NetRatings Inc.

"E-Commerce just becomes commerce…it will be just another type of sales activity."

Doug Nelson, President, Seabright Group

"Electronic Commerce will become an essential part of every company's strategy; companies won't separate it from the rest of the business."

Gay Slesinger, Principal, iMarket Strategies

"What is the big deal about the little 'e' in e-commerce and the 'dot' in dot.com? Soon it will be apparent even to the dot.commers in the consumer space that e-commerce is just a newer type of sales and marketing channel. Since corporations from Wal-Mart to Wall Street already have embraced the Internet, e-commerce is already mainstream. After all, we don't say incorporated companies are 'inc-dots,' do we?"

Brian Kellner, Development Manager, Zoho Corporation

"Electronic Commerce will be more pervasive and it will be an expectation. The 'e' will be removed from e-commerce."

Rolf Scherrer, Intern, Bank of the West

"Commerce is the same as it was 300 years ago. People sell and buy products—whether it's from a wagon pulled by horses or the Internet powered by Cisco and Sun. I think it's important to build a robust business model and work on market share."

2. The Hybrid E-Conomy

Although we are already mired in the New E-Conomy, we are just at the beginning of the changes, as brick and mortar companies race to be successful online, and dot.coms try to dethrone established companies' brands. More consolidation, hybrids, partnering, and new business models will shift the mix and balance of power.

Clyde Foster, CEO, eConvergent

"There will be a more seamless merger of online and offline worlds. Brick and mortar companies will get better at online business, and dot.coms will get better at traditional business and profitability. Economies of scale will result for both worlds."

Peter Sisson, Chief Strategy Officer, wine.com

"More dot.coms will partner with brick and mortar companies. There are few companies that can sustain a pure-play Internet brand. Also, brick and mortar companies will get better at their online efforts and become stronger competitors to some of the dot.com first movers.

"There will be continued consolidation in the B2C market-places. Although it depends on the size of the category, each one can typically support just one or two strong players."

Lisa Sharples, Chief Marketing Officer, Garden.com

"A multichannel approach will be used for all e-commerce companies, including retail. The line will blur between who's an e-commerce company and who isn't."

Rip Gerber, Chief Strategy Officer and Vice-President of Marketing, Commtouch

"The age of the large conglomerates is over. Ten years from now, the Fortune 500 will be irrelevant. Those that survive will either be invisible giants running the infrastructure for everyone else or those that will unquestionably own their customers through passion-invoking brands and impenetrable customer relationships."

Todd Elizalde, Director of E-Commerce, Cisco Systems

"In the next few years, there will be fewer dot.coms, and many more successful, large, established companies."

Maria Luisa Rodriquez, Co-Founder and Director, e-co consulting

"There will be an integration between online and offline businesses, along with some hybrids."

Don Davis, Director of Worldwide Business Development, Ricoh of Silicon Valley

"There will be tremendous consolidation. Some businesses will continue to go into business with the intent of being acquired. Brick and mortar companies may also purchase dot.coms that are in their market space."

Constance Wilde, CEO, Aton International, Inc.

"The key to survival for the small to mid-size business in the New E-Conomy will be strategic partnerships. The sheer volume of information and the rate of change make it extremely difficult for the individual owners of smaller businesses to stay far enough ahead to anticipate new trends. Savvy business owners who cultivate active partnerships with suppliers and outsource companies will have the best chance of thriving in the years ahead."

Mark Osburn, Management Analyst, Santa Clara Valley Transportation Society

"Just as technology will continue to grow and modify society, regulation and taxation will continue to be serious considerations. In the phase of bureaucracy that we are in, large corporations will create consolidation, and adapt the government / economic / technology complex to a level never before seen."

3. Everything and Everyone is Connected

In the not-too-distant future, the use of the Internet will be routine, rather like electricity, as the comfort level with the technology and this method of doing business e-volves. Our work and personal lives will not only be more connected because of the evolving technology infrastructure, but they'll be more integrated as well. Processes and functions we use in the workplace will make their way into our homes. A totally Internet-enabled world where every IP appliance can coordinate an exchange transaction with or without a human guide is right around the corner.

Brooks Fisher, Vice-President of Corporate Strategy and Marketing, Intuit Inc.

"The nature of work will be transformed. Telecommuting will be the norm. We won't need as much space for retail businesses. Parks and open space can be reclaimed."

Sean Kaldor, Vice-President of E-Commerce, NetRatings Inc.

"TV and wireless will become a more active part of the Internet world…creating an 'Internet lifestyle,' which will be more casual and inherent. The Internet becomes the social activity."

Mohit Mehrotra, Vice-President and General Manager, American Express Corporate Services Interactive

"In the near future, conducting business online will become the norm. There will be a much higher level of comfort in conducting business online, from both the company's and the customer's point of view."

Maria Luisa Rodriquez, Co-Founder and Director, e-co consulting

"In the future, customers will decide when and where they want their goods. They will be able to buy daily items (food, pharmaceutical, etc.), and make the Internet part of their daily routine."

Barbara Jones, Director of Customer Service, Cisco Systems

"The customer of the future will live in an Internet-integrated environment—extending to the home. Ideas such as smart home appliances like smart refrigerators, or cars that alert you to the maintenance schedule—all controllable through the Internet—are just around the corner."

Dylan Tweney, Writer and Consultant, Tweney Media

"There will be more e-commerce in general and people will be more comfortable with it. We will also see e-commerce in more contexts—embedded in Web applications and in Internet devices."

Steven Robinson, Senior Project Manager of E-Commerce, Saltmine

"E-Commerce will become a much more personalized and accepted way of doing business. It will become second nature to buy products or services with mobile devices anytime, anywhere."

4. Customers Rule

With the Internet, customers have gained considerable power to choose with whom they will do business, as well as where and when. The need for intense customer focus and exemplary customer service will continue into the future as customers remain central to the growth of e-commerce.

Ashu Roy, CEO and Chairman, eGain

"Web sites will become 'customer interaction centers,' where customers can access information and buy goods and services on a 'self-service' basis."

Doug Nelson, President, Seabright Group

"Customers will get more and more comfortable using technology to mediate the sales process, meaning that buying and selling online through all sorts of access devices will be commonplace. This should be a huge wake-up call for companies, for they must keep up with the customers and be able to serve them accordingly."

Bill Daniel, Senior Vice-President of Products, Vignette

"The place from which you buy things will blur. Customers will expect that companies provide a choice—which may be tough to do from an infrastructure standpoint."

Bob Cross, President, Venture Capital Online, Inc.

"If not used wisely, the tools of the Internet merely enable marginal vendors to provide empty promises slicker and faster—and they call it e-commerce. In the long run, it won't work, because the customer is still king, and the Internet doesn't change that. Although the Internet can indeed change processes and channel structures, it doesn't change customer expectations. Even in the virtual world of the Internet, customers still vote with their feet."

Dave Deasy, e-Business Consultant

"Competition will continuously increase, and the winning differentiator will be customer service. The bar will continue to be raised in terms of customer expectations."

Ellen Reid, President, Smarketing.com

"With the speed of information being conveyed with the Internet, it is incumbent upon every Web site owner to express their message quickly, succinctly, and understandably. If not, the site visitor will move on to the multitudinous other sites that are of interest to them. If you don't speak your message, you will lose market share."

Stefan A. Vermeulen, Manager of New E-Business, KPN Business Communications

"Effective multichannel marketing and consolidation between old and new practices will be the focus in the future. The Internet will not be perceived as a sole channel by customers, but they will think in terms of mobile business, desktop commerce, and personal selling."

5. Better, Faster, and Maybe Cheaper

With continued learning and experimentation, companies will build better products and services by utilizing the multiple capabilities of their own companies and also their partners. Price may still be a determinant in customers' buying decisions, but value received is becoming more important than price by itself. New ways to conduct business enabled by technology will lead to many new opportunities for companies, with improved choices for customers and more efficient payment mechanisms for the exchange of value between parties.

Brooks Fisher, Vice-President of Corporate Strategy and Marketing, Intuit Inc.

"The nature of money will change. The physical need for it will disappear. This removes the administrative headache from buying things."

Peter Ostrow, CEO, Testmart

"Companies will get better at usability, navigation, and e-commerce in general. There will be better products to buy."

George Roman, CTO, diCarta

"There will be simpler payment schemes which will make it easier for people to buy goods and services. Customers will have higher expectations with sites as well—every interaction must be a positive experience."

Barbara Jones, Director of Customer Service, Cisco Systems

"There will be systems that integrate the products of many companies so that customers can order with one transaction. Once a pattern is established, then it becomes even more efficient.

"More payment systems will be possible over the Internet, such as accounts receivable, accounts payable, and other B2B accounting functions."

Brian Kellner, Development Manager, Zoho Corporation

"There will be more knowledge about e-commerce, and an improved rate of implementation."

6. Business Models and Value Webs

Just when you thought things were settling down with business models, be prepared for more changes. Improvements in efficiency of the supply chain and logistics, disintermediation, and continuing complex are part of the future.

Alan Naumann, President and CEO, Calico Commerce

"There will be more collaboration than ever, and it will be much more effective. We will apply what we've learned from manufacturing supply chains, and extend successful partnering through to the customer."

Norm Hullinger, Vice-President of Sales and Operations, Egghead.com

"The level of service for the 'last mile' will increase significantly. Express carriers such as UPS, FedEx, etc. will be faster and less expensive."

Andrew Krainin, Senior Vice-President of Marketing, Sameday.com

"A new set of supply chains are forming that move products directly from manufacturers to the customer (both B2B and B2C). These new systems will decrease transaction costs and bypass layers of the distribution chain."

Peter Ostrow, CEO, Testmart

"There will be a consolidation of choice…complex business models will fall by the wayside. If a business can't be defined by basic traditional techniques, then it won't work."

Paul Brazina, Executive Director, Electronic Commerce Institute-LaSalle University

"The key to e-commerce profitability will be an efficient and effective system to distribute products and services."

7. New Standards and Rules Create Opportunity

There has been much controversy and discussion about privacy and security and how it affects e-commerce. Quite often, new regulations and laws can be perceived as just more bureaucracy that gets in the way of doing business. However, as security issues are mitigated and standards are commonly deployed for security and privacy, new opportunities will actually be created for business.

Mark Walsh, Chairman and Chief Strategy Officer, VerticalNet

"Anonymity on the Internet will disappear. With advances in technology and electronic signature legislation, the privacy barriers start to disappear. It will be easier for companies to acquire and maintain information about customers in order to sustain lifetime customer relationships."

Brooks Fisher, Vice-President of Corporate Strategy and Marketing, Intuit Inc.

"With improved security and recent changes in legislation such as e-signatures, virtual has become 'real.' This is one of the last holdouts where infrastructure was still needed. With that barrier removed, businesses can come online much faster."

Peter Ostrow, CEO, Testmart

"There will be open standards for procurement, which means the elimination of tiered pricing. This will be a big step toward true globalization."

Kaj Pedersen, Vice-President of Engineering, Lycos Quote.com

"The Internet has become the method by which many financial firms retrieve and advertise their services. With this come issues that relate to security and a company's ability to disseminate information. With the increase in demand for online trading and financial services, the winners will be those who can exploit the opportunity for real-time services, within a secure environment."

George Roman, CTO, diCarta

"There will be an explosion of digital signature technology, which will open up new markets and make it easier to provide more services through the Internet."

Mohsien Hassim, Manager of Information Risk Management, KPMG South Africa

"Success of any e-business venture will strongly depend on good project management, a well developed business plan, and a properly structured business strategy. But in all of this, information security is key. Without it, the security of the company's data may be at risk, and the company may not survive. Remember that with Web presence, the whole world is at your doorstep—including hackers."

8. E-Volving End-to-End Infrastructure

Many advances have been made in integrating front office and back office systems both in a company and through the ASP/BSP model. Technologies that improve speed, collaboration, or integration of processes will be a requirement for survival and growth in the future.

Alan Naumann, President and CEO, Calico Commerce

"Enabling technologies will allow companies to do much more online...such as turbo-charging existing selling channels, doing one-to-one Internet selling, and creating net marketplaces and exchanges."

Ashu Roy, CEO and Chairman, eGain

"The network effect of the Internet that allows businesses to collaborate will continue, and that will mean economic efficiencies."

Clyde Foster, CEO, eConvergent

"The biggest opportunity for companies will be the integration of all customer touch points in a reactive and proactive way. This means a tightly linked infrastructure that ties marketing and customer relationship management together."

Andrew Krainin, Senior Vice-President of Marketing, Sameday.com

"New technologies will improve the speed and efficiency of existing supply chains. Internet-based systems dramatically reduce the cost and complexity of connecting enterprises, to make collaborative planning and optimization the rule rather than the exception."

Norm Hullinger, Vice-President of Sales and Operations, Egghead.com

"There will be more CRM tools and better back end systems, allowing companies to identify customers and tailor customer service individually."

Dylan Tweney, Writer and Consultant, Tweney Media

"The Web will be a lot more interactive. In the future, it will be more than just a publishing medium for content."

9. The New Face of Marketing

As companies continue to wrestle with issues about online and offline branding, we are entering a new era of personalization. Marketing will be faced with implementing new approaches in the Internet-enabled world.

Jim Sterne, President, Target Marketing of Santa Barbara

"We are entering the age of proactive or anticipatory customer service. Companies will target customers and send personalized FAQs to serve their customers."

Atul Vashistha, CEO, neoIT.com

"Marketing will change. There will be a need to be more precisely targeted, more precisely customized. Niche players may actually have an advantage in the future if they have solid customer relationships in the markets they know. Also, brand will matter in the end, but companies will have to find innovative ways to build brand loyalty because there are very low switching costs."

Russ Cohn, CEO, Brigade Corporation

"I believe that there will be less selection and less free stuff online. Also, I think there will be less 'unjustified' customer service."

Mohit Mehrotra, Vice-President and General Manager, American Express Corporate Services Interactive

"Companies need to consolidate services into the 'single desktop' online environment, and complement them with high quality service. That's how new brands will be created."

Lisa Sharples, Chief Marketing Officer, Garden.com

"The bar will be raised with regard to personalized, one-on-one marketing through the Web—especially for brick and mortar companies."

Christina Cheney, President and CEO, Simmedia

"Due to all of the consolidation and changes in business models, companies will have to be much more strategic than tactical—especially when it comes to marketing and business development."

10. New Dimensions for Growth and Evolution

As today's leaders make decisions about tomorrow's growth, there are many factors at work in this new environment that will make a huge impact. Technologies such as wireless and portable computing will provide more ways to access the Internet and will require companies to provide content accordingly. The world marketplace means greater demand for products and services, and companies need to figure out how to build businesses across geographic boundaries. We are faced with much growth in the next few years. Whether it happens slowly or quickly, we all need to be armed with the lessons we have learned so far to be better prepared to meet all the challenges of the brave new world.

Mark Walsh, Chairman and Chief Strategy Officer, VerticalNet

"E-Commerce changes in general will take longer than we think; legacy behavior does not change overnight."

Anwar Akel, Alexandria, Egypt

"To die is losing the ability to change—not the loss of breath."

Mark Resch, President and CEO, CommerceNet

"Adoption of the Internet will continue to rise—with or without the speculative enthusiasm of Wall Street. There is surprising vigor around the world, and much enthusiasm for e-commerce. Clearly, these are the early days—even in North America only about 10 percent of the manufacturers have true e-commerce presence on the Internet.

"E-Commerce will continue to behave like a complex, adaptive system. There will be no single global control point or mechanism; the tangle of non-hierarchical interaction will continue. The sophistication of global electronic commerce presence will increase, and companies' behavior will change with experience. The dynamics of the system make it unlikely that optimum equilibrium will occur in the near future."

Bill Daniel, Senior Vice-President of Products, Vignette

"There will be an increase in the number of people who interact with the Internet and conduct e-commerce using wireless devices."

Jorden Woods, Chairman and CTO, Global Sight

"Mobile, wireless access to the Internet will be commonplace, that will greatly accelerate globalization (no wait to get wired). And with that, global standards for the wireless Internet will emerge."

Atul Vashistha, CEO, neoIT.com

"Competitors are no longer just the companies 'next door.' There will be many global competitors, and companies who are not even physically in your regions."

Maria Luisa Rodriquez, Co-Founder and Director, e-co consulting

"There will be many different access modes to the Internet... including TV, portable devices, and wireless. The challenge will be creating the infrastructure to support the customer relationship from all those modes."

Dylan Tweney, Writer and Consultant, Tweney Media

"E-Commerce applications will be incorporated into wireless devices. Companies will have to maintain separate content streams for these devices."

Dan Hazen, System Support Consultant, Hewlett Packard

"Companies should foster symbiotic relationships with competitors to provide comprehensive solutions to customers across geographies, time zones, and cultures.

"CEOs should plan on investing a percentage of revenue each year to morph the business model. ROI should not be measured on a short-term basis unless extinction is on your agenda."

Cesar Plato, Founder, muybueno.net

"Internet companies will eventually realize the importance of reaching out to people online as well as offline, by organizing events where people could meet face to face. The best business is personal business. This is very important in ethnic markets. Businesses need to focus not on who you know, but who knows *you*."

Herman E. Guanlao, Executive Vice-President and General Manager, Intercaps Philippines, Inc.

"E-Commerce is about technology, capital, and knowledge—all unavailable to poor countries. However, e-commerce can bring about a new world economic order where people of the world are connected and aware that we live in one world and are brothers and sisters in search of an equitable and better quality of life for all. Technology may finally have a chance to save the world."

I wish to thank all the people who made predictions and contributed quotes for this chapter. These people from the real world will help shape our Internet-enabled future in the next few years, and I am looking forward to sharing the experience with them.

E-Volutionary Tactics

→ A number of the old-fashioned principles that worked in the Industrial Age will work in the Internet Age. You don't have to start over.

→ Don't relax, we are just at the beginning of the changes brought about by the Internet Age. Figure out how you can transition your company to be successful online, maintaining the brand you currently have in the physical world or de-throning the brand of the current incumbent.

→ Treat the use of the Internet the same as a standard commodity—like electricity.

→ Deliver intense customer focus and exemplary customer service; share value among all your partners.

→ Run many experiments and continue corporate learning to create better products and services.

→ Reexamine your business models and be prepared for continual evolution and change.

→ Support government and private sector activities to bring about global standards in security and privacy.

→ Whether you run your internal IT shop or outsource this function, integrate your front and back office systems to deliver improved speed, collaboration, and integration of processes.

→ Deliver on mass customized products and services.

→ Be prepared to embrace new paradigms as they become pervasive in society and help deliver increased value to the customer.

Change Is Constant, Change Is Good

FROM OUR GLIMPSE of the real world in the last chapter, it is clear that

vast changes will still be happening well into the future. The old adage:

"The only thing that's constant is change" certainly applies to the world

of ECM and the Internet in general.   ▶ ▶

Even the ideas and information in this book will have changed by the time the book is published and distributed. But don't be disheartened, because you will always be able to go to the book's Web site at E-Volve-or-Die.com, and also to my Web site at ECnow.com, to read up on the latest developments. These Web sites focus on capturing what is changing about ECM and how you can apply it to the real-time business problems that you face every day.

Dealing with Constant Change

As the leaders of today's businesses, who must grow and manage your companies into the future, you need to make change your friend. As a CEO or top executive of your company, you must act as the chief change agent, or CCA (now there's a good job title). If *you* are not committed to making the changes, if *you* don't walk the walk of the talk you talk, there is little hope that anyone else in your company will either. Effective change has always started at the top, and it always will. It goes hand in hand with leadership style, among other things. Says Love Goel, CEO of Personify, Inc., "To implement change in a company, it takes cash, integrity, respect for people and leadership. The CEO today is more important than ever, and it's his or her leadership that will challenge people to think differently, to take risks, to get people exhilarated and eager to make change happen. Strong and committed leadership is what creates the momentum for change."

Everyone in the company must be involved in implementing change. The larger the organization, the longer it can take to make change happen. However, it doesn't have to be that way. Many large companies, such as General Electric, Ford, and Hewlett-Packard, have been able to implement widespread changes in a rather short period of time in this New E-Conomy. What does it take? "Some of the same business basics used for years still apply," says Tom Popek, Principal of Strategic Internet Consulting. "All the familiar business principles—such as empowerment, involvement, motivation, incentives, rewards, buy-in, commitment, walking the talk, ownership, 'just do it'—all these strategies can be effective, as long as the top executives drive it." Change may actually begin on the grassroots level, with self-directed teams presenting ideas for change to their managers and so on through the top of the organization. Implementing change should be part of everyone's job description, regardless of organizational structure or hierarchy. It is the only way for the company to be able to cope with change and become successful at evolution and growth.

Catalysts of Change

How do you know when changes are needed? Is the need for change determined by your customers, your shareholders, your investors, your employees, or your partners? Any of these constituencies has a say in the growth of your company and the strategies you will employ. Financial metrics and the bottom line are of keen interest to your shareholders, investors, and employees, and a downward trend in these metrics is usually the first catalyst for change. Your customers and your ability to meet their needs and expectations are also key catalysts, because they will have an ultimate impact on your bottom line.

The way you interact and collaborate with your partners will also make a difference in how you serve your customers, whose relative happiness and satisfaction will impact your bottom line. "In the online world, customers can check you out without your knowing about it. If they go to your competitor instead, then you may eventually see some impact on your revenues. The basic metrics for survival and reasons for change are the same as they have always been—revenue, profit, and cash. In order to decide what changes need to be made, you need to look across your whole enterprise," according to Tom Popek, Principal, Strategic Internet Consulting. Because the need for change can be influenced by so many different constituencies, it is important to be able to maintain and monitor your business relationships with all.

Change Management

In the course of identifying what changes need to be made, you may have to look at legacy systems, legacy processes, and legacy people. If any of these is holding you back from realizing your vision, it's a good place to start the change management process. To determine other areas of your business that might be candidates for change, ask yourself these questions:

▲ Does your core business still make sense?

▲ Where are your customers (today's and tomorrow's)?

▲ Who are your partners?

▲ How do you sell and where?

▲ Where are you resource-constrained?

▲ What is your business strategy?

▲ How could you be organized differently to better satisfy your customer?

These changes need to be reflected in your vision. Thinking back to Chapter 3, "The Plan Is the Thing," you'll remember that the single vision and corporate goals (and metrics that measure their success) are the catalysts for change—the catalyst to create the holistic Internet-enabled entity (which is an empowered self-running entity).

Managing change in a company is a matter of managing people and their behavior. No matter how your company is organized, it will be necessary to get people involved in the change process. The philosophy of experimentation and *rewarding* failure equally with success works best during times of widespread change. According to Love Goel, CEO of Personify, "There has to be an openness of communication of how and what to change. People need to be empowered to discover and share together what needs to be done. There are no rules and no manuals and no handy Tom Peters books involved in this. It should be a roll-up-your-sleeves and dig-in environment!" It is up to the executive leadership to establish the collaborative and open environment for change to happen. Coupled with monitoring systems that can detect needed changes and whether they are working, the Internet provides the means for companies to establish much better tracking systems internally, as well.

Empowering people and encouraging teamwork may work in some organizations as long as there are incentives. "Good people will always do good things. They will collaborate and do whatever it takes to do good work, but it surely helps if you provide them incentives," says Narry Singh, Vice-President of Global Trading, Rapt Inc.

Trends That Create the Need for Change

The holistic Internet-enabled entity owes its e-volution to the rapid technology changes of recent years (that's the Internet-enabled part...). In response to the opportunity and creativity spawned by these advancements, companies have made tremendous changes in how they do business. We are only at the beginning of what will really occur. The majority of companies today are still structured around the concepts carried forth from the last business revolution, from the Agricultural Age to the Industrial Age. In the remainder of this chapter, we will present some possibilities to consider.

Narry Singh, Vice-President of Global Trading, Rapt Inc., sees five major drivers that will require widespread changes in companies:

▲ The next-generation Internet (600 times faster than the Internet is right now) will require big changes in applications.

▲ Third-generation wireless technologies will enable a vast array of products and services, as well as the need to interface to them from other platforms.

▲ Next-generation supply chains mean suppliers are "unchained" and free to establish new value relationships with customers and other suppliers.

▲ Trading hubs will enable new types of online collaboration and marketplaces (1,000 are already in existence today).

▲ Governments will increasingly get involved in regulation and policy-making, requiring compliance from the commercial sector.

When considering these technology and business advances, you can look at them as opportunities or challenges. They represent both. If your company is able to not only see the opportunity, but also implement change in a comprehensive way, you will truly be able to e-volve the company.

Managing the Future

This book has focused on the evolution process for companies and what is required to transform your company into a holistic Internet-enabled entity. You have now examined what is required to deploy and manage e-commerce in your organization. The evolution process must go on into the future. If companies don't e-volve, they will die.

You have looked at the real world and some predictions about what is in store. What will the future really be like? No one knows for sure, but I want to take you on a fantasy tour of the e-commerce (business) world in the year 2025. Whether this little tour provokes you or stimulates your creativity, one thing is for sure: It involves *change*.

E-Commerce in the Year 2025

The year is 2025...please reset your (mental) watches. I am speaking to you, the reader, from the future.

Let me update you on what has happened with technology and some of the customs and business practices that are common now. First, holographic technology was perfected about ten years ago. Therefore, when I encounter other humans, it's hard to know whether they are physically present in the room and vice versa, so I say "Greetings, near and far!" Any humans physically present respond by saying, "Greetings!" in return.

Five fundamental building blocks are at work in the year 2025:

- ▲ Knowledge workers and their personas
- ▲ Object-based ECOsystems
- ▲ The semantic Web
- ▲ Bio-integration and IT
- ▲ Collaboration

A Day in the Life of Mitchell... Year 2025

Greetings, near and far! I just flew in specially today from the moon—I took the moon shuttle. Yesterday I celebrated my nephew's eighteenth birthday. You probably know George because he was actually the first cloned human. Now that he's eighteen, he has an opportunity to change the genetic makeup of his system (change his DNA). Recently enacted laws allow humans to do that when they turn eighteen. If I were George and could make that decision, I think I would go for the full head of hair option!

While I was on the flight, I was able to increase my productivity. I have a working persona that does work for me, and that persona did three different transactions. It did some consulting work in Hong Kong, conducted in Mandarin. It did some business planning in Paris, speaking French. And then it did some Web marketing work in Etheria (not a physical location), which was done in byte-talk. At one of the locations (Hong Kong), the client was interested in hiring my consulting persona on a full-time basis, so I converted the work persona into an employee persona. This is a way for me to create an increased revenue stream, and I was pretty happy about that. As a result, I was able to pay taxes and deposit transactions in four different nation-states, and I deposited funds into ten different accounts that are set up with ten different investment strategies that interest me. (See Figure 14.1.)

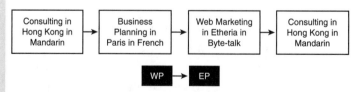

Figure 14.1

Work personas can be in more than one place at a time.

One of the things that helped me to prepare for today is that I sent my scanning persona out to look at the Web to absorb all the latest news and current events. One of the things the scanning persona uncovered was that today is the 100th anniversary of one of Babe Ruth's spectacular baseball records. The scanning persona got together with my work persona and formed a 48-hour company. This company created a holographic 4-dimensional baseball card. The work persona sent out a request to 15,000 customer-personas, who said they were interested in buying the product and three Business Service Providers (BSPs) who said they would collectively be able to build the product for me. They built it and sent it to their virtual stores. So within 48 hours, we built and sold 15,000 holographic cards to the customers who wanted them. The revenues were split equally among the parties, but more importantly, I planted the seed for future relationships. (See Figure 14.2.)

Figure 14.2

Virtual companies can be created instantly and dissolved again when the mission is complete.

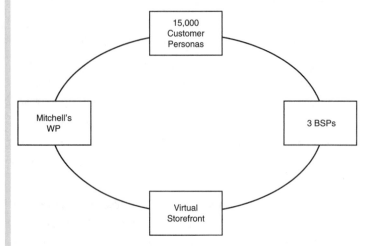

One of the things I did when I landed here was check into a medical e-point of service station for bioscanning. I stuck my finger into the scanning device, and it scanned my whole body, took a look at the outside environment and elements, and found that the pollen count (compared to the moon) was a lot higher and there were bacteria and viruses in the air that my body was not accustomed to. I elected to have a 72-hour immunity gene inserted into my DNA so I would be able to withstand the environment and not be susceptible to the virus. I paid for this service using the magnetic card that I inserted into the bioscanning system, and all money and transactions happened in the background, transparent to me.

I did enjoy a little bit of R & R when I checked into my hotel. I did some exercises in the gym, and I had my meal replicated to fit the characteristics of the environment I am in. In today's world, I generally work about 20 hours per week, and the rest of the time I spend physically and holographically with my friends. When I went to bed last night, my alpha chip (that was inserted into my brain two years ago) merged the information from my various personas, and the right amount of information was downloaded. (See Figure 14.3.) In my dream sleep, the information was synthesized so that I was able to wake up as a more enlightened person.

Not a bad day!

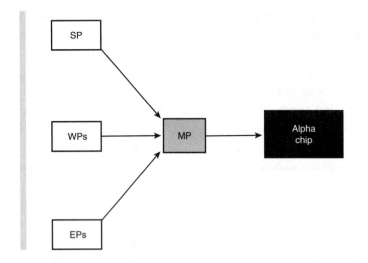

Figure 14.3

The managing persona synthesizes information from other personas and uploads it into the alpha chip in your brain.

Let's look at some of the concepts at work today, in 2025. A Knowledge Worker is a person who spends a lot of time and energy integrating business with knowledge from the Internet, and regardless of geographic boundaries, he can add value to a company or entity. Knowledge workers work from multiple locations around the globe. (Back in the year 2000, they were called "consultants.") We have human-hybrid workgroups now; knowledge personas, employee personas, and work personas all work together to collaboratively deliver in a much more exciting environment, and they can deliver much more power and information to companies.

Today, knowledge workers have lifetime equity and long-term vesting. You don't lose, because working personas and employee personas have the information, and it is never lost; it remains with, and can grow with, the company. As people provide employee personas, you get increased revenue streams. There's also an increased functionality service model; I have the opportunity to go to my employee personas and give them more information that I have learned over time, and I can ratchet up the amount of value I add to the company (and receive more money from the company accordingly).

One of the things we recently talked about was the security issue dealing with personas. When I give a work persona to a company, the company gets an employee persona that is then theirs and not really mine. If the employee persona is to be effective, it must learn information that is confidential to the company; information that I should not know about. So, it's possible to have employee personas on one side of a persona firewall; information coming into the company is seen by these personas, but it has to be monitored by managing personas when the information goes outside the firewall. The company has managing personas and worker personas and knowledge workers—all who can share internal information—but the information from my employee persona can't send me information unless it's been scrutinized and scrubbed by the managing personas.

Figure 14.4

Security is in place to guard against unintended transfer of information among personas.

The building block and trend here is that knowledge workers and personas are the keys to living and thriving in virtual organizations, and that allows knowledge workers to perform non-human-chaperoned tasks. A number of things have been enabled by this trend, and my worker personas have been able to do a number of things I could not have done otherwise if my physical presence was required. Back in the 1970s and '80s when the steel and auto industries downsized, people lost their jobs forever. In the 1990s when knowledge workers in the military lost their jobs, they could fit into society; however, they essentially started over. Today, knowledge workers can leave a piece of themselves behind to collect income while they try new things.

> *Knowledge workers and personas are the keys to living and thriving in virtual organizations in 2025, and that allows knowledge workers to perform non-human-chaperoned tasks.*

The second building block of 2025 is object-based ECOsystems. The definition: Components that come together to deliver basic business functionality. Back in the year 2000, Java, XML, ASPs, and UML were the precursors of what we have today. The ECOsystem today is comprised of many different business elements. They include consumer objects (scanning personas of individuals that represent their wants, needs, and ability to spend); Business Service Providers (BSPs), who have universal access to deliver different types of information; business managing personas, who manage what's happening inside the company; and knowledge workers and their personas. That is the virtual business world today.

In this virtual world, BSPs run everything. They understand your business and solve problems for you; they are the ultimate in outsourcing business processes. Things are designed and assembled in real-time in the appropriate business model.

The evolution of the object-based world began in 1990 with Java, in 2005 UML and Java were integrated for process design, and in 2010 programs designed themselves. In ancient times of the Agricultural Age, tools were put in the hands of people. In the Industrial Age, tools and machines were freestanding. In the Software Economy from 1980 to 2005, machines were run by humans who added value to the processes. In the Info-Process Economy from 2005 to 2020, digital machines were built from e-processes. In the ECOsystem (ECO stands for "e-commerce object") of today, software learns to design itself. (See Figure 14.5.)

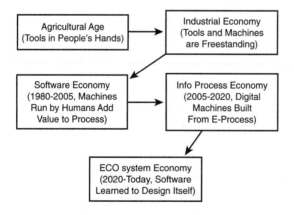

Figure 14.5

The business and technology e-volution timeline.

In the year 2001, the ASP was surrounded by a series of services. You had the ability to do payments or accounting or warranty or financial services. Today, it's an integrated core set of services that can provide specific business functions that together produce results that people are interested in. Now objects find themselves through networks, and they do it virtually. Back in

2001, we had companies like Priceline and eWanted, and consumers named their price for a certain product. Companies would come back and respond as to whether they could meet that price or deliver that product or service. Today, instead of the consumer saying they want to buy something, businesses say they want to make something, and it all happens automatically. It's a different system of supply and demand.

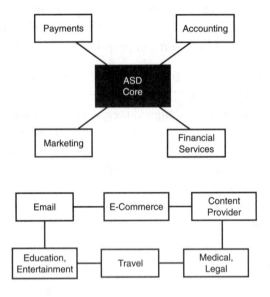

Figure 14.6

The original ASPs in 2000 were surrounded by discrete services.

Figure 14.7

Today's ASPs consist of integrated services.

The third building block is the semantic Web. Today the Web understands itself, learns from interactions, and there's no such thing as a Web page; things are presented conceptually. Back in the year 2001, information was mostly static, published by humans, semantically read and placed, and things were not presented within context. Spiders were often used to gather information. In the year 2025, Web documents have disappeared. The Internet in real-time understands who you are and what you are and can sense the information that has both the content and the context for things you are interested in. The network has become neural. To have a neural network (that is, a "brain"), you must have a way to store information, communicate, and process. Today, computers have 25 times the capacity of a human brain. (Moore's Law became extinct in 2005.) We e-volved to three-dimensional chips in the year 2005, and computer capacity now doubles every six months.

The Internet uses semantic patterns just like a brain (See Figure 14.8.). It creates relationships from new information and learns from its experience, and it solves problems exponentially. We have scanning personas that go out and scan information from the Internet, retrieving it based on our personal profiles and our ad-hoc desires and giving that information to us in summarized form. There's also a digital human interface. About ten years ago, an alpha chip was created to be biologically implanted in one's brain so that you can actually store information. These are needed because given the high capacity of computers, we need a way to keep up with the machines! Our managing personas coordinate the uploading and maintenance of these alpha chips, synthesizing information that we need during our dream sleep.

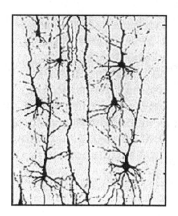 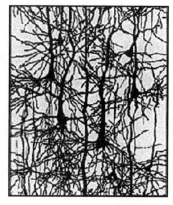

Figure 14.8

The Internet uses synaptic patterns like a brain, learning from experience.

The intelligent Internet is the backbone of our civilization. Back in 2001, Cisco, Dell, and many other companies touted the benefits of their customer care Web site. With it, customers helped themselves through the Internet site, often saving a tremendous amount of time and money. The goal of their sites was to have the computer do more and more for the customer while eliminating human intervention. Today, it's very difficult to tell the difference between the humans and the Internet. We all have our personas to go out there and collaborate with various business objects, negotiating our wants and needs. Our scanning personas then become consumers and buy things for us.

At the turn of the century, we started cloning sheep. We were also able to mend bones by installing metal pins. The next step was the ability to replicate limbs with prosthetics, fix eyesight, install pacemakers. This was the start of the development of biological components that were able to extend our lives. Today, we have the fourth building block: the integration of biotech and IT. Biotech was able to merge the biological and logical, and we figured out how to manipulate molecular and cellular structures. From a logical perspective, we are able to understand DNA. The integration of these two enables us to create artificial ears, eyes, and other parts and replace them with new parts. We built storage devices from molecular polymers. We also were able to take neurons and craft them onto silicon wafers. In the area of computational research, we were able to make computers simulate biological circuits. From the integration side, we started seeing cornea implants, cochlear implants for the deaf, partial spinal cord implants, and so on. In short, we started experimenting with the human body.

Today, we have full-scale biological computers and networks. Bio-implants and sensors can be used to detect environmental conditions that are negative to us, and we can change our bodies to compensate for this. The first cloned baby is now 18 years old. In the year 2010, designer DNA was programmed by computers, enabling us to temporarily or permanently change our DNA. There are tremendous health care benefits to us today. We are able to do bioscans in a minute, have modifications done on-the-fly, and have everything paid for automatically. Now that we understand the building blocks of humans and the process of nature, we can alter them or modify them permanently or temporarily, and we can integrate computers and humans to become part of the human race.

The last building block is collaboration. Collaboration today is when all the suppliers, partners, companies, customers, and competitors work together to solve the problems and provide for wants and needs. In the year 2000, these were called "strategic partnerships." Today, business incubator requests are globally broadcasted. The ability of BSPs to respond on a global basis and figure out what they can do to solve these issues are known by all. We have not created order-less enterprises, but virtual enterprises. Businesses today are truly built on integrated processes that can understand and learn from each other, and adapt, e-volve, or perish. The core competencies of global firms are interlinked, and enterprises retain employee and customer value. The storefront is really a virtual market maker. Scanning personas are out there expanding their wants and needs, the worker personas collect and aggregate that information and then broadcast the needs to various BSPs who come together to form a business to solve an issue.

We have a lot more active collaboration today—with multiple entities. Retailers are now virtual meeting places, and customers are awareness providers. We have the ability to build exactly what we want, exactly when we need it.

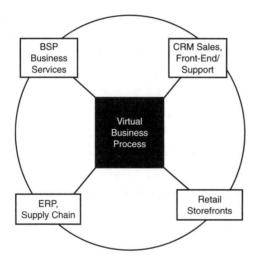

Figure 14.9

Objects find each other through networks, through business incubated requests.

The path of the e-commerce evolution started in the late 1900s, with networked business processes. In early 2000, we had object-based application design. In 2005, knowledge workers and their personas were introduced. The year 2010 saw the creation of the consciousness of the semantic Web. In 2015, biotech and IT started to converge, and in 2020, collaboration became the key to the e-commerce system. Today, we take everything that's digital for granted, because we have become fully digital and interlinked.

In the year 2025, success is about using the digital medium in collaborative relationships. And remember: Be true to your persona!

Back to 2001

Now, let's jump back to the year 2001. With this glimpse of what may happen in the future, you might think about what you can do today to prepare. Everything from year 2025 has some foundation in technology or business concepts now—they are just extrapolated into the future.

1. If the economy will indeed become digital and internet-worked, what are you and your company doing today to take advantage of that? How can you tie in with all your vendors, all your partners, and your employees to become internetworked?

2. If companies have transitioned from the Industrial Age to the Internet Age, why have you not eliminated or changed your current functional units in terms of how you do business? You need to think about how you can do a better job of figuring out how to take advantage of this medium of the Internet as one component of everything your business will be doing.

3. If employees will turn into knowledge workers and personas, what can you do today to make your employees happier? How can you capture the information and knowledge they have so that you can use it over and over? If the employee is the key to success in customer satisfaction, figure out what tools and capabilities you can give them so you can harness their power in a better way than you currently do.

4. The Web will become semantic, and the network will become neural. When that happens, how will you use collaboration to better conduct business? How can you better link the supply chain and value web to enable people to talk to one another and share valuable information?

5. Business incubator requests will drive ad-hoc information to customers, suppliers, employees, and corporations to form virtual and borderless corporations. Are you taking advantage of ASPs and BSPs today? Why buy a $500,000 software package, hire employees to install the package,

and create the infrastructure to make it work, when you can go out and rent it for a lot less money? You should take advantage of the other available tools and services that will solve this problem for you.

Boldly Setting Forth…

I hope that I have given you a lot to think about in these 14 chapters. Now it's time for action. After the E-Volutionary Tactics section that follows, you will find a series of pages labeled by topic. These pages are for you. Write down the steps that you will commit to in order to e-volve your company into the future. Go forth with a sense of excitement, of creativity, and purpose. It will be a wild ride. And remember to forge ahead with my son's single battle cry: "MESS!" Let the real e-volution begin.

E-Volutionary Tactics

→ Change will be with us forever; make it your friend.

→ Managing change requires committed leadership from the top.

→ Create a Chief Change Agent (CCA) in your company.

→ Managing change is also a matter of managing people and incentives in ways that create win-win situations for the employees and the organization.

→ Many catalysts for change reside either within your company or externally; create opportunities for everyone to lend a hand and voice their opinions.

→ The future will be full of opportunity, surprises, and new ways to transform business.

→ Experiment and e-volve, adjusting your strategies and activities based on the lessons learned in your everyday activity and from your experiments.

→ Reorganize all your functions, companies, divisions, and so on to revolve around your customers.

→ We are just at the beginning. Be prepared, because you ain't seen nothing yet!

What is your e-commerce (business) vision?

_____

_____

_____

_____

_____

_____

_____

_____

_____

_____

List five corporate goals that will help you carry out this vision.

_____

_____

_____

_____

_____

_____

_____

_____

_____

_____

_____

What are the metrics that every person in your company will know and
be measured by, that will help you carry out your vision?

_____

_____

_____

_____

_____

_____

_____

_____

How will you e-volve your organization for the future?

_____

_____

_____

_____

_____

_____

_____

_____

_____

How will you manage change and continue to e-volve your company?

_____

_____

_____

_____

_____

_____

_____

_____

_____

_____

What new opportunities will you pursue?

_____

_____

_____

_____

_____

_____

_____

_____

_____

_____

What new business models will you use?

_____

_____

_____

_____

_____

_____

_____

_____

_____

What are your customer touch points?

_____

_____

_____

_____

_____

_____

_____

_____

_____

What functions and processes will you outsource or change?

_____

_____

_____

_____

_____

_____

_____

_____

_____

How will you improve your customer service?

_____

_____

_____

_____

_____

_____

_____

_____

_____

_____

_____

What is your globalization plan?

_____

_____

_____

_____

_____

_____

_____

_____

_____

_____

How will you handle marketing?

_____

_____

_____

_____

_____

_____

_____

_____

_____

_____

PART

V

Appendixes

A Case Studies 273

B Recommended E-Commerce Glossaries 297

C Resources 301

D End Notes 305

Case Studies

MY OBJECTIVE for *E-Volve-or-Die.com: Thriving in the Internet Age Through E-Commerce Management* was to present to you the strategies for e-volving your company into a holistic, Internet-enabled entity. This section showcases three companies that have been able to successfully implement many of the principles discussed throughout this book. The three companies—UPS, Office Depot, and Cardinal Health—have indeed transformed themselves into holistic Internet-enabled entities. I hope these cases will inspire and motivate you to do the same with your company. ▶ ▶

United Parcel Service, Inc. (UPS)

www.ups.com

UPS is an enabler of e-commerce in the package delivery industry. They have been in the package delivery business for 95 years, providing services to businesses and consumers worldwide in more than 200 countries.

Alan Amling, Director of E-Commerce Marketing, provided the content for this case study.

Key Concepts from This Book

Chapter 1   Creative thinking

Chapter 2   Business models

Chapter 3   Planning from the top down

Chapter 6   Vision encompasses world market

Chapter 7   Creating new outsourced services

Chapter 8   Finding new ways to provide more and better customer service

Chapter 9   Employee ownership and commitment

Chapter 14   Change as a part of the culture

History of Transformation

In 1994, UPS began to investigate the potential of e-commerce and started an internal group focused on enabling e-commerce. UPS redefined its core business and found ways to change its structure and processes, forming new businesses to take advantage of new opportunities.

Products and Services

UPS is in the transportation industry. They move goods, information, and funds between individuals and companies. Their operations provide delivery by land and by air, and they offer services at customer shipping centers, as well as online through

Figure A.1
www.ups.com
UPS operates in more than
200 countries worldwide,
does business in 15 different
languages and dialects, and
delivers an average of 13.2
million packages per day. UPS
wanted to undergo a more
fundamental change–to transform their company into an
enabler of global commerce

www.ups.com. They operate in more than 200 countries world-wide, do business in 15 different languages and dialects, and deliver an average of 13.2 million packages per day.

Catalyst for Change

UPS was interested in finding ways to leverage their extensive infrastructure and expertise in basic transportation of goods, services, and information. They wanted to enter new markets and continue to grow. They also wanted to undergo a more fundamental change—to transform their company into an enabler of global commerce.

Vision and Strategy

In 1991, the company's vision was to be "the leading package delivery company." They were able to grow significantly toward that goal, but they weren't satisfied with just that. They wanted a larger challenge for the company. In 1999, they changed their vision statement to "the enablers of global e-commerce." At that time, their company purpose (vision), mission, and strategies were redefined as this:

▲ *Purpose (why they are in business):* To enable global commerce.

▲ *Mission (what they seek to achieve):* To fulfill their promise to constituents by

> Serving their evolving needs.
>
> Sustaining a strong and employee-owned company.
>
> Continuing to be a responsible employer.
>
> Acting as a caring corporate citizen.

▲ *Strategy (their plan of action):* To sustain the core and create their future by

> Investing in the core business of worldwide distribution and logistics.
>
> Building competencies in the integration of goods, funds, and information.
>
> Using technology to create new services; attracting talented people.
>
> Studying customer behavior and anticipating their needs.
>
> Practicing innovation that leads to growth.
>
> Developing an environment that enables them to treat each customer as if he or she were the only one.

Changes Made/E-Volutionary Process

When UPS began the process of transformation, they started at the basic level—taking a hard look at their core competencies and expertise. They also examined the assets in their multifaceted infrastructure, from data communications, to their fleets of trucks and aircraft, to their call centers. They did this analysis and examination with the idea of finding ways to leverage the growing technology and connectivity of the Internet in order to build entirely new subsidiaries of UPS. In the process, they found several gold mines. With additional investment in nformation technology (at the rate of more than $1 billion USD per year), they were able to transform a very sizable company in record time.

Once they had identified opportunities within their own company and finished their internal analysis, they re-examined the external world to learn more about e-commerce, markets, and their customers. After taking a look at what people were doing with e-commerce in the external business world, UPS decided that their own definition of e-commerce was not about technology, but it was about the integration of "bits and bytes with bricks and mortar." They noticed that customers were changing, and the power dynamic was shifting from the sellers (companies) to the buyers (customers). UPS wanted to find ways to provide more access points to that new breed of customer.

UPS also claims that luck and timing helped a great deal. With the surge in e-tailing as well as B2B e-commerce, UPS was in a unique position to meet the increased demand. They were the bridge between the physical and electronic world, with a well-tested and highly reliable infrastructure to serve both worlds. UPS was able to foresee the importance of electronic information to the transportation industry. As early as 1985, they began improving their data networking applications to enhance communications with their customers and increase efficiency. For instance, they built up their IT network and database in order to collect and track more than 200 data elements for every single package they ship. With more than 13 million packages being shipped every day, that's a lot of data! However, their system continues to handle that level of information exchange. Consequently, they were well poised to help the multitude of new B2C online companies who came to rely on UPS for shipping. UPS was able to offer these new companies tracking services as well. It was as easy as setting up a link to the UPS Web site. UPS also offers a set of transportation APIs called the UPS OnLine Tools that allow businesses to integrate tracking, rating, address validation, and a number of other valuable functions into their Web site. Now, through their eLogistics service, small B2C companies (as well as large companies) can have their own virtual logistics department hosted at UPS.

When UPS redefined its core business, the description included the transportation of not only goods, but also funds. They wanted a way to leverage their expertise and infrastructure to transfer funds among entities. UPS has always dealt with COD payments, credit risk assessment, billing systems, and cash flow. With the advent of electronic signatures, it's easier to move such services online and provide that as another service to their B2B customers. UPS has even started UPS Capital, which provides working capital to small businesses. UPS Capital has also applied the Internet to its business, developing online COD receivables management products and cutting customers' COD receivables wait from two weeks to two days.

Business communication services became another new UPS offering. UPS has significant call center expertise and infrastructure to handle the call volume generated by more than 13 million package deliveries daily. Now that more of their tracking requests come in through their Web site than by phone (about 2.5 million requests per day), they have excess call center capacity. They now offer call center services to their customers, integrating the call center services with their customers' business infrastructure.

Several of the new and existing UPS services can now be combined. With the new subsidiaries, UPS now has the potential to lease call center capacity to a customer, handle the logistics and related information exchange for all transactions, and then provide fulfillment and shipping to the customer's customers. UPS is already doing this, and an example of one of their customers is Nike.com. All the back-end systems for Nike.com are provided and managed by UPS, along with order handling at a UPS worldwide logistics center, and then on to UPS fulfillment, and some of the shipping as well (depending on the destination). UPS has, through creative deployment of its core competencies, taken on greater pieces of the value web in B2B e-commerce.

Figure A.2
www.nike.com

All of Nike.com's back-end systems, order handling, and fulfillment are provided and managed by UPS.

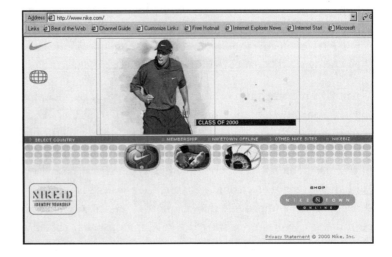

UPS has been able to make tremendous strides because of their open and consensus-based company culture. The company is still 99 percent employee-owned. Executives are willing to listen to ideas from any employee. There are informal and formal ways to bring ideas forward, and employees are encouraged to do this. UPS also seeks good ideas from their customers and partners. It's all about being willing to listen to an idea, regardless of the source, and then having the business savvy and commitment to implement the best ideas. When the e-commerce team started inside the company in 1996, team members from different functional areas were able to get the resources they needed to move forward because the highest levels of management were committed to the cause.

There is also a more formalized process for employees to bring forward ideas. Teams (such as the e-commerce team) are made up of people from different functional organizations such as IT, sales, marketing, and finance. When an idea is ready to go forward, the team members begin the process of identifying the stakeholders affected by the new idea and work to get their buy-in first. The idea makes its way on to the agenda of a marketing or management committee that is most often made up of these stakeholders. When the committee evaluates an idea and makes its decision to move forward, there is a much greater likelihood that the idea will be approved. This truly represents a self-empowered entity. People tend to support what they helped to create, and every employee is really a stakeholder (and in the case of UPS, they are shareholders as well). This open consensus-based process helps UPS make significant changes in a very short period of time.

In their transformation, UPS also restructured their organization from a functional-based structure to one that is centered on process. They now have organizations that focus on the customer information management process, the product management process, the customer relationship management process, the business information and analysis process, and the package management process. These changes did not happen overnight because the organization was very large. However, the reorganization is already starting to pay off. Development time for new projects has decreased significantly. The focus on process seems to help—at least so far.

Main Lessons

UPS has done a remarkable job of leveraging their core competencies for the new world of e-commerce. They have figured out ways to deliver their core business services in new ways, while leveraging their tremendous infrastructure assets.

They haven't forgotten where they came from, and they have managed to preserve their company culture. It has served them very well in promoting the creative thought necessary to come up with new ways to do business and grow the company.

They were brave enough to change the vision, starting at the top, and committing themselves to it from the top all the way down through every employee of the company. They managed to do it quickly by making changes in their processes and organizational structure.

UPS has been aggressive in finding new revenue streams with existing and new customers. They understand not only their customers and related needs, but they have also figured out ways to deliver more value. They have expanded the roles they can play in the overall value web by leveraging their infrastructure and expertise.

Roadmap for Continuing E-Volution

The company culture of UPS will serve them well going into the future. UPS has a clearly defined vision and set of strategies that are understood and embraced by all employees to help them maintain momentum and focus.

They have a mechanism and process in place to encourage and act on creative ideas brought forward by their employees, customers, and partners. UPS will continue to find new ways to provide other services for their customers by leveraging the assets they have and investing in new ways to integrate the online world with the brick and mortar world.

Office Depot

www.officedepot.com

Office Depot is a distributor of office products and business services. Their primary markets are mid-sized to large corporations, small businesses, and consumers.

Monica Luechtefeld, Executive Vice-President of E-Commerce, supplied the content for this case study.

Key Concepts from This Book

Chapter 1   Using creative thinking for combining online and offline business

Chapter 2   Business models; the value web

Chapter 3   Creating an empowered entity; involving employees in the vision

Chapter 4   Customer touch points; customer stratification

Chapter 5   Recognizing the importance of content

Chapter 9   Employee incentives

Chapter 10   Using other channels to bring customers to a Web site

Chapter 11   Security and privacy concerns

Chapter 12   Recognizing the new buying patterns of customers as an opportunity

History of Transformation

In 1995, Office Depot started implementing their e-commerce initiatives from the top down. Part of the strategy was to integrate the e-commerce group within the company, rather than setting up a standalone dot.com. Ultimately, all 1,500 of their field sales force went through e-commerce training, along with training on Office Depot's EC initiatives. As a result of these initiatives, their online revenue has grown from $350 million USD in 1999 to an expected $800 million USD by the end of 2000.

Figure A.3
www.officedepot.com

Office Depot is the world's largest office products distributor, with 855 retail superstores in the U.S. and Canada, and 123 additional international stores. The primary reason for transforming Office Depot was desired growth in their current market, and expansion into new marketplaces.

In 1999, an Office Depot ventures fund was established to invest in new EC initiatives for the small business market.

Products and Services

Office Depot sells a wide variety of office products, including pens, copiers, computers, peripherals, software, and furniture. They are the world's largest office products distributor, with 855 retail superstores in the U.S. and Canada and 123 additional international stores. They also sell online through their Web sites. Their annual sales in 1999 were $10.3 billion USD, representing a 14 percent increase from the year before.

Catalyst for Change

The primary reason for transforming the company was desired growth in their current market and expansion into new marketplaces. By becoming familiar with their customers' buying behaviors and business operations, they saw the need to change their business models, their product/service mix, their organization, and their overall business strategy.

Vision and Strategy

When Office Depot began their transformation, the vision for the company was to be the most successful office products company in the world. The overall company strategies that support the vision are listed here:

- ▲ Superior customer satisfaction
- ▲ An associate-oriented environment
- ▲ Industry leading value
- ▲ Ethical business conduct
- ▲ Shareholder value

This environment formed the foundation for developing new initiatives within the company, one of which was e-commerce. For this, they developed a more specific business strategy based on their keen understanding of their customers' needs now and for the future. Their new business strategy is to merge the on-line and offline worlds to satisfy customers in their two main market segments—large business and small office/home office (SOHO) business. In the large company segment, penetration and adoption of Office Depot's Internet services has continued to pay off. In the SOHO market, companies have generally not spent the time, money, and energy to make this happen. However, Office Depot believes that the SOHO marketplace will ultimately surpass the automation efforts of large companies by going 100 percent online to run their businesses. Office Depot will build tools and partner with companies to deliver these services. They will be prepared for this market shift. So their strategy was to grow both market segments when those segments were ready for the corresponding online offerings. Once Office Depot defined this new strategy, they set out to transform the company accordingly.

Changes Made/E-Volutionary Process

Office Depot developed a thorough understanding of their customer base and their changing behaviors, and then they reorganized the company by customer segment during their transformation. They evaluated sales history by segment to develop a stratification scheme. The new e-commerce strategy required the company to view customers horizontally rather than vertically. Once the company completed that analysis, several new ways to serve their customer base became obvious, requiring the company to integrate their infrastructure assets with the online environment.

It was clear that the majority of Office Depot's large corporate customers were beginning to run components of their businesses online. Office Depot assumed correctly that these large companies would be willing to buy their office products online as well. The next step was for them to offer direct server-to-server connections to their customers to speed up the procurement process even more. Today, 87,000 customers are connected privately to Office Depot's servers, with more than 390,000 total users. For each of those customers, Office Depot creates a personalized welcome screen with the customer's corporate logo, and it also offers content such as personalized messages from Office Depot's sales team, a bulletin board with news about logistics issues, and other informational content. Procter and Gamble and WorldCom are examples of customers that are connected this way. In addition, Office Depot has partnered with the major purchasing technology companies like Commerce One, Ariba, Metion, and Purchase Pro. Office Depot's strategy is to be interoperable with these corporations and to make it easy for their customers to connect.

Office Depot has a goal to make this area of business 40 percent of their revenues. They are currently adding 1,000 customers per week to their online system. At that rate, they are on track to meet and possibly exceed that goal.

After their success among their large customers, Office Depot was ready to tackle the next layer in their stratification scheme: the SOHO market. In 1998, they started focusing on this segment. Small business customers will eventually run their businesses online, but they have been slower to adopt those technology solutions than large businesses have. The reasons for this include fewer startup resources, lack of knowledge about how to do business online, and concern about security and privacy. However, the small business market is huge, so Office Depot decided to find other ways to capture this lucrative market segment as part of their overall strategy. Some small businesses are beginning to use service providers of various types (ISPs and ASPs), so Office Depot intends to partner with some of those service providers to gain the attention of small businesses. They also partner with companies such as AOL and Microsoft's bCentral for marketing purposes in an effort to reach more small business customers.

Another way to reach this market is through Office Depot's retail locations, where small businesses are more likely to do their shopping for office supplies. When small businesses recognize that it can be a timesaver to shop online, that segment will grow. So Office Depot is partnering and rolling out in-store seminars to educate their customers on how to do that. The ultimate goal is for customers to come into their stores and learn about "Business in a Box"—a suite of online services that includes finance, human resources, payroll, and of course, procurement of office supplies and equipment. By using in-store demos, Office Depot offers the opportunity for small business customers to be educated about how it works, how security and privacy can be addressed, and how the customer can save money. It's all about delivering value to the customer, and that is why Office Depot has been so successful in this area.

Rolling out programs such as this to their retail stores takes careful planning and implementation. It's a matter of integrating the retail channel with the online channel on many fronts, including inventory compatibility, marketing information, and sales. The ultimate goal, of course, is to offer customers choices on how they want to buy business products without creating confusion. An online customer, for example, should be able to return an item to a retail location for a refund without any hassles. Similarly, a retail customer should be able to order online from inside the store and have goods delivered wherever they need them.

Combining retail and online operations also involves some management issues. Individual store managers need to be credited with sales however they occur. Because employees are evaluated on the same metrics and incentives, including meeting the sales and e-commerce initiatives, their compensation should be administered accordingly.

Office Depot's competitive advantage arises from its extensive infrastructure as well as their vision. They have an integrated warehouse distribution system with its own trucks and drivers. They have the capability to deliver goods on a next-day basis. Their large mainframe back-office system can handle the scale and volume they need to expand their customer base and offer more services. With their network of more than 850 retail stores, they have a built-in marketing and distribution platform to bring tomorrow's business solutions to their business customers today.

Main Lessons

Every person in the organization should think about e-commerce, and this was one of the goals of the original e-commerce initiatives at Office Depot. It is a company goal to be e-commerce-enabled, and this goal is tied to employee compensation.

Office Depot is committed to understanding their customers' buying behavior and changing needs. By anticipating future needs and developing ways to deliver products and services in a value-added environment, Office Depot will continue to grow with their customers. Because they have developed a strategy and then reorganized the EC initiatives according to the stratification of their customer base, they are well positioned to be market leaders in their major markets.

Leveraging their retail distribution infrastructure to provide more services to customers and driving traffic to their online stores promises to be very effective for Office Depot. Also, expanding the value web by finding complementary service providers enables them to provide more value to their small business customers and help their overall growth.

Roadmap for Continuing E-Volution

Partnering with customers—as well as competitors—will be a key strategy for Office Depot going forward. Finding additional ways to leverage their infrastructure and implementing these plans quickly will enable them to keep e-volving, as well. Most important is their commitment to keeping employees involved in growth by providing focus and meeting the company's e-commerce objectives. An employee that is valued will create value for the company and its customers.

Cardinal Health

www.cardinal.com

Cardinal Health is a distributor of products and services to the health care industry. They serve three primary markets: hospitals, retail, and pharmaceutical manufacturers.

Kathy White, Executive Vice-President and CEO, supplied the content for this case study.

Key Concepts from This Book

Chapter 1	Thinking outside the box
Chapter 2	Business models to fit the changing needs of the market and industry
Chapter 4	Listening to customers and leveraging customer touch points
Chapter 9	Self-directed workgroups
Chapter 12	Getting ideas from customers
Chapter 14	Change as a part of company culture and as a competitive advantage

History of Transformation

The founder of Cardinal Health, Bob Walter, grew the company through strategic acquisitions over the last 15 years. During this growth period, Cardinal Health was able to maintain profitability. They consistently ranked number 13 in shareholder return among the Fortune 500. Today, they are a $30 billion USD company.

Cardinal's acquisitions included other regional health care distributors, along with specific types of manufacturers whose products could augment Cardinal's offerings. Bob Walter has an uncanny ability to find and execute great deals with acquisition candidates, and he is always on the lookout for technology innovators. That strategy has been the secret to Cardinal's competitive advantage. When they acquired Allegiance, Cardinal was able to leapfrog into the e-commerce world with the advanced technology implementations Allegiance brought with them. These implementations will enable hands-free procurement in all their market segments, as well as integration among their market segments, which is the current e-commerce strategy for Cardinal.

However, Cardinal does not stop there. By involving all employees in the company, they continue to innovate and find ways to provide additional services to their customers, and they expand their role in the value web of their industry. This entrepreneurial philosophy is akin to a teenager waiting to grow up, and they are being very successful in the meantime.

Products and Services

Cardinal Health provides a wide array of services that support the health care industry. Their customers are pharmaceutical manufacturers, medical products manufacturers, hospitals, and health care providers. For manufacturers, Cardinal Health provides product development, specific types of manufacturing, packaging, distribution, marketing, and sales services. For health care providers and hospitals, they offer similar services, as well as products that help improve operational and clinical performance. Cardinal Health also works in partnership with pharmaceutical and biotechnology companies to develop unique dosage and packaging for drugs used by retail pharmacies, hospitals, physicians, and surgery centers. For hospitals and health care providers, Cardinal develops and manufactures pharmaceutical supply and dispensing systems. On the procurement and inventory management side of things, Cardinal also helps develop integrated technology solutions.

Figure A.4
www.cardhealth.com
Cardinal Health provides a wide
array of services that support
the health care industry.
Cardinal Health is one of those
companies where change has
become part of their culture.

Catalyst for Change

Cardinal Health is one of those companies for which change has become part of their culture, along with anticipation of their customers' needs for innovative solutions. In fact, their company purpose, as posted prominently at their Web site says, "The people of Cardinal Health are driven by a common purpose: To help our customers across the health care industry find answers to the challenges they face." Because of this corporate philosophy, there wasn't a single event or business reason that caused Cardinal's entry into the e-commerce world. It was just part of their continuing evolution. They had been transforming their company continuously and leveraging the capabilities of their acquired companies.

Few companies excel at acquisitions. Cardinal is probably one of those who has been able to use acquisitions as a successful growth strategy. Acquisitions can create much organizational upheaval. If there is a sequence of acquisitions, the company can be in the mode of constant change. It's also difficult to find the right acquisition candidate that has the assets and a compatible culture to smoothly assimilate the people into the acquiring organization. Bob Walter has been able to do both of these things very well during the screening process, before the actual acquisition. His philosophy toward newly acquired companies is to leave them alone as long as they are hitting their financial targets. The entrepreneurial environment of Cardinal and the strategy of constant change have helped move the company from $1 billion just four years ago to $30 billion USD today.

Vision and Strategy

Cardinal Health was not in the practice of making broad vision statements that promised to do everything for everybody. Because of their entrepreneurial environment, their vision was inherently reflected in their culture, even if not articulated or written on a plaque. Their vision is to innovate, and to make sure that they do what they say they will do. That vision is put into practice every day at Cardinal Health. After their e-commerce transformation began, another more specific vision evolved: "To be known as the predominant procurement and information engine offering in the health care industry." To refine that a little further, the company used focus groups to obtain feedback resulting in these elements, which were then added to their overall vision:

- ▲ A passion for performance
- ▲ Agility in business
- ▲ Responsiveness to the marketplace

Their strategy for the business is to combine top-down planning with bottom-up ideas. An idea can come from anyone in the company or customer base, and the idea will have a chance to be heard and considered. The top-down planning considers the big picture and the world outside of Cardinal Health. Through effective and strategic acquisitions, the company continues to expand. The internal planning involves everyone in the innovation process finding ways to grow their infrastructure in response to customer needs.

Changes Made/E-Volutionary Process

During Cardinal Health's growth period over the last 15 years, they focused on expanding the distribution side of the business, which is about 70 to 80 percent of their revenues today. This was accomplished through acquisition. In 1993, the objective was to acquire manufacturing expertise, so specific manufacturers were acquired. The manufacturing side of the business makes up the other 20 to 30 percent of their business today. There are different competitive differentiators in the distribution and manufacturing businesses, which necessitate different business strategies. In the distribution business, "any truck can deliver the same product," so differentiation comes through technology innovation or e-commerce. In the manufacturing business, it is still possible to differentiate on product, and the method of delivery isn't as important (not yet anyway). Therefore, the focus of Cardinal Health's initial e-commerce transition was the distribution side of the business.

Cardinal Health makes it their business to understand the business and information technology problems that their customers have. They regularly send out teams of people from both the technology and the business side of the company to hospitals, clinics, and pharmaceutical manufacturers to discover ways to develop new services and ways to integrate existing services. The focus of these teams is to use creative ways to take the physical solution and move it to the electronic world. By using this strategy, Cardinal Health had a head start on developing their initial e-commerce offerings.

From these "field trips" and other customer input, Cardinal Health developed two online offerings, *eprocurement* and *entelligence*, that would be part of their dot.com incarnation, Cardinal.com. They developed the *eprocurement* tool to help bring efficiency and consolidation to the procurement process for their customers. It essentially allows customers access to the products all the way back through the warehouse. *entelligence* was developed after studying hospital issues such as contract compliance, the need to consolidate orders across multiple hospitals, and the lack of hospital resources to do these tasks. One of the future online tools will link pharmaceutical dispensing machines in hospitals to the other back-end systems to manage the whole process online. Another project, which will bring in the manufacturing side of Cardinal Health, will be a full-service online system for pharmacies, which will link many parts of the value web including the procurement, manufacture, packaging, labeling, and distribution of drugs. To make this happen, Cardinal Health has to rely on technology as the integrator of their internal systems to link the capabilities of all their business units that were previously separate entities. However, this is something they should be able to handle easily judging by their speedy implementations so far.

Prior to their e-commerce initiatives, Cardinal Health had built a customer technology center in Chicago called the Information Concept Center (ICON). The purpose was to have a place for salespeople to meet with customers and do demos of services and products. They average 2,000 customer visits per month at the center. Near the end of the development phase for Cardinal.com, they decided to use ICON to get customer feedback on user interface, functionality, and most importantly, pricing for their online offering. They wanted to do this before the rollout, and the timing was such that they were able to engage these feedback participants as the first customers of Cardinal.com.

Cardinal Health launched Cardinal.com in February of 2000. Within two months, they were doing $5 million USD per month in revenue. As of August 2000, the level was up to $13 million USD per month. Their rollout started with 100 customers they had identified through their focus groups at the ICON center who enrolled. Cardinal Health also moved people over from an existing e-commerce system and database that Allegiance had in place. The company's sales force implemented the rollout to

Figure A.5
www.cardinal.com/tours

Cardinal Health has to rely on technology as the integrator of their internal systems, to link together the capabilities of all of their business units that were previously separate entities.

key customers after a brief training session. Now 25 percent of their online business comes from new customers. That is pretty fast rollout for an incumbent brick and mortar company.

From May 1999 to May 2000, during the dot.com rise and fall, the marketing and branding programs of Cardinal Health changed slightly in response to some new dot.com competition, such as NeoPharma. As with all industries during this period of time, analysts were praising dot.coms and criticizing incumbent brick and mortar companies. In response, Cardinal Health did some internal brainstorming and branding surveys among their customer base and came up with four key points that became the focus of their marketing implementation:

▲ Procurement

▲ Information integration

▲ Service extension

▲ Education

All four of these were key components to realizing their initial vision, especially for the distribution business. At a company level, they also gathered opinions from customers about what Cardinal Health represents in the overall market. This resulted in additional elements for their vision:

▲ A passion for performance

▲ Agility in business

▲ Responsiveness to the marketplace

After this exercise, they had validation of their vision directly from their customers. It helped strengthen their commitment to continue their transformation despite what the analysts were saying.

Cardinal Health has always had a small company philosophy even though they employ more than 36,000 people. The founder, Bob Walter, has managed to maintain an entrepreneurial culture with little to no bureaucracy. There is a sense of urgency within the company as if they are always behind the competition, the market, or the technology curve—even though they are actually in the lead. They have streamlined decision-making, and good ideas are encouraged from any employee. These ideas receive limited scrutiny, and good ideas are funded and supported throughout the company.

The organizational management philosophy emphasized self-supervised workgroups. Teams are set up for special projects and to come up with new innovations for the company. People come from different functional organizations within the company, and the work is results-driven without interference from politics or personality conflicts. The approach is to take average people and put them in such situations where they can grow, develop, and become leaders. Cardinal Health and their management team believe in the value of employees as human beings, and acknowledge that employees want opportunities to grow and be creative. When working on these teams, people are encouraged to think creatively. Every idea is taken seriously, and people have a chance to speak and be heard. Employees are also encouraged to interface with customers, and they are empowered to do so. Coupled with the open and creative environment, the employees have a chance to make real changes that shape the future success of Cardinal Health.

Main Lessons

Cardinal Health discovered a new way to use an asset. Their customer center in Chicago was originally set up for sales and demonstrations, but they used it to gather important customer feedback on future initiatives such as Cardinal.com. This is an example of how companies should examine all internal assets and processes to find ways to be more customer-centric.

Despite the lack of a clearly articulated vision and strategy, Cardinal Health was able to emerge as a leader in their industry. Because of their willingness to experiment and take some risks, they were able to find innovative ways to be more competitive. Key to their success was taking time to learn from the experiments, and also involving their employees in the effort.

Their culture of embracing continuous change has been a huge factor in their evolution. Because the company has successfully completed so many acquisitions and continues to be entrepreneurial, they have learned how to manage change on a continuing basis. Every employee in their organization is involved and encouraged to think outside the box and come up with ideas. It's a culture of change, but also one of continuous innovation focused on their customers.

Roadmap for Continuing E-Volution

Experimentation and encouraging employees to think outside the box will serve Cardinal Health well while going forward. Maintaining the open, entrepreneurial environment of their culture will be key to their future success. Being a "teenager" works well as long as growth is greater than 50 percent per year. When growth slows down (and in all companies it does), a top-down strategic planning methodology will be best for Cardinal Health. This top-down methodology can indeed work in an entrepreneurial environment, as demonstrated by UPS and Office Depot.

Cardinal Health always has several innovation initiatives in progress, of which all are well funded and have commitment from the top. They are looking for future ways to integrate technologies, such as wireless, into their growing array of products and services and to achieve their hands-free procurement goal.

Continuing to be customer-centric, and spending time and money to learn about their customers, are also key parts of their roadmap. With the existing ICON center, they have an extremely valuable customer feedback infrastructure they can leverage in new ways going forward.

Using self-supervised workgroups as a vital part of their organizational management philosophy will result in continued empowerment and development of their workforce. Coupled with an open communications environment and customer focus, their internal organization will act as its own engine for evolution and growth of the company.

B

Recommended
E-Commerce Glossaries

THE PROLIFERATION of terminology related to e-commerce continues

at an incredible rate. In the interest of including the most up-to-date

information possible, I have decided to direct you to online resources

rather than providing a list of terms here that would be quickly out-

dated. Therefore, I evaluated some of the current glossaries of terms

available and chose those that are the best for readers of this book.

▶▶

One of the best online glossaries/encyclopedias is TechWeb, located at **www.techweb.com/encyclopedia**. TechWeb contains more than 14,000 definitions of computer terms and concepts, and they update it frequently and invite site visitors to submit new terms as well.

A number of private companies who are e-commerce service providers offer glossaries at their sites. These vary by type of company and industry. For example, see Order Trust at **http://www.ordertrust.net/html/aec_glossary.html**. You can find others by using your favorite search engines and entering "e-commerce glossary" as the search term.

General-purpose encyclopedias, such as Encyclopedia Britannica, also have some e-commerce terminology, but not to the extent of some of the others mentioned here. In addition, they charge subscription fees for online access to their encyclopedia.

The best advice I have is that you find one source that fits your industry needs and help keep it up-to-date by submitting requests and suggestions for updates.

You can also view a glossary of terms at this URL: **http://www.e-volve-or-die.com/glossary.htm**.

C

Resources

THE ECNOW.COM WEB SITE provides a list of noteworthy resources on electronic commerce and marketing. Resources include books, articles, conferences, seminars, and Web sites of interest. The following screen shot shows the most current list available at the time of publication, but you should note that this list changes frequently. Consult this list online for the most recent information. To do so, go to **http://ecnow.com/resources.htm** and click on the sites you find interesting. ▶ ▶

Figure C.1
http://ecnow.com/
resources.html

A list of resources used for this book can be found at ECnow.com.

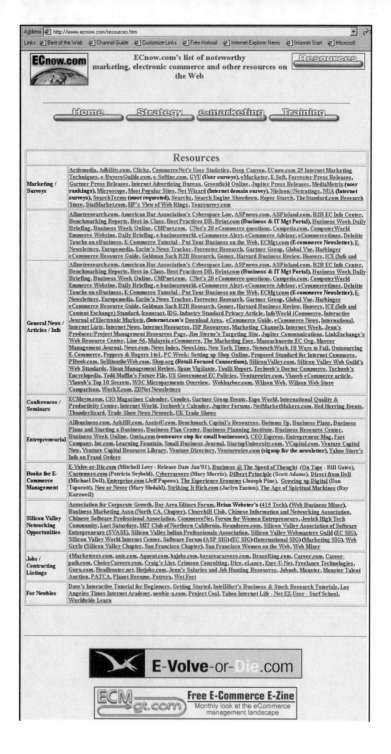

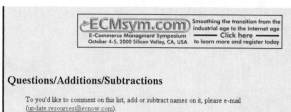

Questions/Additions/Subtractions

To you'd like to comment on this list, add or subtract names on it, please e-mail (update.resources@ecnow.com).

Strategy | Training | Speaking | e-marketing | Overall Services
Resources | Examples | ECMgt.com eZine | ECM Training
Home Page | Contact Info / Feedback | * Start Today * | Site Map

ECnow.com (http://ecnow.com)
1-408-257-3000 (Phone), 1-603-843-0769 (eFax)
E-mail: General (Mitchell.Levy@ecnow.com), Webmaster (webmaster@ecnow.com)

This is a great way to do research on ECM and to keep up with what's happening in the e-commerce space. In addition, I encourage you to sign up for 20–25 online newsletters because they fully address what's happening.

There are several categories of information, as shown in the figure. The first category, "Marketing and Surveys," includes articles, tools, and other tips on using the Web for market research as well as effective marketing techniques for the Web. The "General News and Articles" category includes databases of articles, publishers of e-commerce magazines and trade journals, general business and e-commerce articles, and pertinent online newsletters.

For the "Conferences/Seminars" section, I have listed those that have a strong e-commerce emphasis. The "Entrepreneurial" section includes a lot of information on funding, starting, and operating new businesses. The next section is a list of some of the best books on various aspects of e-commerce management, including those that are inspirational stories or case studies. "Books for Thinking Outside the Box" are the best sources of information and ideas on creative thinking. The next two sections focus on networking and job opportunities, and at the end is a section containing very basic information for people who are new to e-commerce.

I invite your ongoing contributions to this resource list. If you know of any exciting resources to add, please send the information to **update.resources@ecnow.com**.

End Notes

Please go to **http://e-volve-or-die.com** to view all contributors' bios and longer company descriptions.

Chapter 2

Interactive Week, "New Application Gives Vendor Hope", August 3, 1998. Used with permission.

Companies providing quotes for this chapter include:

Keynote Systems
www.keynote.com
Keynote is the world's largest supplier of Internet performance measurement, diagnostic, load testing, and consulting services to companies with e-commerce Web sites.

Sameday.com
www.sameday.com
Sameday.com offers the unique technology to enable rapid-response product distribution.

SAQQARA
www.saqqara.com

SAQQARA helps sellers maximize their B2B e-commerce results through best-of-breed product content management and exchange solutions.

Chapter 3

Fast Company, "Getting It Done", by Paul Roberts, June 2000, p. 148–152. Used with permission.

Companies providing quotes for this chapter include:

Seabright Group
www.seabrightgroup.com

Seabright Group creates dynamic, online learning communities that enhance understanding, training skills, building brands, and driving sales.

Zoho Corporation
www.zoho.com

Zoho is the premier online hospitality marketplace.

Chapter 4

Companies providing quotes for this chapter include:

American Express
www.aexp.com

American Express is a diversified, worldwide travel, financial, and network services company.

Brigade Corporation
www.brigade.com

Brigade provides "Everything behind the help button"™—a full outsourced solution for Internet customer support.

eConvergent
www.econvergent.com

eConvergent helps e-businesses and large enterprises establish and build lifelong customer relationships.

Intuit Inc.
www.intuit.com

Intuit creates the world's best-selling personal, small business, and tax preparation software and web-based solutions.

Net Perceptions, Inc.
www.netperceptions.com

Net Perceptions is an innovator of solutions that translate business knowledge into profitable action.

TestMart
www.testmart.com

TestMart is the first choice for products and services in the precision instrument marketplace as a result of our unique value offering—comprehensive unbiased content combined with robust online commerce.

Chapter 5

Companies providing quotes for this chapter include:

Net Perceptions, Inc.
www.netperceptions.com

Net Perceptions is an innovator of solutions that translate business knowledge into profitable action.

NetRatings, Inc.
www.netratings.com

NetRatings is a media and market research company that provides the Nielsen/NetRatings services.

Tweney Media
www.tweney.com

Tweney Media is a writing and content consulting firm in San Mateo, California.

Vignette Corporation
www.vignette.com

Vignette is the leading supplier of e-business application software.

Chapter 6

"Global E-Commerce: Taking Your Business Global on the Web," course material from Jorden Woods and GlobalSight Corporation, 2000. Used with permission.

Companies providing quotes for this chapter include:

Cisco Systems
www.cisco.com
Cisco is the worldwide leader in networking for the Internet.

CommerceNet
www.commercenet.com
CommerceNet sets the business agenda for global e-commerce.

e-co consulting
www.e-coconsulting.com
e-co consulting helps companies create business value in the European community.

GlobalSight Corporation
www.globalsight.com
GlobalSight is the leading provider of enterprise software for accelerating global e-business.

WineShopper.com
www.wineshopper.com
WineShopper.com is a revolutionary new Web site designed to provide access to the largest selection of wines available anywhere. (Acquired by wine.com in August 2000.)

Chapter 7

Companies providing quotes for this chapter include:

Calico Commerce
www.calico.com
Calico Commerce is a leading provider of software that enables corporations to control e-business selling.

Commtouch

www.commtouch.com

Commtouch is the worldwide leading provider of outsourced email and messaging solutions for destination sites, service providers, and corporations.

diCarta

www.dicarta.com

diCarta is the online contract management company.

eGain

www.egain.com

eGain helps companies establish profitable, long-term customer relationships through superior customer service.

NaviSite

www.navisite.com

NaviSite, a leading managed application hosting provider, offers the facilities, equipment, and expertise needed to launch and sustain a company's Web business.

Chapter 8

Companies providing quotes for this chapter include:

Cisco Systems

www.cisco.com

Cisco is the worldwide leader in networking for the Internet.

Commtouch

www.commtouch.com

Commtouch is the worldwide leading provider of outsourced email and messaging solutions for destination sites, service providers, and corporations.

eGain

www.egain.com

eGain helps companies establish profitable, long-term customer relationships through superior customer service.

Egghead Software
www.egghead.com

Egghead.com offers purchasing needs for computer products, electronics, office products, or from a variety of leisure categories such as sporting goods and travel.

Garden.com
www.garden.com

Garden.com provides the ultimate destination for gardening information, products, and services in the gardening industry.

Target Marketing
www.targeting.com

Target Marketing of Santa Barbara offers Internet marketing strategy consulting to Fortune 500 companies and Internet startups.

Chapter 9

Companies providing quotes for this chapter include:

Loudcloud
www.loudcloud.com

Loudcloud builds and runs high-performance Internet infrastructure environments for businesses.

neoIT™
www.neoit.com

neoIT™ addresses the scarcity of IT resources through its global online marketplace for outsourcing IT projects.

Personify
www.personify.com

Personify is the leading provider of e-business software that helps companies accelerate growth and increase profitability by measuring, analyzing, and optimizing customer-focused service metrics.

Chapter 10

Companies providing quotes for this chapter include:

Simmedia.com
www.simmedia.com
Simmedia is an Internet business strategy and UI design architecture firm that builds the front-end for e-business applications.

The Ward Group
www.ericward.com
The Ward Group helps content-oriented sites get linked, reviewed, and announced strategically.

Chapter 11

Companies providing quotes for this chapter include:

Becker and Poliakoff, P.A.
www.becker-poliakoff.com
Becker and Poliakoff, P.A. provides innovative, pragmatic, and cost-effective business solutions.

CommerceNet
www.commercenet.com
CommerceNet sets the business agenda for global e-commerce.

Kirkpatrick and Lockhart LLP
www.kl.com
Kirkpatrick and Lockhart LLP is a national law firm with approximately 600 lawyers in Boston, Harrisburg, Los Angeles, Miami, Newark, New York, Pittsburgh, San Francisco, and Washington.

TechRisk.Law
www.techrisklaw.com
TechRisk.Law is a law firm focusing on technology and e-commerce risk management.

TRUSTe
www.truste.org
TRUSTe is an Internet privacy seal program.

Chapter 12

Companies providing quotes for this chapter include:

Rapt Inc.
www.rapt.com
Rapt is a leading provider of solutions for Dynamic Commerce Management, targeting companies that buy and sell high volumes of goods in fast-moving markets.

Ricoh Silicon Valley
www.rsv.ricoh.com
Ricoh of Silicon Valley is a new subsidiary of Ricoh Company Ltd. composed of three separate but interrelated business and research centers.

Ventro
www.ventro.com
Ventro builds and operates companies that transform the supply chain in businesses around the world.

VerticalNet
www.verticalnet.com
VerticalNet provides end-to-end e-commerce solutions targeted at distinct business segments through three Strategic Business Units: VerticalNet Markets, VerticalNet Exchanges, and VerticalNet Solutions.

Chapter 13

All quoted companies that are interviewed in the book are listed.

Chapter 14

Companies and people providing quotes for this chapter include:

Dave Deasy, former COO of hpshopping.com, is an independent consultant and speaker for e-commerce strategy and implementation.

Personify

www.personify.com

Personify is the leading provider of e-business software that helps companies accelerate growth and increase profitability by measuring, analyzing, and optimizing customer-focused service metrics.

Rapt Inc.

www.rapt.com

Rapt is a leading provider of solutions for Dynamic Commerce Management, targeting companies that buy and sell high volumes of goods in fast-moving markets.

Strategic Internet Consulting

Strategic Internet Consulting helps businesses to leverage the Internet's power to increase revenue, reduce spending, and develop new business models.

Index of Names

3Com, 29

ActivMedia Research, 185
Affinia, 34
Akel, Anwar, 239
AllAdvantage, 173
Allegiance, 288, 292
Amazon.com, 16, 27, 34, 73, 92, 110, 145-146, 184, 213
American Express Corporate Services Interactive (Mohit Mehrotra), 68, 231, 238
Amling, Alan (UPS), 162, 274
Andreessen, Marc, 27
   Loudcloud, 121
AOL, 33, 205, 285
Arbinet Global Clearing Network, 37
Ariba, 14, 28, 37, 284
At Once, 120
Aton International, Inc. (Constance Wilde), 230
Autobytel, 27

Bank of the West (Rolf Scherrer), 228
Barnes and Noble, 148
bCentral, 285
Becker and Poliakoff (Mark Grossman), 196
Bezons, Jeff, 146
Bluelight.com, 14, 158
Boeing, 36
Boo.com, 49
Brazina, Paul (Electronic Commerce Institute-LaSalle University), 235
Brigade Corporation (Russ Cohn), 71, 227, 238

Caldwell, Kaye (CommerceNet), 196, 198
Calico Commerce, 14, 123
   Alan Naumann, 122, 127, 234, 237
Cardinal Health, 17, 287-295
Cargill, 37

Carsdirect, 27
CDNOW.com, 34, 78, 86
Charles Schwab, 72, 161, 165
Chemdex.com, 85
Cheney, Christina (Simmedia.com), 183-184, 187, 239
Cisco Systems, 14, 54, 56, 102, 123, 152, 257
   Barbara Jones, 143-144, 231, 234
   Todd Elizalde, 106, 138, 229
Clarke, Leo (TechRisk.Law), 196, 197, 199-200, 202, 206
Clarksdale, 27
Clickquick.com, 34
Cohn, Russ (Brigade Corporation), 71, 227, 238
Commerce One, 28, 36-37, 284
CommerceNet, 206
   Kaye Caldwell, 196
   Mark Resch, 101, 110, 239
Commtouch, 120, 129
   Rip Gerber, 122, 229
Cross, Bob (Venture Capital Online, Inc.), 232

DaimlerChrysler, 37
Daniel, Bill (Vignette), 94, 232, 240
Davis, Donald (Ricoh-Silicon Valley), 213, 219, 229
Deasy, Dave, 143, 150, 232
   hpshopping.com, 138, 152
Dell, 27, 54, 67, 115, 125, 152, 161, 173, 200, 257
DGNonline, 120
DiCarta (George Roman), 130, 234, 236
Digital Market, 30
Digital River, 120
Double Click, 200

E*Trade, 31

e-co consulting (Maria-Luisa Rodriguez), 104, 109, 113, 229, 231, 240

e-STEEL.com, 85

EasyJet, 160

eBay, 14, 22, 27, 94

eBenefits.com, 120

eChemical, 36

ECMgt.com, 21, 94, 225

ECnow.com, 21, 172

eConvergent (Clyde Foster), 70, 228, 237

eGain (Ashu Roy), 128, 147, 232, 237

Egghead.com, 14, 48
    Norm Hullinger, 141, 151, 234, 237

eLance, 14

Electronic Commerce Institute-LaSalle University (Paul Brazina), 235

Elizalde, Todd (Cisco Systems), 106, 138, 229

emarketer.com, 102

Enron, 163

EqualFooting.com, 36

Ernst & Young, 39

eSchwab, 27, 31, 161

eSteel, 158

eWanted, 256

Excite At Home, 205

ExciteClassifieds.com, 89

Exodus, 120

FedEx, 38, 234

Fisher, Brooks (Intuit Inc.), 69, 77, 230, 233, 236

Flextronics, 120

Ford, 19, 37, 246

Forrester Research, 183

Foster, Clyde (eConvergent), 70, 228, 237

The Gap, 152

Garden.com, 86
    Lisa Sharples, 143, 148, 229, 238

Gardner, Neil (NaviSite), 128

General Electric, 51, 246

Gerber, Rip (Commtouch), 122, 229

Global Frontier, 120

GlobalSight (Jorden Woods), 101, 111, 240

GM, 37

Goel, Love (Personify, Inc.), 166, 246, 248

GroceryWorks, 35

Grossman, Mark (Becker and Poliakoff), 196, 197, 202-203, 206

Guanlao, Herman E. (Intercaps Philippines, Inc.), 241

Hallmark, 36, 152

Hanna, Gwen (Homebid.com), 227

Hassim, Mohsien (KPMG South Africa), 236

Hazen, Dan (Hewlett Packard), 240

Hefner, Lori, 206

HelloAsia, 49, 58

Hewlett Packard, 246
    Dan Hazen, 240

Homebid.com (Gwen Hanna), 227

Horowitz, Ben (Loudcloud), 161

hpshopping.com, 16
    Dave Deasy, 138, 152

Hullinger, Norm (Egghead.com), 141, 151, 234, 237

I2, 220

IBM, 37

iMarket Strategies (Gay Slesigner), 228

Intercaps Philippines, Inc. (Herman E. Guanlao), 241

Intuit Inc., 39, 78
    Brooks Fisher, 69, 77, 230, 233, 236

iSyndicate.com, 94

Jones, Barbara (Cisco Systems), 143-144, 231, 234

Kaldor, Sean (NetRatings Inc.), 84, 227, 231

Kellner, Brian (Zoho Corporation), 55, 227-228, 234

Keynote Systems (Dan Todd), 33

Kinko's, 216

Kmart, 158

Kozmo.com, 38

KPMG South Africa (Mohsien Hassim), 236

KPN Business Communications (Stefan A. Vermeulen), 233

Krainin, Andrew (Sameday.com), 26, 41, 235, 237

Lands' End, 32, 91, 150, 152

LandsEnd.com, 139

Larsen, Steve (Net Perceptions), 73, 86

Lockheed Martin, 36

Loudcloud
    Ben Horowitz, 161
    Marc Andreessen, 121

Luechtefeld, Monica (Office Depot), 281

Lycos Quote.com (Kaj Pedersen), 236

MacArthur, General, 60

Mail Order Gardening Association, 144

Mehrotra, Mohit (American Express Corporate Services Interactive), 68, 231, 238
Mercata, 14
Metcalfe, Robert, 29
Metion, 284
meVC (Carol Wu), 196
Microsoft, 200, 205
Microsoft's bCentral, 285
Mondus.com, 115
muybueno.net (Cesar Plato), 241

Napster, 206
Naumann, Alan (Calico Commerce), 122, 127, 234, 237
NaviSite (Neil Gardner), 128
Nelson, Doug (Seabright Group), 48, 228, 232
neoIT.com (Atul Vashistha), 158, 160, 163, 238, 240
NeoPharma, 293
Net Perceptions (Steve Larsen), 73, 86
NetRatings Inc. (Sean Kaldor), 84, 227, 231
Netscape, 27
Nike, 125
Nike.com, 278
NoBrainerBlinds, 186
Nordstrom, 32
nua.ie, 102

Office Depot, 17, 281-287, 295
OpenRatings.com, 37
Oracle, 39, 220
Osburn, Mark (Santa Clara Valley Transportation Society), 230
Ostrow, Peter (Testmart), 75, 233, 235-236

Pedersen, Kaj (Lycos Quote.com), 236
PeopleSoft, 39
Perry, David (Ventro), 213-214, 220
Personify, Inc. (Love Goel), 166, 246, 248
Philips, 102
Plato, Cesar (muybueno.net), 241
Polaroid, 75
Popek, Tom (Strategic Internet Consulting), 246-247
Premiere Choice Award, 36
Priceline, 14, 22, 256
Procter and Gamble, 122, 284
Purchase Pro, 284
PurchasingCenter.com, 34

Rainmaker (Michael Tilson), 66
Rapt Inc., 14
    Narry Singh, 158, 217, 220, 222, 249
Recording Industry of America, 206
Referit.com, 34
Reid, Ellen (Smarketing.com), 233
Resch, Mark (CommerceNet), 101, 110, 239
Ricoh of Silicon Valley (Donald Davis), 213, 219, 229
Ritz Camera, 33
Ritzcamera Online, 34
Robinson, Steven (Saltmine), 231
Rodriguez, Maria-Luisa (e-co consulting), 104, 109, 113, 229, 231, 240
Roman, George (DiCarta), 130, 234, 236
Roy, Ashu (eGain), 128, 147, 232, 237

Safeway, 35
Saltmine (Steven Robinson), 231
Sameday.com, 38
    Andrew Krainin, 26, 41, 235, 237
Santa Clara Valley Transportation Society (Mark Osburn), 230
SAP, 39
SAQQARA (Don Swenson), 31
Sara Lee, 125
Scherrer, Rolf (Bank of the West), 228
Schoolpop.com, 34
Schwab, 72, 161, 165
Seabright Group (Doug Nelson), 48, 228, 232
searchenginewatch.com, 180
Sharples, Lisa (Garden.com), 143, 148, 229, 238
Simmedia.com (Christina Cheney), 183-184, 187, 239
Singh, Narry (Rapt Inc.), 158, 217, 220, 222, 249
Sisson, Peter (Wine.com), 112, 227, 229
Slesinger, Gay (iMarket Strategies), 228
Sloan, Alfred, 51
Smarketing.com (Ellen Reid), 233
Solectron, 120
Steer, David (TrustE), 196, 197, 199-201
Sterne, Jim (Target Marketing of Santa Barbara), 238
Strategic Internet Consulting (Tom Popek), 246-247
Sullivan, Danny, 180
Sun Microsystems, 26
Swenson, Don (SAQQARA), 31

Target Marketing of Santa Barbara (Jim Sterne), 238
TechRisk.Law (Leo Clarke), 196
Testmart (Peter Ostrow), 75, 233, 235-236
Tilson, Michael (Rainmaker), 66
Todd, Dan (Keynote Systems), 33
Toshiba, 102
Toys 'R' Us, 37, 213
Travelocity, 67
TrustE, 199
    David Steer, 196
Tupperware, 77
Tweney Media (Dylan Tweney), 83, 231, 238, 240
Tweney, Dylan (Tweney Media), 83, 231, 238, 240

United Airlines, 77
UPS, 17, 38, 222, 234, 274-280, 295
    Alan Amling, 162
US Steel, 158

Vashistha, Atul (neoIT.com), 158, 160, 163, 238, 240
Ventro, 14
    David Perry, 213-214, 220
Venture Capital Online, Inc. (Bob Cross), 232
Vermeulen, Stefan A. (KPN Business Communications), 233

VerticalNet, 14, 28, 37
    Mark Walsh, 212, 221-222, 235, 239
Vignette, 94
    Bill Daniel, 94, 232, 240
Vstore.com, 34

Walsh, Mark (VerticalNet), 212, 221-222, 235, 239
Walter, Bob (Cardinal Health), 287, 289, 293
Ward, Eric (The Ward Group), 185-186
WebVan, 38, 146
Welch, Jack, 51
White, Kathy (Cardinal Health), 287
Wilde, Constance (Aton International, Inc.), 230
Williams-Sonoma, 77
Wine.com, 14
    Peter Sisson, 112, 227, 229
Woods, Jorden (GlobalSight), 101, 111, 240
WorldCom, 284
Wstore.com, 115
Wu, Carol (meVC), 196, 197, 199, 206

Xerox, 85

Yahoo, 27, 76

Zoho Corporation (Brian Kellner), 55, 227-228, 234

Index

A

access, outsourcing, 126
ads, as part of content, 86
advertising, 187. *See also* marketing
affiliate marketing, 34-35
alignment process (organizational structure)
    overview of, 157
    vision statement, 158
ASPs (application service providers),
    39-40, 121

B

B2B enterprises, content on sites, 85
back office processes. *See* business processes
benchmarks (customer service metrics),
    143-144
benefits and risks (global business operations),
    101-103
biotechnology, future predictions, 257-258
branding (online), marketing, 183-184
brands, role in marketplace, 221
BSPs (Business Service Providers), 39, 121
business, importance of basics (quotations),
    227-228
business context, planning Internet-enabled
    companies, 49
business infrastructure partnerships, 39-40
business metrics (markets), 221-222
business models, 25-26
    customer-centric, 159-162
        quotations, 232-233
    customers
        definitions of value, 30-31
        effect on delivering value, 76-77

early Internet models, 26-27
economic environment (quotations),
    228-230
Internet integration, 15-18
    creative thinking, 18, 20
    to Internet-enabled companies, 16
    trial and error, 18
Internet-enabled world, 230-231
partnerships, 31-32
    adaptation to change, 41-42
    business infrastructure partners, 39-40
    distribution partners, 35-36
    economic factors, 40-41
    fulfillment partners, 37-39
    marketing partners, 33-35
    selection criteria, 32-33
    supplier partners, 36-37
quotations, 234-235
value webs, 28-30
business partners. *See* partnerships
business plan, customer service in, 146
business processes
    changing, planning Internet-enabled
        companies, 54
    customer service, 147-148
    customer value, planning Internet-enabled
        companies, 54-56
    customers' effect on, 74-76
    global business operations, 110-111
    outsourcing. *See* outsourcing
    transition to new organizational
        structure, 163
Business Service Providers (BSPs), 39, 121

C

case studies
  Cardinal Health, 287-295
  Office Depot, 281-287
  UPS, 274-280
catalysts of change, 247
changes in e-commerce
  catalysts of, 247
  future predictions, 250-261
  management of, 248-249
  organizational involvement, 246-247
  trends toward, 249-250
  Web sites for updated information, 246
channel marketing skills, 187
channel partnerships, 35-36
Children's Online Privacy Protection Act
  (COPPA), 197
click and mortar companies, defined, 33
click-wrap agreements (contract law), 202
collaboration
  future predictions, 258-259
  markets, effect on, 220
collaborative management, transition to new
  organizational structure, 166-167
Commerce Service Providers (CSPs), 121
communications
  customer touch points, 70-71
  importance of, transition to new
    organizational structure, 162-163
company infrastructure (customer service),
  150-151
content
  customization (global business operations),
    108, 110
  as differentiator, 91
  evaluation, 92-94
  importance of, 83-84, 95
  organization and design, 88, 90
  sources, 94-95
  updates, 92
  value to customer, 84, 86-88
  Web sites, 179
continous planning process (Internet-enabled
  companies), 58-59
contract law, 199, 202
  international business, 200
control, outsourcing, 126
conventional marketing, combined with
  Internet marketing, 185

COPPA (Children's Online Privacy Protection
  Act), 197
copyright, legal issues, 201-202
creative thinking, Internet integration, 18, 20
CRM (Customer Relationship Management),
  69-70
CSPs (Commerce Service Providers), 121
currencies (global business operations), 107
customer service
  in business plan, 146
  employee incentives, 144-145
  expectations, 137-139
  infrastructure, 150-151
  maintenance of, 152
  metrics, 143-144
  online processes, 147-148
  partners, role of, 145
  people skills, 141-142
  place within organization, 140-141
  single customer information database,
    148-149
  stratification, 147
  training employees for, 140-142
customer-centric business models, 159-162
  quotations, 232-233
customers
  business model, effect on (delivering value),
    76-77
  business processes, effect on, 74-76
  changing roles of, 66-67
  content customization for (global business
    operations), 108, 110
  definitions of value, 30-31
  expectations of e-commerce, 13-14
  feedback from, 67-68
  market focus on, 214
  outsourcing, effect on, 127-128
  personalized interactions with, 73-74
    delivering value, 78-79
  power of, 65-66
  relationship management, 69-70
  research on, 30-31
  retaining, 68-69
  stratification, 71-73
  touch points, 70-71
  value, planning Internet-enabled
    companies, 54-56
  value of content to, 84-88
customs (global business operations), 106

D

database for customer information, 148-149
delivery process (global business operations), 106
deployment (global business operations), 114-115
designing content, 88, 90
differentiator, content as, 91
direct marketing, 183
distribution partnerships, 35-36
domain names, choosing, 177-178

E-F

e-business. *See* e-commerce
e-commerce. *See also* Internet-enabled companies
  changes. *See* changes in e-commerce
  customer expectations, 13-14
  defined, 12
  Internet integration, 15-18
    creative thinking, 18, 20
    to Internet-enabled companies, 16
    trial and error, 18
  transition to Internet Age, 12-13
  trends, 20-23
ECnow.com Web site, marketing resources available on, 171-172
economic environment (quotations), 228-230
economic factors, partnerships, 40-41
EDI (Electronic Data Interchange) systems, 26
email
  direct marketing, 183
  signature tags (marketing), 180
employees
  customer service incentives, 144-145
  training for customer service, 140-142
  transition to new organizational structure
    collaborative management, 166-167
    legacy people, 164
    self-directed work groups, 165-166
    transforming people, 164-165
enforcement (legal issues), 198, 200
evaluation
  content, 92-94
  outsourcing, 131
  planning Internet-enabled companies, 58-59
expensive mass (customers), 72
experimentation, role in marketplace, 218-219

flattened hierarchy organizational structures, 159
front office processes. *See* business processes
fulfillment partnerships, 37-39
future predictions
  changes in e-commerce, 250-261
  quotations, 239-241

G-H

give-aways (marketing), 179
global business operations, 99-100
  benefits and risks, 101-103
  business processes, 110-111
  changes to, 115
  currencies, 107
  delivery process, 106
  deployment, 114-115
  legal issues, 105-106, 200
  localization, 108, 110
  partnerships, 112-113
  "thinking globally," 104
  translation, 107-108
  vision statement, 103
gold rush, Internet compared to, 212-213
GPS (Global Positioning System) devices, privacy issues, 201

hierarchical organizational structures, 159
history, Internet business models, 26-27
holistic Internet-enabled companies. *See* Internet-enabled companies
horizontal organizational structures, 159

I-J

incentives, customer service, 144-145
individual customer interactions. *See* personalized customer interactions
Industrial Age, transition to Internet Age, 12-13
infrastructure (customer service), 150-151
intellectual property (legal issues), 201-202
interactions with customers. *See* personalized customer interactions
international business. *See* global business operations
international treaties (legal issues), 203

Internet
    compared to gold rush, 212-213
    integration, 15-18
        creative thinking, 18, 20
        to Internet-enabled companies, 16
        trial and error, 18
    markets. *See* markets
Internet Age
    customer expectations, 13-14
    transition to, 12-13
Internet marketing. *See* marketing
Internet-enabled companies, 16. *See also*
    planning Internet-enabled companies
Internet-enabled world, 230-231

K-L

knowledge workers, future predictions,
    253-254

language issues (global business operations)
    localization, 108-110
    translation, 107-108
laws. *See* legal issues
legacy people, transition to new organizational
    structure, 164
legal issues, 195-196
    contract law, 202
    current status of laws, 197-198
    effect on companies, 205
    global business operations, 105-106, 200
    intellectual property, 201-202
    international treaties, 203
    privacy, 200-201
    regulation and enforcement, 198, 200
    resources for information, 206
    taxation, 203-204
localization (global business operations),
    108-110

M

mainstream accounts (customers), 72
management of outsourcing, 129-130
management styles, collaborative
    management, 166-167
market research from Web site, 184
marketing
    content as, 86
    conventional combined with Internet
        marketing, 185

direct marketing, 183
domain names, choosing, 177-178
email signature tags, 180
give-aways, 179
importance of, 187-188
market research, 184
mass customization, 173
online branding, 183-184
online newsletters, 182
permission marketing, 173
personalization, 173
quotations, 238-239
resources available on ECnow.com
    Web site, 171-172
search engine optimization, 180, 182
skills needed for, 185-187
URL promotion, 180
viral marketing, 172
Web sites
    basics, 175-177
    content, 179
    as passive marketing devices, 174-175
    usability, 178
marketing communications skills, 186
marketing partnerships, 33-35
markets, 211-212
    brands, role of, 221
    business metrics, 221-222
    collaboration partners, 220
    customer focus, 214
    development, 219-220
    experimentation, role of, 218-219
    Internet compared to gold rush, 212-213
    new products and services, 214
    new types of, 215
    opportunities, finding, 215-216, 218
    warning about losing, 222
mass customization (marketing), 173
master schedule, planning Internet-enabled
    companies, 53
Metcalfe's law, 29
metrics
    business metrics (markets), 221-222
    customer service, 143-144
    success measurement, planning
        Internet-enabled companies, 51-52
mission statement. *See* vision statement
multilingual issues. *See* language issues

N-O

newsletters (online), marketing, 182

object-based ECOsystems, future predictions, 254-256
online marketplaces, 36-37
online newsletters (marketing), 182
online processes. *See* business processes
opportunities, finding in marketplace, 215-218
organization of content, 88, 90
organizational involvement, implementing change, 246-247
organizational structure, 155, 157
  alignment process
    overview of, 157
    vision statement, 158
  commitment to vision statement, 167
  transition to, 162-163
    collaborative management, 166-167
    legacy people, 164
    processes, changing, 163
    self-directed work groups, 165-166
    transforming people, 164-165
  types of, 159-162
outsourcing, 119. *See also* partnerships
  control and access, 126
  customer service, 127-128
  deciding what to outsource, 124-126
  determining need for, 123
  evaulation, 131
  examples of outsourced services, 120-121
  management of, 129-130
  service providers, 121-122
  vendor selection, 128-129

P

partnerships, 31-32. *See also* outsourcing
  adaptation to change, 41-42
  business infrastructure partners, 39-40
  customer service, role in, 145
  distribution partners, 35-36
  economic factors, 40-41
  fulfillment partners, 37-39
  global business operations, 112-113
  marketing partners, 33-35
  markets, effect on, 220
  planning Internet-enabled companies, 57-58
  selection criteria, 32-33
  supplier partners, 36-37

payment mechanisms (quotations), 233-234
people management, organizational changes, 248-249
people skills (customer service), 141-142
permission marketing, 173
personalization (marketing), 173
personalized customer interactions, 73-74
  delivering value, 78-79
personas (future predictions), 253-254
planning Internet-enabled companies
  business context, 49
  continuous process, 58-59
  customer value, 54-56
  importance of, 47-49
  objective of, 61
  partners, 57-58
  processes, changing, 54
  roadmap (master schedule), 53
  stakeholders, 56-57
  success measurement, 51-52
  tactical phase, 59-60
  vision statement, 50-51
portals, partnership selection criteria, 32
predictions for the future (quotations), 239-241
privacy
  legal issues, 200-201
  quotations, 235-236
processes. *See* business processes
product marketing skills, 186
public relations skills, 186

Q-R

regulation (legal issues), 198, 200
research on customers, 30-31
retention of customers, 68-69
risks and benefits (global business operations), 101-103
roadmap (master schedule), planning Internet-enabled companies, 53

S

search engine optimization (marketing), 180-182
security (quotations), 235-236
self-directed work groups, transition to new organizational structure, 165-166
semantic Web, future predictions, 256-257
service level agreements (customer service), 147

service providers for outsourcing, 121-122

services, newly available, 214

shipping (global business operations), 106

signature tags (marketing), 180

skills, needed for marketing, 185-187

stakeholders, planning Internet-enabled companies, 56-57

"stickiness" of sites, 90

stratification (customer service), 147

structure of organization. *See* organizational structure

success, measuring (planning Internet-enabled companies), 51-52

supplier partnerships, 36-37

supply chains, defined, 26

T

tactical phase, planning Internet-enabled companies, 59-60

target accounts (customers), 72

taxation (legal issues), 203-204

teams (self-directed work groups), transition to new organizational structure, 165-166

technologies (quotations), 237-238

"thinking globally," 104

third-party oversight programs, 199

touch points (customers), 70-71

tracking deliveries (global business operations), 106

training for customer service employees, 140-142

transforming people (transition to new organizational structure), 164-165

transition to new organizational structure, 162-163

collaborative management, 166-167

commitment to vision statement, 167

legacy people, 164

processes, changing, 163

self-directed work groups, 165-166

transforming people, 164-165

translation (global business operations), 107-108

treaties (legal issues), 203

trends in e-commerce, 20-23, 249-250

trial and error (Internet integration), 18

U-V

UCITA (Uniform Computer Information Transactions Act), 197

updating content, 92

URLs

domain names, choosing, 177-178

marketing, 180

usability of Web sites, 178

value

customers' definition of, 30-31

delivering to customers

effect on business model, 76-77

on personalized basis, 78-79

value webs, 28-30

economic factors of partnerships, 40-41

quotations, 234-235

VAT (Value Added) tax, 204

vendor partnerships, 36-37

vendors for outsourcing, selection, 128-129

viral marketing, 172

virtual value webs. *See* value webs

vision statement

aligning organizational structure with, 158

commitment to during transition, 167

global business operations, 103

planning Internet-enabled companies, 50-51

W

Web sites

branding, 183-184

content, 179

domain names, choosing, 177-178

market research from, 184

marketing basics, 175-177

as passive marketing devices, 174-175

search engine optimization, 180, 182

updated e-commerce information, 246

usability, 178

WIPO (World Intellectual Property Organization), 199

word-of-mouth marketing, 172

work groups, transition to new organizational structure, 165-166